Early Modern Matters of Life and Death

Aaron Greenberg, PhD

BIOGRAPH LLC

Published by bioGraph
Chicago, IL
bioGraphbook.com

First bioGraph trade paperback edition April 2020

For information about discounts for bulk purchases,
please contact info@bioGraphbook.com

Designed by bioGraph
Cover Design by lefthandedscissorz
Manufactured in the United States of America
1 2 3 4 5 6 7 8 9 10

Printed on 90gsm acid-free paper

Library of Congress Control Number: 2020936130

ISBN: 978-1-951946-06-7 (paperback)
ISBN: 978-1-951946-07-4 (eBook)

What's the matter, sir?
I'll tell thee: life and death!

William Shakespeare
*True Chronicle History of the Life
and Death of King Lear* (1606)

Acknowledgments

This book would be deader than dust without the guidance of Will West, Laurie Shannon, and Kasey Evans. I owe a lifetime of gratitude to Heather Dubrow for fanning the first sparks, and I thank Michael Witmore for sharing Shakespearean metaphysics. I salute the departments of English and Comparative Literary Studies at Northwestern, especially Jeffrey Masten, Nathan Mead, Susan Phillips, and Samuel Weber. For fostering the life and death import of my work, I thank Feinberg School of Medicine's Center for Bioethics and Medical Humanities.

At Northwestern, my students in "Shakespeare's Social Networks," "Life-Writing," and "A Long History of Longevity" helped me revive ancient ideas for new audiences. At the School of the Art Institute of Chicago, students in "(Still) Life-Writing" helped me reimagine matters of life and death through artists' eyes. For inviting me to present these matters, I thank the American Comparative Literature Association, the Newberry Library, and the Renaissance Society of America. Excerpts of Chapter 4 appear in *Shakespeare's Things* (Routledge, 2020), edited by Brett Gamboa and Lawrence Switzky.

Above all, thanks to AJ Greenberg for saving this labor from the post-partum neglect of its author.

Table of Contents

Reasoning With Life

This book reasons with life, as Duke Vincentio enjoins Claudio to do in Shakespeare's *Measure for Measure* (1604). Steeling Claudio for execution, the duke arraigns a personified subject "that bears the name of life" whom he scorns as "a thing" that only "fools would keep"; a mere "breath" at the mercy of myriad forces, including the aging and diseased mortal body that sustains it, planetary influence, and the state. "Thou art not noble," the duke tells life, but "nursed by baseness"; "not thyself" but the product of "a thousand grains" issuing "out of dust"; not "happy" but racked with fear of death (3.1.5-41).[1] The duke's dissection of "life" exposes crises around the meanings of that term in early modern England. To begin: if one can reason with life, then life must be reasonable—yet the duke's interpellated life seems tragically irrational.

Seventeenth-century writers remade the ancient distinction between rational, sensitive, and vegetative lifeforms. On the one hand, authors including Richard Overton, John Milton, and Margaret Cavendish conceived these lifeforms on a continuum, separated by degree but not by

---

[1] William Shakespeare, *Measure for Measure*, in *The Norton Shakespeare*, ed. Stephen Greenblatt et al. (New York and London: Norton & Company, 2008). All subsequent citations of Shakespeare's plays come from this edition.

kind. On the other hand, orthodox Anglicans believed rational human life to be exempt from the mortality pertaining to nonhuman, embodied lifeforms. This begs the question of Claudio: asked to dissociate from life so as to reason with it on the other end, what kind of life is his? In what sense can Claudio be said to live while under the duke's persuasion he makes himself "absolute for death" (3.1.5)?

The duke debases life to make its loss tolerable but also to recalibrate Claudio's ethical orientation toward it, to make life "sweeter" by not hankering after it. The duke, who is disguised as a friar, appears to offer a Christian consolation that Claudio reductively summarizes as an echo of Christ's message in the book of Matthew: "I humbly thank you. To sue to live, I find I seek to die, and seeking death, find life" (3.1.41-43).[2] However, the duke says nothing about Providence, the immortal soul, or the afterlife, and his reasoning seems secular, materialistic, and even nihilistic. I will unpack the implications of these and other tensions in the meaning of early modern English "life," that "sensible warm motion" (3.1.120) to which Claudio continues to cling. Suffice it here to remark the duke's proliferation of competing meanings and values inherent in the deceptively simple four-letter word.

In the four centuries since Shakespeare lived, the term "life" has become an increasingly overdetermined,

---

[2] Cf. the book of Matthew, 16:25 Authorized (King James) Version. All subsequent citations of the bible come from this translation.

and hence indeterminate, palimpsest. The term's received meanings remain foundational to current cultural, scientific, and political discourses that ignore its complex semantic history at their peril. Early modern discourses around life afford indispensable perspective on issues of vital concern today, including biopower, medical ethics, state sovereignty, and dehumanization. In her genealogical historicization of Shakespeare's *Lear*, Margreta de Grazia has suggested that "while we are quite sophisticated in understanding versions of what we presently are—we have little sense of what the alternatives once might have been."[3]

I aim to revive in early modern sources potential alternatives to present conceptions of life. At the same time, I concur with Nikolas Rose, who has proposed to move beyond "the now familiar tropes of genealogy and 'histories of the present' [that] seek to destabilize a present that has forgotten its contingency," and instead "to emphasize continuities as much as change," because "today, to destabilize our present does not seem such a radical move."[4] My contention is that the political ecology of living, dead, and (in)animate beings in early modernity elucidates the claims of humanism and human exceptionalism that evolved in the period and that still inform present-day anthropogen-

[3] Margreta De Grazia, "The Ideology of Superfluous Things," in *Subject and Object in Renaissance Culture*, ed. Margreta De Grazia et al. (Cambridge: Cambridge University Press, 2002), 17-42; 34.
[4] Nikolas Rose, *The Politics of Life Itself: Biomedicine, Power, and Subjectivity in the Twenty-First Century* (Princeton and Oxford: Princeton University Press, 2009), 4-5.

esis, "the becoming human of the living being," which Giorgio Agamben has argued is never fully accomplished "but…always under way…every time and in each individual [who] decides between the human and the animal [and] between life and death."[5] This early modern political ecology was in many ways different from our own, but there are instructive continuities, and even the discrepancies serve to bring our twenty-first-century worldviews into sharper focus. I look to the early modern past not to locate the budding germs of an ostensibly mature present, then, but to discover still-latent seeds of historical developments yet unrealized.

This project does not focus exclusively on Shakespeare or even on strictly literary seventeenth-century texts, but I turn frequently to Shakespeare for his astonishingly concise articulation of the issues I flesh out with the work of his contemporaries. With that caveat, a few more passages from Shakespearean locales will set the stage for what follows. In the Forest of Ardenne in *As You Like It* (1600), the shepherd Corin asks the courtly clown Touchstone how he likes "this shepherd's life," eliciting from Touchstone a philosophical discourse on the forms and qualifications of life.[6]

---

[5] Giorgio Agamben, *The Open: Man and Animal*, trans. Kevin Attell (Stanford: Stanford University Press, 2004), 79.

[6] While it is often referred to as "Arden," it is rendered "Ardenne" in *The Norton Shakespeare*, 1649.

> Truly, shepherd, in respect of itself, it is a good
> life; but in respect that it is a shepherd's life, it
> is naught. In respect that it is solitary, I like it
> very well; but in respect that it is private, it is a
> very vile life. Now in respect it is in the fields, it
> pleaseth me well; but in respect it is not in the
> court, it is tedious. As it is a spare life, look you,
> it fits my humour well; but as there is no more
> plenty in it, it goes much against my stomach
> (3.2.11-19).

Living up to his name, Touchstone provides criteria by which to assess the relative values of life. The shepherd's life inherently may be "*a* good life," but it is not *the* good life, and when Touchstone compares it with other kinds and forms of life, it devolves from being good to being nothing at all. The shepherd's life is good because it is solitary, that is, safe from the encroachments of society and free to expand and to associate with nonhuman lifeforms. In the words of the exiled Duke who is also living in the forest, "our life, exempt from the public haunt, finds tongues in trees, books in the running brooks, sermons in stones, and good in everything" (2.1.15-17). But Touchstone also finds the shepherd's life abhorrent, even disgusting, because it is private, referring not to a private inner life "exempt" from the public but to life that is privative, deprived and dispossessed.[7]

---

[7] Hannah Arendt has remarked "the strict and even cruel privacy" by which "life processes manifest themselves," in *Human Condition*

Such privacy, as the poet Andrew Marvell suggested, is more akin to death than to life: "The grave's a fine and private place," he reminded his coy mistress. Unlike the "spare life" that has just enough, Touchstone's private life is inadequate, indicating, if not death, then a biological subsistence bereft of the higher capacities (such as rationality or immortality) by which early moderns distinguished human from nonhuman life, and life worth living from life that "none but fools would keep." In Touchstone's litany of lifeforms, as in Duke Vincentio's consolation, life unfolds as a pluralized singularity that is both subject and object (he likes it, and it pleaseth him), both present and absent (it is not in the court, but it is in the fields). These features reflect a culture where sovereignty instituted sociopolitical order in part by authorizing certain claims of anthropogenesis while disallowing others; where emergent forms of power took unprecedented interest in the collective life of populations; and where some resisted by proliferating unauthorized and unorthodox definitions of human life and by defending the inherent value, liberties, and rights of individual embodied lives.

Shakespeare's Edgar tells his suicidal father Gloucester that "life's a miracle" (*True Chronicle Historie of the Life and*

(Chicago: University of Chicago Press, 1998), 117. Julia Reinhard Lupton has also shown that this usage of "privacy carries the negative sense of deprived or privative, subtracted from the public realm by the sheer intensity and shame of bodily function," in *Thinking With Shakespeare: Essays on Politics and Life* (Chicago and London: The University of Chicago Press, 2011), 5.

Death of King Lear, 20.55), but in the pagan world of the play, where power is exercised by making characters live and not letting them die, Edgar's piety rings hollow. "Life's but a walking shadow," for Macbeth, "a poor player that struts and frets his hour upon the stage, and then is heard no more. It is a tale told by an idiot, full of sound and fury, signifying nothing" (*Macbeth*, 5.5.23-27). One might expect this bleak view from a tyrannical regicide, but how to account for the duke's similar view in *Measure for Measure*, or even Touchstone's assessment that life becomes "naught" when it is qualified as "a shepherd's life"? Is it possible to reconcile such apparent nihilism with the more general sense that Shakespeare's work affirms rather than denies the meaning and value of life? In any case, the absent presences of life, the zones of indistinguishability between the living, the dead, and the (in)animate, and the alternating exaltation and debasement of life are all characteristic of the early modern English worldview.

The anamorphic binaries of Touchstone's life also reflect a culture that worked continuously to "reason with life" by defining it against what it is not. "O life, no life, but lively form of death," Hieronimo cries in Thomas Kyd's *Spanish Tragedy* (3.2.1-4). "No, no, no life!" King Lear wails after Cordelia's death. "Why should a dog, a horse, a rat, have life, and thou no breath at all?" (*True Chronicle Historie*, 24.299-301). Such expressions redress what Donna V. Jones has identified as the "difficulty [of] the word 'life' itself" in twenty-first-century critical thought, which she attributes to the lack of a word for expressing "the unity of life and death." Jones aims to recover that unity through Michel Foucault's insight about the work of nineteenth-century anatomist Xavier Bichat, which shows that "death is dispersed within life," and that "life" has come to stand for "the set of dynamic functions that resists the death intrinsic to it."[8]

Foucault's claim is that "from the Renaissance to the end of the eighteenth century, the knowledge of life was caught up in the circle of life folded back upon and observing itself; from Bichat onwards it is 'staggered' in relation to life, and separated from it by the uncrossable boundary of death."[9] I reevaluate such schematic metanarratives that are useful but often gainsaid by early modern texts, not only to situate an epistemic break at least three centuries before Foucault placed it, but also to draw attention to a fertile plot in the history of life and death, an entangled bank of ideas teeming with latent pluripotency, of which Bichat's anatomy is just one possible mode.

Montaigne, for instance, reminded himself and readers of his essays that "you are in death during the time you continue in life; for you are after death when you are no longer living...and death doth more rudely touch the

---

[8] Donna V. Jones, *The Racial Discourses of Life Philosophy: Négritude, Vitalism, and Modernity* (New York: Columbia University Press, 2010), 3.

[9] Michel Foucault, *The Birth of the Clinic: An Archaeology of Medical Perception*, trans. A.M. Sheridan Smith (New York: Vintage, 1973), 145-146.

dying than the dead, and more lively and essentially."[10] Like Duke Vincentio, Touchstone, Lear, and Hieronimo, Montaigne indicates that early modern life was no more a self-same subject and object of knowledge than is post-nineteenth-century life. On the contrary, early modern life formed a larger unity with death and (in)animacy, such that the disarticulation of these ontological categories, which seems perhaps self-evident today, was fiercely contested in seventeenth-century England.

The poet, politician, and explorer Walter Raleigh explained the unity of this political ecology as he posited that the law of nature applies not only to humans but to all living creatures.

> But this definition is not generall, but of
> the naturall law in things of life. The law of
> nature in generall, I take to be that disposition,
> instinct, and formall qualitie, which God in his
> eternall prouidence hath giuen & imprinted
> in the nature of euery creature, animate, and
> inanimate. And as it is diuinum lumen in men,
> inlightning our formal reason; so is it more then
> sense in beasts; and more then vegetation in
> plants.[11]

Everything that lives is animate, in other words, but

---

[10] Michel de Montaigne, "That to Philosophize is to Learn to Die," in *The Complete Works*, trans. Donald M. Frame (New York, London, and Toronto: Alfred A. Knopf, 2003), 67-82; 78.

[11] Walter Raleigh, *The History of the World* (London, 1614), 272.

not everything that is animate also lives. Where Raleigh emphasized a God-given natural law common to all human and nonhuman beings, seventeenth-century writers increasingly emphasized the differences between human life and inanimate nature. In his *Experiments in Chyrurgerie* (trans. 1642), for instance, Wilhelm Fabry, the pioneer of German surgery, described "inanimate creatures, as Trees, and the like."[12] At the end of the period I investigate, Margaret Cavendish proposes a philosophical vitalism in part to counteract the progressively rigorous demarcation of the ecology of living and (in)animate things.

> For we cannot in Reason conceive that Man
> should be the onely Creature that partakes of
> this soul of Nature, and that all the rest of
> Natures parts, or most of them, should be soul-
> less, or (which is all one) irrational, although
> they are commonly called, nay believed to be
> such. Truly…no particular Creature can claim a
> prerogative in this case before another; for there
> is a thorow mixture of Animate and Inanimate
> Matter in Nature….I do not deny that a Stone
> has Reason, or doth partake of the Rational
> Soul of Nature as well as Man doth...but yet
> it has not animal or humane sense and reason,
> because it is not of animal kind; but being a
> Mineral, it has Mineral sense and reason.[13]

---

[12] Wilhelm Fabricius Hildanus, *Gulielm, Fabricius Hildamus, His Experiments in Chyrurgerie*, trans. John Steer (London, 1642), 65.
[13] Margaret Cavendish, *Observations upon Natural Philosophy* (London,

Versions of this worldview have survived through the present. The twentieth-century Russian-Ukrainian geochemist Vladimir Ivanovich Vernadsky, for instance, echoed Cavendish when he described human beings as "walking, talking minerals."[14] While I recognize the rhetorical and conceptual overlap between the distinct senses in which Cavendish and Vernadsky understood human minerality or mineral humanity, I also suggest that every such articulation of anthropogenesis reflects the historically specific epistemological and sociopolitical orders that it constitutes. Human life meant something different for Cavendish than it meant for Vernadsky or than it means for anyone alive today.

What is Our Life?

"What is our life?" Raleigh asked in his poem "On the Life of Man" (1612). It is "a play of passion," he answered, adding that in "[o]ur mothers wombes...we are drest for this short Comedy," which we perform on "earth the stage" for "the spectator" in heaven, and that the "graues that hide vs from the searching Sun/Are like drawne curtaynes when the play is done."[15] Raleigh's answer only prolifer-

---

1666), 45-46.

[14] Russian scientist Vladimir Ivanovich Vernadsky, quoted in Lynn Marguilis and Dorion Sagan, *What Is Life?* (Berkeley: University of California Press, 1995), 49.

[15] Walter Raleigh, "On the Life of Man," *The Poems of Sir Walter Raleigh*, ed. Agnes M. C. Latham (London: Routledge and Kegan Paul,

ates more questions. Whose life is the antecedent of the possessive plural "our"? If the subjects that are dressed in flesh-costumes are disembodied souls, why does Raleigh imagine them buried in graves like bodies, especially if "our" refers to his fellow Anglicans? (Chapter 3 aims to answer to this last question.)

Like the "one man [who] plays many parts," described by Shakespeare's Jacques, for whom "all the world's a stage" (*As You Like It*, 2.7.138-141), the subject of Raleigh's "our life" seems to retain a constant identity as it passes through its vegetative state in the womb, its performance on earth, and its privacy in the grave. This conflicts with Duke Vincentio's account of a life that is not "[it]self" but rather pluralized into "a thousand grains...of dust." Raleigh's constant subject also contradicts the Cartesian conception of life emergent in the seventeenth century, which rigorously differentiated the vegetative life of plants (and indeed of human fetuses) from the rational, ensouled life that is capable of performing itself.[16]

The polymathic physician Thomas Browne, whose

1951), 51-52.

[16] See Garrett A. Sullivan Jr., *Sleep, Romance and Human Embodiment: Vitality from Spenser to Milton* (New York: Cambridge University Press, 2012), 23. "What has been neglected in literary and cultural studies... is Descartes' profound transformation of the relation of the human to other forms of life—a transformation that is a conceptual precondition for Descartes' privileging of the cogito. Without banishing the vegetable and sensitive souls, Descartes could not have located the human being in thought alone."

work infuses the chapters that follow, remarked that "we enjoy a being and life in three distinct worlds"—first, in our mother's wombs; second, in the "scene of the world, [where] we rise up and become another creature, performing the reasonable actions of man," and finally, in "the last world," where, free of "this slough of flesh," we live the disembodied eternal afterlife of the soul.[17] Obscured by the seemingly universal inclusivity of Raleigh's "our" and Browne's "we" are the multitude of lives and lifeforms that were excluded from full participation in English life, including our twenty-first century lives, then still unbegotten and unborn. On the one hand, their inclusion of the vegetative life within English wombs belied the hegemonic ideology that privileged "reasonable" lives over the sub-human lives belonging to plants, animals, and (in)animate things, as well as to pre-rational and irrational humans.

On the other hand, that Browne and Raleigh included and identified with life in the womb attests to Foucault's thesis that the seventeenth century witnessed "a progressive generalization and redefinition of the concept of vegetative life," a redefinition that, among other consequences, enabled "the modern State…to include the care of the population's life as one of its essential tasks, thus transforming its politics into biopolitics."[18] I flesh out and anatomize this provisional critical skeleton through close

---

[17] Thomas Browne, *Religio Medici and Christian Morals*, ed. Geoffrey Keynes (London and New York: T. Nelson, 1940), 67.

[18] Agamben paraphrasing Foucault, *The Open: Man and Animal*, 15.

readings of primary seventeenth-century sources that undertake anthropogenic decisions about which lives are allowed to bear what Duke Vincentio calls "the name of life."

If the subjects that possessed Raleigh's "our life" were plural, then, was the "life" (not "lives") they collectively possessed singular? As Jonathan Gil Harris has observed,

> Writers in the Middle ages and the Renaissance tend not to speak of 'life' but of 'lives.' This plural form generally appeals to those of us who wish to resist making 'life' a universal abstract exchange value. But what exactly do we pluralize when we speak of 'lives' rather than 'life'—singular living entities, individual conceptions of 'life,' otherwise homogenous taxonomic categories?[19]

The deceptive inclusivity of the "life" described by Raleigh and Browne substantiates Harris' concern about "life" in its singular form. Melinda Cooper has expressed similar concern that "in the absence of any substantive critique of political economy, any philosophy of *life as such* runs the risk of celebrating *life as it is*. And the danger is only exacerbated in a context such as ours, where capitalist relations have so intensively invested in the realm of bio-

---

[19] Jonathan Gil Harris, "Twenty Questions," in *Animal, Vegetable, Mineral: Ethics and Objects*, ed. Jeffrey Jerome Cohen (Washington, D.C.: Oliphaunt Books, 2012), 289-295; 289.

logical reproduction."[20] Another pitfall of discussing "life" in the singular is the false sense that the meaning of "life" is universally self-evident.

Agamben has observed that "[life] never gets defined as such" in Western culture—"And yet, this thing that remains indeterminate gets articulated and divided time and again through a series of caesurae and oppositions that invest it with a decisive strategic function in domains as apparently distant as philosophy, theology, politics, and—only later—medicine and biology."[21] This book pursues early modern "life" at the intersection of all these domains, not to define it precisely but to reveal the competing values arising from a proliferation of definitions; not to show that the meaning of "life" was philosophical and theological before it became secularized, politicized, and scientificized, but to analyze its subtle interdiscursivity, to show that early modern meanings of "life" were always already political, and that its current meanings, many of which are shaped by seventeenth-century ideas, are still philosophical and theological. This plural polyvalence can be lost when "life" is conceived as a singularity.

Synthesizing the theories of Michel Foucault and Carl Schmitt, Agamben has argued that sovereign power institutes political order by defining a particular, state-sanc-

---

[20] Melinda Cooper, *In Vivo: Life as Surplus: Biotechnology and Capitalism in the Neoliberal Era* (Seattle: University of Washington Press, 2011), 42.

[21] Agamben, *The Open: Man and Animal*, 13.

tioned form of human life that is distinct from other forms of "bare life" that are excluded from full citizenship but included in the political order as "the obscure background from which the life of the higher animals gets separated."[22] Aristotle's tripartite division of the soul into (1) vegetative life shared by humans, plants, and animals, (2) sensitive life common to humans and animals, and (3) rational life belonging to humans alone was one of many apparatuses that facilitated early modern anthropogenesis.[23]

I investigate how seventeenth-century re-definitions of human life instituted new cultural forms and worldviews, if not yet new sociopolitical orders. I examine a range of published acts of anthropogenesis that reinforced or challenged the authorized orthodoxies regarding which lives are morally and politically relevant, which are endowed with rights, which are to be preserved and prolonged, and which cannot be killed with impunity.[24]

---

[22] Ibid., 14. See also Daniel Juan Gil, *Shakespeare's Anti-politics: Sovereign Power and the Life of the Flesh* (New York: Palgrave Macmillan, 2013), 10.

[23] See Jeffrey Nealon, *Plant Theory: Biopower and Vegetable Life* (Stanford: Stanford University Press, 2016), 36-37.

[24] See Agamben, *Homo Sacer: Sovereign Power and Bare Life*, trans. Daniel Heller-Roazen (Stanford: Stanford University Press, 1998), 139. "It is as if every valorization and every 'politicization' of life (which, after all, is implicit in the sovereignty of the individual over his own existence) necessarily implies a new decision concerning the threshold beyond which life ceases to be politically relevant, becomes only 'sacred life,' and can as such be eliminated without punishment. Every society sets this limit; every society—even the most modern— decides who its 'sacred men' will be."

The always ongoing and variable seventeenth-century acts of anthropogenesis foreground the proliferation of lifeforms that were either included or excluded from English culture, society, and politics. I therefore try to reason with the meanings of early modern English life without overlooking the countless lives that pluralized and were unified by it, including the lives of Christians and pagans, Protestants and Catholics, natives and settlers, the old and the young, flora and fauna, humans and minerals.

Gil Anidjar has observed that "the dominant understanding of life since the eighteenth century at least, has conceded [that life is biological]. We have relinquished and abandoned ourselves to biology. Life is now first of all biological," which means not only that life has increasingly come under the control of scientists, physicians, and other biotechnicians, but also that "life" has been evacuated of its "history" and "meaning."[25] The elision of life's historical meaning is everywhere on display in our culture—for example, in the ubiquitous items of clothing and accessories manufactured by the $100 million lifestyle brand, The Life is Good Company, each bearing the mantric trademark Life is Good.® The brand's irreproachable optimism and celebration of life obfuscate critical questions from the history of the term's meaning: whose life is good? What kinds of life are good, and are some lifeforms better than others? Is life inherently and always good, and if not,

---

[25] Gil Anidjar, "The Meaning of Life," *Critical Inquiry*, vol. 37, no. 4 (Summer 2011): 697-723; 709.

what distinguishes life that is good from life that is not (or no longer) good?

"The sanctity of life is not the universal it now seems," according to Anidjar, but rather the result of a "sacralization, which…divided the being of a more expansive, and still discernable realm…and extended this division down to that which confronts us today under the name life."

> [This sacralization] fashioned and figured
> life, it condensed and reduced it into a highly
> determined realm, instituting and institutionalizing
> a particular division of being that was to become
> life itself, the attributes of which would come
> to be called and identified as biological. Always
> political, this sacralization constitutes one thread
> or moment in a biotheological surge that has
> not only made this or that life sacred but has
> identified life (and its others), lifted and isolated it,
> elevated it above all.[26]

Paradoxically, then, the modern Western view of the sanctity of life is concomitant with the reduction of the meaning of "life" to the sphere of biology. The "life" that has been elevated as the *summum bonum*, as a signifier that can mean virtually anything and everything, in fact represents only a portion of life's historical meaning. Jones has observed that "we seem now to have fully demystified life, though [as late as the early modern period] it was held to

---

[26] Ibid., 698.

be not only a marvelous but wholly mysterious thing."[27] Notwithstanding its demystification, "Life remains today a term of celebration and critique; it provides a perspective and is the basis of all perspective."[28] Robert Mitchell has likewise remarked "in the work of many in the sciences and the humanities…a sense of life as *provocation*… life [not as] a self-evident fact that can be taken for granted but rather a source of perplexity that demands new modes of conceptual and practical experimentation."[29] While this book works to demystify "life" by critically historicizing it, I show throughout how "life" tends to elude efforts to define, instrumentalize, or otherwise control it. I thus preserve "life" as a border concept that provokes and inspires without ever fully being grasped. What "life" provokes in seventeenth-century texts and in their present-day readers are often surprising sociopolitical alliances and ideological positions.

A brief recapitulation of some of the alliances that have formed recently under the banner of "life" will be useful here, not only to suggest historical continuities with the seventeenth century, but also to disclose potential blind spots and biases of our vantage point. The national organization and movement known as Black Lives Matter was created following the 2012 acquittal of the vigilante

---

[27] Jones, *The Racial Discourses of Life Philosophy*, 2.

[28] Ibid., 5.

[29] Robert Mitchell, *Experimental Life: Vitalism in Romantic Science and Literature* (Baltimore: Johns Hopkins University Press, 2013), 2.

George Zimmerman, who killed seventeen-year-old Trayvon Martin. Martin's death revived widespread public scrutiny of extrajudicial killings of Black people by the police and others. The movement aims to resist the dehumanization of Black lives that has stripped them of basic rights, including the right to life and the right not to be killed with impunity.

The slogan "All Lives Matter" has since emerged in backlash, claiming that Black Lives Matter is itself racist and that it overlooks the value of all human lives. "All Lives Matter" has in turn been criticized for its universalistic whitewashing of the injustices committed against Black lives in particular. Supporters of the "Blue Lives Matter" slogan, vociferating the worth of the lives of police officers, have likewise fueled national controversy with their false equivalence between, on the one hand, those who willingly risk their lives by donning a blue uniform, and on the other hand, those whose lives are made vulnerable by the color of their skin. That the question of whether Black lives matter or all lives matter became a litmus test for candidates during the 2015-2016 presidential campaign epitomizes the politicization of biological life that is central to our culture.

In the first episode of the HBO political talk show *Real Time* following the election of Donald Trump, the comedian and political commentator Bill Maher announced that

it is "a bad time to be an animal or a plant."[30] He was referring specifically to Trump's plan to gut the Environmental
Protection Agency. Having just cited Colorado's legaliza-
tion of assisted suicide and imagining the shock of someone waking up from two years in a coma to discover the
state of our country, however, Maher was also subtly allud-
ing to the vegetative and sensitive life of human beings.
His remarks exhibit an ecological awareness that situates
human life among all the other lifeforms with which it
coexists in mutual interdependence, an awareness that
has been dulled by the post-Cartesian worldview and the
"culture of life," which conceive humans as independent
from the natural environment. I work to recover from
seventeenth-century texts a conceptual lexicon for what I
think is Maher's implicit point: that the way we politicize
the biological life of human beings is inseparable from the
way we politicize nonhuman lives, such that as long as it is
"a bad time to be an animal or a plant," it cannot be a good
time to be human.

"Life is winning again in America," Vice President Mike
Pence declared in his speech at the 44th annual "March for
Life" in Washington, D.C., on January, 27, 2017. "That is
evident in the election of pro-life majorities in the congress of the United States of America," Pence continued,
"but it is no more evident in any way than in the historic
election of a president who stands for a stronger America,

---

[30] "Real Time With Bill Maher," HBO, Season 14, Episode 38,
November 11, 2016.

a more prosperous America, and a president who I proudly say stands for the right to life, President Donald Trump." Pence looked back 240 years to the truths declared self-evident by the American founders, "that we are, all of us, endowed by our creator with certain unalienable rights, and that among these are life." Then he looked forward to his current task: "To heal our land and restore a culture of life we must continue to be a movement that embraces all, cares for all, and shows respect for the dignity and worth of every person….Be assured, be assured, along with you we will not grow weary, we will not rest, until we restore a culture of life in America for ourselves and our posterity."[31]

Browne and Raleigh have prepared us to be suspicious of such seemingly universal inclusivity that tacitly devalues, and excludes from the right to life, those lifeforms that are not considered "persons," not "endowed by our creator," or simply not American. In what follows, I excavate the seventeenth-century roots of the "culture of life" to which Pence aspires, a culture described by Jane Bennett as "a cluster of theological beliefs linked to a set of public policies."[32] For instance, the beliefs that "life is radically different from matter" and that human life is exceptional from all other lifeforms have led to legislation to artificially prolong the lives of patients in a Persistent Vegeta-

---

[31] "Vice President Mike Pence [sic] remarks at March for Life," C-SPAN. https://www.youtube.com/watch?v=fJB5W1-E6B0.

[32] Jane Bennett, *Vibrant Matter: a political ecology of things* (Durham and London: Duke University Press, 2010), 86.

tive State (PVS), to restrict access to abortion, and to block funding for stem cell research.[33]

To defend what he calls the Judeo-Christian sanctity of life ethic, Richard Weikart has attributed recent criticism of the "culture of life" to secularization, materialism, and specifically, to an intellectual class fashioned by the likes of Nietzsche and Darwin. Remarkably, Weikart is troubled that an "attack on anthropocentrism is becoming mainstream in our 'culture of death.'"[34] He agrees with his opponents, then, that the way humans relate to other lifeforms is correlated with an orientation toward life and death. But he departs from thinkers such as Bennett, whose ecocritical materialism recognizes "vitality distributed along a continuum of ontological types" in order to unsettle the notion "that humans are special in the sense of existing, at least in part, outside of the order of material nature."[35] Whereas Weikart eschews a debasement of human life that he thinks would make it no better and no less mortal than the lives of plants and animals, Bennett has argued that such debasement is already enacted by hierarchical sociopolitical structures circumscribing life, and she therefore welcomes not the debasement of human life but the elevation of nonhuman lives.

Close reading texts that captured versions of such polem-

---

[33] Ibid.

[34] Richard Weikart, *The Death of Humanity and the Case for Life* (Washington, DC: Regnery Faith, 2016), 4.

[35] Bennett, *Vibrant Matter*, 37.

ics over life as they unfolded in seventeenth-century England affords sharper and broader perspective on discourses surrounding "our life" today. However, to approach the early modern history of life and death requires deciding whether and how to regard the past as alive or dead. It goes without saying that seventeenth-century authors are long dead, but this assumption is problematic. To presuppose that one reads the work of the dead from the perspective of the living is to elide the unity of life and death that was intrinsic to the early modern worldview; to blind oneself to the ongoing life of the dead, which shapes and disrupts our own lives; and it is to presume that the textual media through which past lives have reached the present are themselves dead.

For John Milton, by contrast, "books are not absolutely dead things, but do contain a potency of life in them to be as active as that soul was whose progeny they are; nay, they do preserve as in a vial the purest efficacy and extraction of that living intellect that bred them."[36] This is more than mere metaphor considering the real sense in which early modern texts have a life that not only survived their authors but will also survive their twenty-first-century readers. Rather than side absolutely with the living while seeing past lives as unambiguously dead, therefore, it is more accurate and more generative to identify the ways in which the living are deprived of "life" and the ways in which the dead remain alive.

---

[36] John Milton, *Areopagitica*, in *Complete Poems and Major Prose*, ed. Merritt Y. Hughes (New York: Macmillan, 1957), 716-749; 720.

A Method for Making the Dead to Live

Early Modern Matters of Life and Death works toward an historical ethics and ethical historicism. Beyond this introduction, I do not explicitly remark the often glaring analogues between current debates in our culture and seventeenth-century discussions of life; even so, the analysis of early modern texts demands a self-reflective look at the (dis)continuities between *our* life and the life of the past. Stephen Greenblatt began *Shakespearean Negotiations* (1988) with "the desire to speak with the dead," which he called "a familiar, if unvoiced, motive in literary studies," the profession of "literature professors [i.e.,] salaried, middle-class shamans." Greenblatt admitted to hearing only himself during such conversations, "but my own voice was the voice of the dead, for the dead had contrived to leave textual traces of themselves [that] make themselves heard in the voices of the living."[37]

Jonathan Gil Harris has critiqued new historicism for precisely such "monologic" and "monotemporal" notions of life that regard the past as dead. "When we see the past as a singular time whose life is no more," Harris has suggested, "we might feel obliged to honor it. But this honoring is simultaneously a distancing designed to keep life

---

[37] Stephen Greenblatt, *Shakespearean Negotiations*, 1; Cf. Steven Shapin, *The Scientific Revolution* (Chicago and London: The University of Chicago Press, 1996), 14. "There is perhaps no more hackneyed historical intention than the wish to 'make history come alive,' yet it is something very like that desire that animates this book."

and death separate. Thus, in the case of literary history, we quarantine the past in hermetically concealed necropoles called periods whose organizing principle is context."[38] The very subject matter of my project neutralizes the risk of falling into a "monologic" and "monotemporal" view of life; and while I restrict my scope to roughly six decades in seventeenth-century England, I correct for the limitations of context by interweaving language and ideas sourced from a vast and diverse array of texts. In this I am indebted to the work of historian Keith Thomas, who has characterized his own method as a collaging of strategically collected and carefully arranged quotations.

> In this book [*The Ends of Life* (2009)] I have cited contemporaries so liberally that at times my text comes close to being a collage of quotations. *Collector, non auctor, ego sum* ('I am the collector, not the author'). I have some sympathy with the German cultural critic Walter Benjamin (1892-1940), whose ideal was a work consisting entirely of quotations, put together so skillfully that it could dispense with any accompanying text.[39]

One pitfall of this method is a dearth of the immediate contexts of the selected excerpts, that is, the texts

---

[38] Jonathan Gil Harris, "Four Exoskeletons and No Funeral," *New Literary History* 42 (2011): 615-639; 617-18.

[39] Keith Thomas, *The Ends of Life: Roads to Fulfilment in Early Modern England* (Oxford and New York: Oxford University Press, 2009), 5.

in which they were embedded. Among the payoffs are a broader view of the period's cultural landscape and a greater adherence to the modes by which early moderns themselves produced and digested texts. "The Renaissance was fundamentally a notebook culture," Brian Vickers has noted, "its greatest literary productions displaying what has been called a *stile a mosaico.* Many passages in Montaigne or Rabelais, Bacon or Burton, Chapman or Webster, are tissues of quotations held together by a thin thread of argument."[40] The following chapters are populated with a plurality of early modern voices, some in disagreement, some echoing others with nuanced inflection, and I try without editorializing to afford them room to resound.

I emulate both Benjamin's quotation-collaging and his principle of selection. "To articulate the past historically does not mean to recognize it 'the way it really was' (Ranke)," he wrote. "It means to seize hold of a memory as it flashes up at a moment of danger [that] affects both the content of the tradition and its receivers."[41] Specifically, the danger Benjamin saw was the instrumentalization of history and its present-day readers as "tool[s] of the ruling classes."[42] The past is threatened by our inabil-

---

[40] Brian Vickers, introduction to *Francis Bacon: The Major Works*, ed. Brian Vickers (Oxford and New York: Oxford University Press, 2002), xlii.

[41] Walter Benjamin, "Theses on the Philosophy of History," in *Illuminations: Essays and Reflections*, ed. Hannah Arendt (New York: Schocken Books, 1968), 253-264; 255.

[42] Ibid.

ity to perceive its relevance, he believed, for "every image of the past that is not recognized by the present as one of its own concerns threatens to disappear irretrievably."[43] Those living in the present are threatened, in Benjamin's view, when hegemony misappropriates tradition for political ends. I ward off this threat to the past by unearthing early modern ideas whose relevance to "our life," often overlooked, is undeniable once it is seen. Present relevance is not my criterion for selecting evidence, however I call attention to texts that have caught my attention as proleptic responses to "danger" in the present.

I navigate a middle way by which "to speak with the dead," somewhere between the extreme solipsism of hearing only my own voice and the extreme gregariousness of quotation-collaging that would bury the argument under a cacophony of unchecked voices. In the dedicatory epistle to *Urn Burial* (1658), Thomas Browne articulated a model for relating to the "dead" past that I take as a point of departure for studying early modern lives. Addressing his patron Thomas Le Gros, the gentleman from whose land was unearthed the ancient cache of eponymous urns, Browne expressed his wish that the urns "might have the effect of Theatrical vessels...to resound the acclamations and honour due unto" Le Gros. He observed, however, that they "have no joyful voices; silently expressing old mortality, the ruins of forgotten times, and can only speak

---

[43] Ibid.

with life" when living interlocutors speak on their behalf.[44] The risk of thus reducing historical dialogue between the living and the dead to a unilateral biocentric monologue is less pronounced for literary historians who have the advantage of conversing with artefacts inscribed with their own voices, but this only makes it more incumbent on readers of old texts to clarify the terms of the conversation.

Browne supposed that "none here can pretend relation" to the urns, meaning that neither Le Gros nor any living English person can credibly claim to have descended from those whose remains they contain, and more generally, that the living cannot claim to relate to the dead. The living "can only behold the Reliques of those persons, who in their life giving the Law unto their predecessors, after long obscurity, now lye at their mercies." By foregrounding the dominance of the living over the "obscurity" of the dead, deigning to "mercifully preserve their bones, and pisse not upon their ashes," Browne effectively obscured the hierarchical relationship between himself and Le Gros.

While I reject his biocentric, monologic, and mono-temporal view of the past as dead, I follow Browne's lead in remembering the dead without honoring them. He appreciated that the dead did not "so desperately...place their reliques as to lie beyond discovery, and in no way to be seen again; which happy contrivance hath made com-

---

[44] Thomas Browne, *Hydriotaphia, Urn Burial, in The Works of Sir Thomas Browne*, vol. 4., ed. Geoffrey Keynes (New York: William Edwin Rudge, 1929), 5.

munication with our forefathers, and left unto our view some parts, which they never beheld themselves."[45] Rather than note that parts of the past remain inaccessible to the those who did not live through it, Browne underscored his access to "some parts" of the dead, presumably their bones, which were inaccessible to them while they lived. This serves as an emblem of my method for unearthing the textual remains of seventeenth-century English lives. What I can see that they could not is not their bones, but how their words resonate for posterity four centuries hence; where their utterances are situated in a long history and within a vast context of contemporary utterances; and which prejudices, unspoken assumptions, and ideologies are implicit in their words.

I do not suggest that early modern authors meant something other than what they wrote, as Heidegger suggested of everything Nietzsche wrote, that it was "unwittingly paraliptical."[46] But I suggest that just as the historical embeddedness of the living creates blind spots that prevent full access to the present (which is too proximate) and to the past (which is too distant), so too the specific historicity of early modern lives precluded them from a comprehensive view of their own meanings. This is espe-

---

[45] Ibid.

[46] David Wittenberg, paraphrasing Heidegger, *Philosophy, Revision, Critique: Reading Practices in Heidegger, Nietzsche, and Emerson* (Stanford: Stanford University Press, 2001), 67.

cially clear in a recurring structure that I trace across all four chapters, where authors entertained heterodox ideas before promptly disavowing them.

Such ideological "fort und da" was played out with ideas that were so pressing that writers could not leave them unsaid, but so dangerous that they could not endorse them. I show that early moderns disavowed ideas such as autochthony, life-prolongation, mortalism, and vitalism with excessive affect, often with disgust, fear, and repugnance. This partly reflects an overcompensation in resisting the lure of forbidden ideas. It also indicates a pragmatic decision not to identify as, for example, autochthonous or mortalist, because (as Chapter 1 and Chapter 3 show) such identification made one liable to be deemed irrational, to be dehumanized, and even to be killed with impunity. For our purposes, the affective rejection of certain ideas exposes "some parts" of early modern English life that those who lived through it either could not or would not see.

Decomposition of Chapters

Early Modern Matters of Life and Death proceeds thematically across texts published between the 1590s and the 1650s. Chapter 1—"Born of the Earth"—unearths the idea that certain lives spring from the earth, which ancient Athenians proudly claimed to distinguish themselves from immigrants. Early modern English colonial ideologues revised autochthony to dehumanize, uproot, and justify the extermination of native populations in Ireland and the Americas. Jeffrey Jerome Cohen has suggested that "[t] he life of the past emerges in stories thought surpassed, rising from stone and from earth."[47] This chapter details how early modern Anglicans relegated autochthonous lives (lives emerging from stone and earth) as part of the surpassed past, while at the same time they characterized, often by innuendo, certain still-living populations as autochthonous. Linking indigenous populations to the earth called into question their humanity, while consigning them to the "dead" past threatened their status as living people with a right to life.

Despite the ubiquity of autochthony today in Francophone Africa, Belgium, the Netherlands, and elsewhere, anthropologist Peter Geschiere has observed that to modern Anglophones the term "may appear somewhat exotic and even quaint."[48] Early modern Anglicans also regarded autochthony as exotic and quaint, but they persistently invoked it to discredit it anew, betraying their anxious fascination with this relic of the past. When Browne and others called autochthony "repugnant," they did so not only to slander foreign peoples and to bolster English

---

[47] Jeffrey Jerome Cohen, *Stone: An Ecology of the Inhuman* (Minneapolis and London: University of Minnesota Press, 2015), 201.

[48] Peter Geschiere, *The Perils of Belonging: Autochthony, Citizenship, and Exclusion in Africa and Europe* (Chicago and London: University of Chicago Press, 2009), 2.

territorial sovereignty abroad, but also to inoculate themselves against the danger of becoming or being identified as autochthonous.

Historians including Christopher Pelling and Marcel Detienne have traced the resurgence of autochthony in modern contexts, leaping from antiquity to the late nineteenth century and thus eliding the concept's early modern metamorphosis.[49] The critical tendency to overlook both early modern and Anglophone manifestations of autochthony is a significant oversight, I argue, because the concept was transformed in early modern England by its encounter with Christian and colonialist ideologies. Modern iterations do not neatly derive from or align with early modern autochthony, but the latter may shed light on present-day African discourses of autochthony, which according to Geschiere, generally "refer to a colonial model rather than to a precolonial one."[50] While autochthony was neither central nor explicitly political in early modern England, it constitutes the "central preoccupation" of modern African politicians endeavoring to determine which people belong to which territories. "Everything boils down to the perverse structure of autochthony," political scientist

---

[49] Christopher Pelling, "Bringing Autochthony Up-to-Date: Herodotus and Thucydides," *The Classical World*, vol. 102, no. 4 (Summer 2009): 471-483; See also Marcel Detienne, "The Metamorphoses of Autochthony in the Days of National Identity," in *Arion: A Journal of the Humanities and the Classics*, trans. Janet Lloyd, Third Series, vol. 16, no. 1 (Spring-Summer 2008): 85-96.
[50] Peter Geschiere, *The Perils of Belonging*, 22.

Achille Mbembe has warned. "The prose of autochthony seems to exhaust the possibilities for the constitution of the subject...a xenophobic way of thinking, negative and circular."[51] As one modern Cameroonian has put it, "You can go to bed as an autochthon and wake up to find that you have become an allogene."[52] Such fear of becoming other, already evident in the early modern "repugnance" toward autochthony, has today arrived closer to home amidst a resurgence of nationalism and heated polemic over the legality of the lives of immigrants and refugees.

Chapter 2—"We Scarce Live Long Enough To Try: Francis Bacon's New Science of Life-Prolongation"— charts an unprecedented medicalization of life in Bacon's *The Historie of Life and Death* (1638). Where autochthony provided ideological support for the exercise of English sovereignty over the lives of non-English populations abroad, Bacon's new science facilitated the exercise of English sovereignty over English lives on English soil.

In stark contrast to the ethos of The Life is Good Company, orthodox Anglicans did not characterize life as inherently good; and in contrast to the paradigm of life-

---

[51] See Achille Mbembe, "A Propos des Écritures Africaines de Soi," *Politique Africaine* (Editions Karthala, 2000), 16-43; quoted in Geschiere, *The Perils of Belonging*, 22.

[52] Peter Geschiere and Stephen Jackson, "Autochthony and the Crisis of Citizenship: Democratization, Decentralization, and the Politics of Belonging," *African Studies Review*, vol. 49, no. 2 (September 2006): 1-8; 6.

prolongation in modern Western medicine,[53] which for better or worse owes a debt to Bacon, Anglicans routinely dismissed the value of prolonged life. Orthodox traditions convinced Bacon's contemporaries that the shortness of human life was an inevitable and irreversible consequence of the Fall, that longevity is pre-determined by Providence, and that a short life well lived is better than a long but unhappy life. Bacon disrupted this worldview as he revised orthodox sources to argue that life is good, that longer life is better, and that it is possible to prolong quality life into advanced and even extreme old age.

This paradigm shift reflects the emergent "culture of life" in seventeenth-century England that it also enacted—a culture where a generalized orientation toward the good of (long) life fostered a kind of *E pluribus unum*, unifying many individual lives into one national life; where life became both a personal property and a national resource, its preservation an act of self-sovereignty as well as a means of state power.[54] *The History of Life and Death* aligns

---

[53] See Norelle Lickiss, "On Facing Human Suffering," in *Perspectives on Human Suffering*, ed. Jeff Malpas and Norelle Lickiss (London: Springer, 2012), 245-260; 250. She argues that twenty-first-century medicine generally prioritizes life extension at the expense of relieving human suffering, "lest the slightest possibility for temporary prolongation of life be lost, and death not be delayed."
[54] See Maria Muhle, "A Genealogy of Biopolitics," in *The Government of Life: Foucault, Biopolitics, and Neoliberalism*, ed. Vanessa Lemm and Miguel Vatter (New York: Fordham University Press, 2014), 80. "While [one] interpretation awards life with an intrinsic power that resists biopower, such as Antonio Negri and Michael Hardt propose,

with Foucauldian biopower in its advocacy of disciplinary practices that prolong embodied life.[55]

While modes of evaluating life were progressively quantified, medicalized, and politicized in seventeenth-century England, they continued to be shaped by the theological and ethical traditions from which they emerged. This matters today amidst growing public interest in and funding for life-prolonging initiatives at major universities, The Mayo Clinic, the Buck Institute, and biotech firms such as Google's California Life Company. Notwithstanding advances of modern science that have met and surpassed Bacon's expectations for life-prolongation—including refrigeration and the ability to sustain life through artificial nourishment—the state of the art has progressed modestly. According to Luigi Ferrucci, director of the Balti-

---

[the interpretation] proposed by Giorgio Agamben, radicalizes the thanato-political aspect in the notion of 'bare life'…,Foucault operates with a notion of life that he does not determine: life is a correlate of the techniques and strategies of power and knowledge. It lacks any ontological status and is itself 'produced' by the power-knowledge constellation."

[55] See Michel Foucault, "Right of Death and Power over Life," in *The Foucault Reader*, ed. Paul Rainbow (New York: Vintage Books, 2010), 258-272; 261-262. Foucault has located the inauguration of biopolitics in the seventeenth century, when sovereignty became invested in bodies: on the one hand, in "the body as machine: its disciplining, the optimization of its capabilities, the extortion of its forces," and on the other hand, "the body…as the basis of the biological processes: propagation, births and mortality, the level of health, life expectancy and longevity, with all the conditions that can cause these to vary."

more Longitudinal Study of Aging that has been ongoing since 1958, "on some of the big questions, such as whether longevity is caused mainly by genes or mainly by lifestyle and environment, we just have no idea at all."[56] Still, many are hopeful, some even certain, as Bacon was four centuries ago, that a future of longer human life is imminent.

Chapter 3—"To Die, To Sleep: Soul-Sleeping Through the English Civil War"—asks what it meant to be mortalist, and more generally to be mortal, in early modern England.[57] I examine the resurgence of mortalism—the belief that the soul dies or "sleeps" with the body until Judgment Day—during the English Civil War, focusing on *Mans Mortalitie* (1643), a politicized theological and philosophical treatise published clandestinely by the Leveller Richard Overton. I identify Anglican motives for rejecting mortalism (and for endorsing what I call immortalism), motives which elucidate the structure of seventeenth-century English worldviews more generally. I then interrogate Overton's motives for defending mortalism, which include critiquing human exceptionalism and its concomitant sociopolitical hierarchies; shifting focus from reward

---

[56] Luigi Ferrucci, quoted in Gregg Easterbrook, "What Happens When We All Live to 100?" *The Atlantic*, October 2014, https://www.theatlantic.com/magazine/archive/2014/10/what-happens-when-we-all-live-to-100/379338/.

[57] Cf. Atul Gawande, *Being Mortal: Medicine and What Matters in the End* (New York: Henry Holt and Company, 2014); and Alfred G. Killilea, *The Politics of Being Mortal* (Lexington: University Press of Kentucky, 1998).

and punishment in the afterlife to ethics and justice in the present life; and convincing readers that they have only one life, which should make them less eager, for example, to forfeit it in battle at the sovereign's command or in religious conflicts with the expectation that the soul will reap the reward of the body's sacrifice.

Roughly three and a half centuries before Foucault characterized the soul as "the effect and instrument of a political anatomy [and] the prison of the body,"[58] Overton intuited that the orthodox displacement of life from the mortal body to the immortal soul enabled sovereign power to control, mobilize, imprison, or dispose of English bodies at will. The insights of *Man's Mortalitie* are urgent today. For instance, in the episode of "60 Minutes" aired on November 20, 2016, American journalist Steve Kroft interviewed Turkish President Recep Tayyip Erdoğan about the recent failed coup in Turkey. Kroft questioned Erdoğan's decision, upon hearing of the coup, to fly to the heart of the conflict in Istanbul where he had encouraged Turks loyal to him to flood the streets in the face of rebel tanks and aircraft. "Were you afraid for your life and the lives of your family members?" Kroft asked. Erdoğan's reply evinced a form of sovereignty analogous to that which Overton opposed: "Steve, in our faith there is a concept: we surrender ourselves to death. If you're the leader, you have to communicate the message of immortality to

---

[58] Michel Foucault, *Discipline and Punish: The Birth of the Prison*, trans. Alan Sheridan (New York: Vintage Books, 1995), 30.

your people; because I believe that if a leader hides behind a rock, then the people will hide behind a mountain."[59]

Under the rule of a parliamentary monarchy, while democracy was still a taboo, Overton already challenged immortalism as inimical to values that subsequently became foundational to modern democracy, including freedom of speech, a free press, religious tolerance, separation of church and state, and the right to life. Today, when life is not just politicized but constitutive of politics, when Americans are compelled to reevaluate and fight anew for democracy, *Man's Mortalitie* remains essential not only as an historical document but as a living protest against encroachments on the rights of individuals to embodied life and liberty.

Chapter 4—"She's Dead as Earth: Reviving Renaissance Vitalism in the Age of Biopower"—takes as its point of departure Lear's declaration that Cordelia is "dead as earth," which he immediately doubts, performing a series of critical tests to check her for vital signs. I argue that Lear's hesitation reflects a more general ambiguity, in the play and in early modern English culture at large, regarding the living, the dead, and the (in)animate. Criteria for distinguishing these categories were in flux during the seventeenth century, and Lear's critical tests suggest that such differentiation required a special kind of skill, authority,

---

[59] "60 Minutes," CBS, Season 49, Episode 9 ("Turkey, The Match of their Lives, Bruno Mars"), November 20, 2016. https://www.youtube.com/watch?v=NEtTh_WUacY.

or decision-making capacity. I read Lear's crisis of sovereignty as a conflict between, on the one hand, the power to decide who lives and who dies, and on the other hand, the technical expertise to discern or the authority to declare what is alive and what is not. Parsing the proliferation of lifeforms and meanings of "life" in *Lear* through its parallel discourses of vitalism and biopower, I argue that the play articulates "life" both as a property of subjects to be fostered or disallowed by the sovereign, and as a virtual property of things that eludes human control.

Like autochthony, long life, and mortalism, vitalism has continued to resurface in new contexts despite having been relegated to the dead past as early as the seventeenth century. As Bennett has noted, "Vitalism has repeatedly risen from the scientific critiques of it."[60] One reason for the revived interest in vitalism today is that its emphasis on "vital processes" provides a framework and vocabulary for describing the infusion of "information, knowledge, or 'mind' into social and natural entities, [which makes] them seem less inert, more process-like: bringing them alive."[61]

---

[60] Bennett, *Vibrant Matter*, 90.

[61] Mariam Fraser, Sarah Kember, and Celia Lury, "Inventive Life: Approaches to the New Vitalism," in *Theory, Culture, and Society*, ed. Mariam Fraser, Sarah Kember, and Celia Lury (London: SAGE Publications, 2006), i. See also Kevin Chang, "Alchemy as Studies of Life and Matter," Focus—Isis, 102: 2 (2011), 322-329; 329. "Today we are witnessing an inverse form of vitalism. Medicine again is chemistry, although science no longer assumes any spiritual causes and steers well clear of the soul. In the Renaissance the vital principle, as the first principle of all things, united chemistry and

Jones has pinpointed why vitalism—and by extension, why a play like *Lear*—matters today:

> We live in a biological age. The ecological crisis has heightened our sensibilities of the intrinsic value of the life of all species and encouraged the development of a biocentric ethics. From a different angle, the ability to generate synthetic acellular life and to prolong the life of a brain-dead human being presents us with new examples of bare life and again raises the question of just what life inescapably is. The question is not only a philosophical problem, as decisions about whether to prolong or terminate life depend on how we understand what life is and what expressions such as "good as dead" or "a life not worth living" should mean. The more successful the manipulation of life (and the more lifelike our artifacts), the greater are the scientific and expert doubts about our intuitive sense that the animate can be distinguished from the inanimate.[62]

---

medicine. Today it is the material compound that governs both sciences. Many would see this as the outcome of the materialization of nature by mechanists since the Scientific Revolution. Yet an idea held dear by Renaissance vitalists—that life unfolds according to a plan implanted in the inner seed of the fundamental unit of organic matter—is no longer myth, but confirmed science."

[62] Jones, *The Racial Discourses of Life Philosophy*, 1.

Thinking through the intersection where sovereign decisions between life and death meet "expert" decisions between the animate and the inanimate, my reading of *Lear* accommodates and qualifies recent work in New Materialism. Diane Coole and Samantha Frost have written that New Materialists seek "forms of vitalism that refuse" the traditional "opposition between mechanistic and vitalist understandings of (dead versus lively) matter." Instead, they undertake to "discern emergent, generative powers (or agentic capacities) even within inorganic matter, and they generally eschew the distinction between…animate and inanimate, at the ontological level."[63] New Materialists maintain that the criteria and authority for deciding and distinguishing between life and death are arbitrary and historically contingent. Coole and Frost have extrapolated from polemics around abortion and euthanasia, for example, that "medical, scientific, or religious accounts of the boundary between life and death are currently becoming further enmeshed with issues surrounding sovereignty because increasingly the state must legislate on matters that were formerly left to God or nature."[64]

---

[63] Diana Coole and Samantha Frost, "Introducing the New Materialisms," in *New Materialisms*, ed. Diana Coole and Samantha Frost (Duke University Press, 2010), 1-43; 9.

[64] Ibid., 23. See Rose, *The Politics of Life Itself*, 8. "As biopolitics becomes entangled with bioeconomics, as biocapital becomes open to ethical evaluation, and as ethopolitics becomes central to our way of life, new spaces are emerging for the politics of life in the twenty-first century."

To grasp sovereignty's increasing enmeshment with accounts of the boundary between life and death, we must return to the early modern origins of this entanglement.

Our lives depend on it.

Born of the Earth

Audiences have seen Prospero and Caliban as colonizer and colonized at least since Octave Mannoni penned *Psychologie de la colonization* (1950), later translated as *Prospero and Caliban: The Psychology of Colonization* (1956). A former French colonial official in Madagascar, Mannoni argued that economics alone cannot explain colonialism; that the typical worldviews of settlers and natives must be weighed.[65] For the last several decades, Prospero and Caliban have been made to represent not only colonizer and colonized, master and slave, but also human and the nonhuman.

Stephen Greenblatt has remarked that Shakespeare's play "utterly rejects the uniformitarian view of the human race...that would later triumph in the Enlightenment and prevail in the West to this day."[66] The modern "uniformitarian" notion that beneath the diversity of cultural trappings human beings are all essentially the same, in other words, contradicts the early modern worldview presented in *The Tempest*, which regards some humans as so radically

---

[65] Trevor R. Griffiths has traced critical attention to the play's colonial theme back to the later part of the nineteenth century. See "'This Island's Mine': Caliban and Colonialism," *The Yearbook of English Studies* 13. Modern Humanities Research Association (1983): 159–80.
[66] Stephen Greenblatt, *Learning to Curse* (New York and London: Routledge, 1990), 26.

alien that their humanity is called into question. It is fitting that the adjective "uniformitarian" originated in the field of geology because *The Tempest* represents the differentiation and hierarchization of lifeforms through a vernacular of "earth." I argue that Prospero's earthly epithet for Caliban, read as part of a larger discourse of autochthony, sheds light on the mutually constitutive relationships between colonizer and colonized, between human and nonhuman, and between sovereignty and the life under its dominion.

An autochthon—etymologically derived from the Greek autos (self, own) and *chthōn* (earth, soil)—is, according to the *Oxford English Dictionary*, "a person indigenous to a particular country or region and traditionally supposed to have been born out of the earth, or to have descended from ancestors born in this way."[67] The concept of autochthony is similar to but not synonymous with indigeneity. Both distinguish natives from strangers and link peoples to their ancestral lands, but autochthony, particularly in its early modern English manifestations, goes further by staking claims and innuendoes about the difference between human life that is worth living and preserving, and nonhuman life that is unworthy of being lived or protected. For early modern English writers, that is, it was not clear if and how a person "supposed to have been born out of the earth" qualified as a person in the strict sense of being human, self-representing or represented by proxy,

---

[67] "Autochthon," n.1, *Oxford English Dictionary*, 2nd ed. 20 vols. (Oxford: Oxford University Press, 1989).

and legally recognized as having certain rights and duties.[68]

Autochthony entered the English lexicon as early as *The dictionary of syr Thomas Eliot* (1538). According to Eliot, "Autocthones [are] people which beganne in the countray that they doo inhabyte, whyche name was gyuen to them of Athenes."[69] Eliot's definition elides autochthony's chthonic element and relegates the concept to the historical past of ancient Athens. The definition remains open-ended in words such as "beganne," which may indicate either a kind of birthright citizenship for "autochthonous" individuals who form a collective with other "people" born in the same country, or alternatively, a proto-ethno-nationalism that defines its "people" by their shared ancestral beginnings. In either case, Eliot's indefinite definition exemplifies autochthony's potential to be widely construed, misunderstood, and instrumentalized.

In his translation of *Plutarch's Lives* (1579), Thomas North likewise omitted "earth" from the definition of autochthones: "The first inhabitants which occupied the contrie of Attica, the which were called Autocthones, as much to say, as borne of them selues."[70] Further overde-

---

[68] See Thomas Hobbes, *Leviathan*, ed. J.C.A. Gaskin (Oxford and New York: Oxford University Press, 2008), 106. "A Person, is he, whose words or actions are considered, either as his own, or as representing the words or actions of another man."

[69] Thomas Eliot, *The Dictionary of Syr Thomas Eliot Knyght* (London, 1538).

[70] Plutarch, *The Liues of the Noble Grecians and Romaines*, trans. Thomas North et al. (London, 1579), 2.

termining the newly-Englished term, North's suggestion that autochthones are self-begetting introduced the dehumanizing function of autochthony that became increasingly (albeit never fully) articulate by the time Prospero addressed Caliban as "earth." That neither Eliot nor North seem especially concerned to unpack or contain autochthony's complexity belies early moderns' intense preoccupation with the concept. While some identified with and as autochthones, others adamantly distanced themselves from the idea, including the poet Edmund Spenser, whose *The Faerie Queene* (1596) grounds an historical fiction of English origins on the triumph of colonists over autochthones; and the physician Thomas Browne, who half a century later deemed autochthony "repugnant" to accepted English worldviews.[71]

This chapter aims to determine what was at stake when early modern people claimed or denied autochthony for themselves and others. Ancient Athenians proudly identified as autochthonous to distinguish themselves from immigrants. Early modern English authors, by contrast, revised autochthony through the lenses of orthodox Anglican theology and colonialist ideology, which magnified its potential to dehumanize, uproot, and even justify the extermination of native populations in Ireland and the Americas. Anglicans endorsed an egalitarianism based on the mortality and earthliness common to all humans:

---

[71] Thomas Browne, *Pseudodoxia Epidemica*, ed. Robin Robbins (Oxford: Clarendon Press, 1981), 441.

according to *The Book of Common Prayer*, "we are mortal, formed of the earth, and unto earth shall we return."[72] However, early modern discourse around earth was hierarchizing as well as egalitarian, in part because, as Carolyn Merchant has remarked, Protestants such as Calvin believed that "God had authorized human dominion over earth."[73] English colonial ideologues, moreover, disavowed earthliness and mortality as essential and common human characteristics, instead projecting these qualities onto colonized peoples.

Such disavowal and projection are at play, for instance, where Spenser's Artegal argues that it is not "wrong" for an "earth…formed" population to die, since "when they die,/They turne to that, whereof they first were made."[74] I argue that the discourse of autochthony, as an ideological construct underpinning colonialism, served to isolate a form of vegetative, earthly life that was deemed less than human and accordingly excluded from the sociopolitical order sanctioned by English sovereignty.

Shipwrecked on the island in *The Tempest*, the aged lord Gonzalo formulates a parodic political theory of sovereignty that echoes almost verbatim a passage from

---

[72] Church of England, *The Book of Common Prayer 1979 Edition* (New York: Oxford University Press, 2008), 482.

[73] Carolyn Merchant, *The Death of Nature: Women, Ecology, and the Scientific Revolution* (New York: HarperCollins Publishers, 1980), 131.

[74] Edmund Spenser, *The Faerie Queene*, ed. A.C. Hamilton (Harlow: Longman Annotated English Poets, 2007), V.ii.39-40. All subsequent citations come from this edition.

Michel de Montaigne's essay "Of the Cannibals," which was translated by John Florio into English in 1603. Gonzalo, who twelve years earlier had helped Prospero and Miranda escape Milan as political refugees after Prospero's dukedom was usurped, imagines himself as the sovereign of a utopian "commonwealth" whose "perfection" would "excel the Golden Age" (2.1.167-168). There would be no commerce, no learning, no titles of social distinction, no wealth disparity, no agriculture or mining, and no work in Gonzalo's commonwealth: "all men idle, all; and women too—but innocent and pure; No sovereignty—(2.1.147-156). Sebastian (King Alonso's regicidal brother) and Antonio (Prospero's usurping brother) mock Gonzalo's naïve idealism, which seeks to govern "by contraries" (2.1.147), to institute order not by actively ruling but by allowing "nature [to] bring forth of it own kind all foison, all abundance, to feed my innocent people" (2.1.162-164).

Pagan origin myths associated autochthony with the same Golden Age imagined by Gonzalo. In Ovid's account, autochthony immediately precedes the Golden Age: "And thus the earth which late before had neyther shape nor hew,/Did take the noble shape of man, and was transformed new./Then sprang up first the golden age."[75] The Roman poet Lucretius likewise remarked of the Golden Age that "the human race was hardier then by far," because

---

[75] Ovid, *Metamorphosis. The Arthur Golding Translation 1567*, ed. John Frederick Nims (Philadelphia: Paul Dry Books, 2000), 1.101-104.

"the earth was hard that formed them."[76] The mocking asides of Sebastian and Antonio accentuate the unviability of Gonzalo's proposed form of (no) sovereignty, which they recognize as a relic from an idealized past that cannot be recovered or reinstituted even in the New World.

Sebastian and Antonio find the present age full of political machinations and socioeconomic hierarchies; they grasp that agriculture and mining are necessary because the earth does not yield a cornucopia of itself, that men and women can neither be "idle," because their labor is needed, nor can they be "innocent and pure," because, not born from the earth, they need to reproduce with each other. The discourse of autochthony does not enter *The Tempest* in the context of Gonzalo's Golden Age sovereignty, then, but rather, I suggest, in the context of an emergent kind of sovereignty that is interested in autochthony as a quasi-human form of earthly life.

This emergent sovereignty aligns with a nascent discourse of biopower that performs acts of anthropogenesis to define life that is human and worth preserving against life that is nonhuman and unworthy of living. If Gonzalo's belief that the island has "everything advantageous to life" (2.1.50) explains his naïve negation of sovereignty, then Antonio's caustic aside to Sebastian—"True; save means to live" (2.1.51)—indicates a new kind of sovereignty whose task is to administer the life of its people by

---

[76] Lucretius, *On the Nature of Things*, ed. and trans. Anthony M. Esolen (Baltimore: The Johns Hopkins University Press, 1995), 5.922-935.

converting what is potentially "advantageous to life" into actual "means to live."[77]

This new sovereignty is again on display when Prospero's shape-shifting servant Ariel presents a banquet with strange shapes and music to confuse the shipwrecked King Alonso and his attendants. After the banquet vanishes as quickly as it appeared, Sebastian surmises that it was "a living drollery" (3.3.21), or a puppet show with live actors. The question of whether or not the shapes were "living" is of a piece with the question of their humanity. Gonzalo wonders if people back in Naples would believe his account of the banquet, because "these are people of the island, who though they are of monstrous shape, yet note their manners are more gentle-kind than of our human generation" (3.3.30-33). As the Italians exercise their imagined sovereignty through rhetorical acts of anthropogenesis, Ariel—who does not identify as "human" (5.1.19)—reappears to chastise Alonso, Antonio, and Sebastian, calling them "most unfit to live" among other humans (3.3.58). Such decisions about fitness to live are constitutive of the sovereignty exercised as biopower. I argue that Caliban, loosely figured as an autochthon, represents a limiting case of this emergent sovereignty because his earthliness calls into question his status as a living, human being.

---

[77] See Hobbes, *Leviathan*, 163. "The nutrition of a commonwealth consisteth, in the plenty, and distribution of materials conducing to life: in concoction, or preparation; and (when concocted) in the conveyance of it, by convenient conduits, to the public use."

For Julia Reinhard Lupton, "Caliban's earthen core recalls the first fashioning of conscious life out of an inert yet infinitely malleable substance,"[78] which aligns Caliban with Adam, the first human according to the creation myth of Abrahamic religions, whose name derives from adamah or earth to signify his autochthonous origin. Caliban's Adamic earthliness presented a problem for seventeenth-century English people who believed that "there was… never any Autochthon, or man arising from the earth but Adam," in the words of Thomas Browne.[79] According to this worldview, which maintains that all living people can trace their lineage back to Adam, Caliban should not exist. His presence on Shakespeare's stage and in the early modern English imagination, however, gave form to anxieties underlying a period of increasing globalization and contact between distant cultures—namely, that there might exist more than one human race, contrary to ortho-dox readings of the book of Genesis, and that the cat-egory of the human might contain radical alterity within its apparent self-same identity.

That Prospero identifies Caliban alone as "earth" sug-gests that the epithet refers not to their common humanity derived from Adam, but rather to Caliban's particular form of life, which borders on the nonhuman even as, Pros-pero admits, it possesses "human shape" (1.2.286). Lupton

---

[78] Julia Reinhard Lupton, "Creature Caliban," *Shakespeare Quarterly* 51 (2000): 1-23; 8.

[79] Browne, *Pseudodoxia Epidemica*, 441.

therefore reads Caliban as emblematic of what Agamben has termed "'bare life,' pure vitality denuded of its symbolic significance and political capacity and then sequestered within the domain of civilization as its disavowed core."[80] Caliban's earthly body indeed resembles a form of life that is included in the sociopolitical order but excluded from any rights belonging to human subjects. On the one hand, as I discuss in detail below, Prospero effectively excludes Caliban from the human race by confining him in a rock and preventing him from reproducing or "peopling" the island with his descendants. On the other hand, Prospero includes Caliban as an indispensable source of labor on the island.

The inherent violence of this inclusion surfaces in Prospero's final acknowledgment of Caliban—"This thing of darkness I acknowledge mine" (5.1.278)—which is not Prospero's recognition of shared humanity but rather his assertion of slave ownership. For Caliban, this acknowledgment amounts to a reiteration of Prospero's power either to keep him alive or to kill him: "I shall be pinched to death" (5.1.279). The rhetorical reduction of Caliban to bare life, to a dehumanized vitality that can be fostered, allowed to die, or made to live, only functions insofar as Prospero isolates Caliban's earthliness as a special case of the earthliness common to other lifeforms including humans.

---

[80] Lupton, "Creature Caliban," 2.

Such a conceptual operation was problematic for early modern English people, who routinely acknowledged the earthliness of their own bodily, spiritual, and political lives. However, the earthliness of English identity, reinforced by national origin myths and orthodox theology, underwent a literal sea change beginning in the sixteenth century when, as Carl Schmitt has remarked, England "dared to take the step from a terrestrial to a maritime existence."[81] Prospero's power over Caliban's bare life hinges, moreover, on the representation of earthliness as a sign or condition of mortality. In *The Tempest*, however, as in early modern English culture generally, "earth" has a range of meanings that destabilize this condition of Prospero's sovereignty. Ariel does Prospero's "business in the veins o' th' earth"

---

[81] Carl Schmitt, *The Nomos of the Earth in the International Law of the Jus Publicum Europaeum* (New York: Telos Press Publishing, 2003), 49. "All pre-global orders were essentially terrestrial," Schmitt argues, but the "originally terrestrial world was altered in the Age of Discovery, when the earth first was encompassed and measured by the global consciousness of European peoples." The new world order resulting from this shift—which Schmitt calls the first "nomos of the earth," referring to the Eurocentric international community of political entities bound by common rules—gave sea powers the upper hand over land powers. Agamben (*Homo Sacer*, 175) revises Schmitt's account of the shifting balance of power among nation-states by attending not only to changing relations between land and political order, but also to "the inscription of bare life (the birth that thus becomes nation) within the two of them." Autochthones, supposedly born from the earth that they inhabit and figured in the early modern imagination as a form of bare life, may therefore be key to understanding seventeenth-century sovereignty and the birth of nations.

(1.2.256, emphasis added), for instance, which invokes a correspondence or analogy between the mineral veins of the (in)animate earth and the veins that circulate life through the human body. "O earth," Ferdinand exclaims, addressing the earth as a living subject to "bear witness" to his love for Miranda (3.1.67-68). To be sure, Antonio articulates the link between earth and mortality where, attempting to persuade Sebastian to kill the king, he describes the sleeping Alonso as "no better than the earth he lies upon if he were that which now he's like—that's dead" (2.1.277-278). Antonio's supposition that life is what distinguishes human bodies from the "dead" earth is vexed, however, by Caliban's earthly form of life.

Notwithstanding their ambivalence about the earth in general and autochthony in particular, early modern English people asserted their bond to the earth to reinforce their status as native-born citizens. As Christopher Hill has shown, the seventeenth century witnessed a resurgence of the myth of the Norman Yoke, which maintained that England was free and autonomous prior to the Norman Conquest of 1066.[82] During the conquest, Norman, Breton, and French soldiers led by William the Conqueror invaded, expropriated, and occupied English soil, yielding mass emigration of the native population and miscegenation between the remaining inhabitants, whose descendants were hence ambiguously both natives and strangers.

---

[82] Christopher Hill, *Intellectual Origins of the English Revolution* (Oxford and New York: Oxford University Press, 2002), 361.

During the English Civil War, the Leveller Gerrard Winstanley published a letter to Parliamentary general Thomas Fairfax, presenting King Charles as the successor of William the Conqueror because both "turned the English out of their birthrights," dispossessing the common people of "this Land of our Nativity."[83] Winstanley's grievances were, first, the privatization of land through enclosure, since "the whole land of England is to be a common treasury to everyone that is born in the land," and second, the law of primogeniture, which secured the inheritance of first-born sons while reducing younger siblings to second-class citizens, such that English commoners, forced "to live among their elder brothers," were no more free in England than they would be in foreign countries such as Turkey or France.[84]

Winstanley explicitly did not propose that England return to the laws and ways of life that existed before the eleventh century, but he insisted that because propertyless commoners no less than landed nobles "adventured their lives to recover England out of bondage," the oppressive legacy of the Norman Yoke should "be cut off with the Kings head" for the benefit of all English natives.[85] The

---

[83] Gerrard Winstanley, *A letter to the Lord Fairfax, and his Councell of War: with divers questions to the lawyers, and ministers: proving it an undeniable equity, that the common people ought to dig, plow, plant and dwell upon the commons, without hiring them, or paying rent to any. Delivered to the Generall and the chief officers on Saturday June 9* (London, 1649), 6-7.
[84] Ibid., 9.
[85] Ibid., 8.

myth of the Norman Yoke thus translated the division between natives and foreign invaders into local schisms between English rulers and their subjects, between English individuals and their own ethnic-national identity, and between English inhabitants and the very soil beneath their feet.

Despite over half a millennium of assimilation following the Norman Conquest, Alan Stewart has observed that early modern English culture "very clearly defined its native population against all 'strangers' or aliens from overseas, and individual English towns and cities defined their citizens against not only overseas strangers but 'foreigners' from other English provinces."[86] One might expect that claiming autochthony would be a way to secure a sense of belonging amidst what Eric Griffin has described as a "stranger crisis" in Elizabethan England,[87] where ambivalence toward immigrants, according to Laura Hunt Yungblutt, was exacerbated by a government that "simultaneously welcomed strangers and felt threatened" by them.[88]

---

[86] Alan Stewart, "'Euery Soyle to Mee Is Naturall': Figuring Denization in William Haughton's *English-men for My Money*," *Renaissance Drama*, New Series 35, Embodiment and Environment in Early Modern Drama and Performance, ed. Mary Floyd-Wilson and Garrett A. Sullivan Jr. (Evanston: Northwestern University Press, 2006), 55-81; 59-60.

[87] Eric Griffin, "Shakespeare, Marlowe, and the Stranger Crisis of the Early 1590s," in *Shakespeare and Immigration*, ed. Ruben Espinoza and David Ruiter (London and New York: Routledge, 2016), 13-36; 14.

[88] Laura Hunt Yungblutt, *Strangers Settled Here Amongst Us: Policies, Perceptions, and the Presence of Aliens in Elizabethan England* (London and

That no early modern English person (to my knowledge) claimed to be autochthonous, however, reflects the culture's suspicion that the term meant far more than that oneself and one's ancestors were born in a particular land.

Compounding their ambivalence toward autochthony, English people often identified as immigrants who, according to traditional origin stories, descended from Trojans that had come up from the Mediterranean to colonize England. In accordance with the theory of geohumoralism—Mary Floyd-Wilson's term for the classical and early modern belief that local and regional differences such as climate and geography directly shape inhabitants' humoral dispositions, and hence their bodies and minds—the myth of Mediterranean origins informed English ethnic and moral identity, such that many appropriated the ostensible qualities of their southern progenitors, including courage, confidence, dignity, and understanding.[89] However, belief in a Mediterranean genealogy waned in early modern England, partly a result of the Protestant Reformation, which severed ties with Rome and with the south more generally, compelling the English increasingly to identify with northerners.

This posed a problem within the geohumoral scheme, forcing the English to acknowledge their kinship to other northern peoples such as the Scythians, with whom they

---

New York: Routledge, 1996), 93-94.

[89] Mary Floyd-Wilson, *English Ethnicity and Race in Early Modern Drama* (Cambridge University Press, 2003), 3.

now "shared a climate, a genealogy, and a set of barbaric traits," including earthliness.[90] When in the sixteenth and seventeenth centuries the myth of Trojan genealogy "rapidly lost ground," according to Floyd-Wilson, English authors were compelled "to acknowledge the implications of their barbaric ancestry." Where the Trojan origin myth informed and hence appealed to aspects of English identity, "the Englishman's autochthonous roots constituted a more estranged relationship with the classical world and humanist studies."[91] I argue, additionally, that the "autochthonous roots" of English people led to other, more contemporary and less scholarly, forms of estrangement—with themselves, their nation, their race, their religion; with the dead buried under British soil, and with the living native inhabitants of colonized foreign lands. The discourse of autochthony, in other words, put English people between a rock and a hard place, serving at once to ground and to undermine their sense of identity.

---

[90] Ibid., 15.
[91] Ibid.

A Brief Long History of Autochthony

Throughout antiquity, autochthony was something of which to be proud. According to the ancient historian Thucydides, Athenians used to adorn their hair with golden grass-hoppers, either because grass-hoppers are musical creatures, "or else, because they would seeme to be Autochtones, boasting themselves not to be brought into that countrie from any other place, but that the place of their abode was also the place of their breeding, even as grasse-hoppers come of the earth."[92] Athenians invoked autochthony to distinguish the biological purity of their homogenous population against other city-states, which they saw as heterogeneously constituted by foreign immigrants. The tragedian Euripides thus had his character Erechtheus boast of Athenian superiority, because "its people do not come from elsewhere, but we are autochthonous. Other cities are founded as if by moves in a board-game, some hauled in from one place and others from another: whoever dwells in a city not his own is like a square peg in a round hole, a citizen in name only."[93]

Unlike early modern authors, ancients did not probe the truth of autochthony on theological and empirical grounds, but both cultures frequently construed it as a belief to be held as if it were true, a metaphor to be taken literally for political reasons. In Plato's *Republic*, for

---

[92] Franciscus Junius, *The Painting of the Ancients* (London, 1638), 161.

[93] Euripides, *Erechtheus* fr. 360 K., quoted in Geschiere, *Perils of Belonging*, 10.

instance, Socrates described autochthony as a "noble lie" or "opportune falsehood," because it foments a collective sense of belonging.[94] Rulers, soldiers, and citizens should therefore be persuaded, he suggested, that their upbringing and education, "their whole experience of it happening to them, was after all merely a dream, something they imagined, and that in reality they spent that time being formed and raised deep within the earth" until "the earth their mother released them, and now it is their duty" to defend "their mother or nurse—and to regard the rest of the citizens as their brothers, born from the earth.'"[95] Historian Nicole Loraux has characterized the idea that humans come from the earth as "ground zero of myth" in antiquity.[96] The notion was also commonplace and orthodox in early modern culture—the poet John Donne, to cite just one example, called man "the noblest part of the Earth"[97]—suggesting that this particular tenet of autochthony was not what vexed English authors.

To be sure, being born of the earth meant something quite different for early moderns than it meant for ancients,

---

[94] Plato, *The Republic*, in *The Collected Dialogues of Plato*, ed. Edith Hamilton and Huntington Cairns, trans. Paul Shorey (New York: Pantheon; Princeton: Bollingen, 1964), 658.

[95] Plato, *The Republic*, ed. G.R.F. Gerrari, trans. Tom Griffith (Cambridge University Press, 2000), 107-108; 414e.

[96] Nicole Loraux, *Born of the Earth: Myth and Politics in Athens*, trans. Selina Stewart (Ithaca and London: Cornell University Press, 2000), 1.

[97] John Donne, *Devotions Upon Emergent Occasions*, ed. Anthony Raspa (New York and Oxford: Oxford University Press, 1987), 11.

as evidenced in *The Celestial Husbandrie, or, the Tillage of the Soul* (1616), a sermon delivered at Paul's Crosse, London, on February 25, 1616, where Anglican preacher William Jackson hammers the point home: "Man of earth is called earth: and I cannot passe this poynt, before I haue fixed your considerations, vpon this obseruation."[98] At first glance, Jackson appears simply to reiterate the script for burial outlined in *The Book of Common Prayer*, which recalls for mourners the mortality and earthliness they share with the dead; but this is a sermon, not a burial, and Jackson's Christianized autochthony functions as more than a memento mori or recollection of mortality. "So then it is earth," he stated. "The difference is this: liuing earth walkes vpon dead earth, and shall, at the last be as dead, as his pauement, that he treads vpon."[99] In other words, Jackson conceived "earth" as the common substrate and zone of indifference between life and death, a view which fed the English perception of autochthones as a race of living dead. Whether or not the earth is "dead" was a matter of debate in the early seventeenth century, as I show in Chapter 4 through Shakespeare's Lear, who cries that he knows "when one is dead and when one lives," as he holds his daughter's corpse, finally concluding, ambiguously, that "She's dead as earth" (24.255-256).[100]

---

[98] William Jackson. *The Celestiall Husbandrie: or, The Tillage of the Soule* (London, 1616), 4-5.

[99] Ibid., 5.

[100] William Shakespeare, *The True Chronicle Historie of the Life and Death*

Jackson's conception of the human and its place within the cosmos is rooted in his Christianized autochthony, which lends itself to a kind of humanist pride before becoming a warning against vanity. Its earthly origins, in Jackson's view, make the human a "sweet abstract, or compendium," that is, a microcosm of the world and all its creatures and things, such that we share "being with stones, life with plants, sence with beasts," and so on. Yet "be not proud," he reminded the audience, because despite this enviable ontological position, "thou art but earth."[101] In addition to its synthesis of humanist, memento mori, and vanitas tropes, Jackson's "man of earth" constitutes a reactionary expression of Christian identity grounded in anthropocentrism and geocentrism, which assumes that the earth is the center of the universe and that man is the center of the earth: "Earth is the lowest of all elements," he observed, "and the Center of the world. Earth must be earth, liuing earth to dead earth."[102] Implicitly endorsing the official condemnation of Copernicus' heliocentric cosmology that was pronounced by the Roman Holy Office the same year that he delivered his sermon, Jackson preserved his belief that humans are central to everything.[103]

Jackson's own ideological investments informed his

---

of *King Lear* (London, 1606).

[101] Jackson, *The Celestiall Husbandrie*, 4.

[102] Ibid., 5.

[103] See Steven Shapin, *The Scientific Revolution*, 24. The "pre-Copernican cosmology was literally anthropocentric."

Christian endorsement of human earthliness, but his proposal that "man may well be called earth" emerged from
a long philological tradition. He therefore reiterated that
earth is also called "Humus" because of the moisture it
receives from the sea, and "Tellus," because it is fruitful. I
return below to the latter etymology, which I suggest links
Spenser's Talus to the earth in book 5 of *The Faerie Queene*;
for now, suffice it to recall that the first etymology (earth
as humus) served to ground human identity in the earth
throughout the medieval and early modern periods. Only
after the classification of eighteenth-century zoologist Carl
Linnaeus did the human come to be identified by its pur-
ported sapience, that is, as homo sapiens, and even then
only through an editorial ambiguity.[104] Previously, mortality and earthliness were generally the salient characteristics
of human beings.

Philologist Georges Dumézil has thus observed that
for most Indo-European languages, "man is 'the terrestrial' (thus Latin homo, from humus) before being 'the
mortal.'"[105] As Isidore of Seville vouched in his seventh-
century *Etymologies*, "The human being is named homo
because he was made from the earth, humus, as it says
in Genesis...It is incorrectly declared that the complete

---

[104] Giorgio Agamben, *The Open: Man and Animal*, trans. Kevin Attell
(Stanford: Stanford University Press, 2004), 25.

[105] Georges Dumézil, *Le Festin d'immortalite: Esquisse d'une etude de
mythologie compare indo-europeenne* (Paris, 1924), xv-xvi, quoted in Loraux,
Born of the Earth, 4.

human being is from both substances, that is the association of body and soul. Properly, homo is from humus."[106]
This claim became increasingly loaded in early modern
English culture as Christians and colonists strived to por-
tray themselves, in Browne's words, as "once removed
from earth," that is, as less earthly than autochthones. But
unlike a number of his contemporaries, Jackson seems
little concerned in 1616 that his representation of human
earthliness might confound or escape its acceptable Christian framework by invoking the worldly discourse of pagan
autochthony.

In the allegorical romance, *Bentivolio & Urania* (1660;
1664), English clergyman Nathaniel Ingelo cited autochthony among a number of "false Principles...perversely
applied" to human beings. There are some, Ingelo related,
who believe that humans are "Autochthones, Intelligent
Mushromes, or else Pre-Adamites born before the Moon
upon some Arcadian Hill," or perhaps descended from
"the Serpentine Brood of Cadmus," the mythological
founder of Thebes who slays a dragon and sows its teeth
in the ground, whence spring the Spartoi or "sown" race
of people. These autochthonous origin stories were unacceptable to Ingelo for at least two reasons. First, because
they contradict his belief that all human life is "derived
from our Common Parents Adam and Eve," as the book

---

[106] Isidore of Seville, *Etymologies: Complete English Translation*, trans.
Priscilla Throop (Charlotte: MedievalMS, 2005), XI.I.4.

of Genesis reports.[107] Second, because they level the distinction between human and nonhuman life, such that the life of autochthonous humans is no more exceptional than that of intelligent mushrooms. And yet, just as early modern Anglicans believed from scripture that man came from the earth, many also readily accepted from an empirical standpoint that inanimate matter such as "dead earth" had the potential to produce vegetative and animal (if not human) lifeforms.

In *The History of Animals*, Aristotle distinguished creatures born to parents from those born spontaneously "from putrefying earth or vegetable matter, as is the case with a number of insects."[108] Many early moderns concurred with Aristotle, including the experimental physicist William Harvey, who discovered the circulation of the blood in the 1620s. It was not until the 1660s that Italian physician and poet Francesco Redi debunked Aristotle's theory with a series of experiments demonstrating that

---

[107] Nathaniel Ingelo, *Bentivolio & Urania: 2nd part* (London, 1664), 145.
[108] Aristotle, *The History of Animals, Complete Works of Aristotle, Volume 1: The Revised Oxford Translation*, ed. Jonathan Barnes (Princeton: Princeton University Press, 1984), 852. See Hiro Hirai, *Medical Humanism and Natural Philosophy: Renaissance Debates on Matter, Life and the Soul* (Leiden, Boston: Brill, 2011), 5-6. "From the traditional Aristotelian point of view, there existed a sharp distinction between living beings (animate) and lifeless things (inanimate). But how can the phenomenon often called 'spontaneous generation' (abiogenesis, i.e., the appearance of life from lifeless matter) be explained in this scheme?"

maggots do not emerge from rotten meat.[109] But ultimately Nathaniel Ingelo was less interested in the technical possibility of earth-born life than he was in establishing that autochthones are neither Christian nor human, and that ultimately they cannot be said to exist.

Not the dubious empirical validity of pagan autochthony, but rather its contradiction of the Pentateuch— the first five books of the Old Testament attributed to Moses—was perhaps the main reason that English authors could not accept it. In *Purchas His Pilgrims* (1613-1625), for instance, a popular collection of travel writing, the cleric Samuel Purchas wrote that "it is most repugnant to a Christian man, knowing the Bookes of Moses concerning Originals, to affirme themselues to be Autocha [sic]," in the manner of the Greeks. "It were better truly to confesse the vnknown originall of Ancestors," Purchas asserted, "then to be carried away with the opinion and error of Earth-bred men."[110] Thomas Browne, to whom the next section turns for an extended close reading, agreed with Purchas that autochthony is "repugnant" and that it

---

[109] See Henry Harris, *Things Come to Life: Spontaneous Generation Revisited* (Oxford and New York: Oxford University Press, 2002); Cf. Jones, *The Racial Discourses of Life Philosophy*, 2. "As late as the early modern period…it was believed, for example, that toads could be generated from ducks putrefying on a dung heap, a woman's hair laid in a damp but sunny place would turn into snakes, and rotting tuna would produce worms that changed first into flies, then into a grasshopper, and finally into a quail."

[110] Samuel Purchas, *Purchas His Pilgrimes In Fiue Books* (London, 1625), 660.

would be better to profess ignorance of one's origins than it would be to claim autochthony. Browne nevertheless entertained the error, even attempting in good faith to reconcile autochthony with accepted English ideologies, or at least to neutralize and appropriate it.

Autochthony at the Apocalypse

More explicitly than his contemporaries, Browne deployed the concept of autochthony to distinguish living from dead races of people, articulating a construct that then served to identify certain still-living autochthonous races as virtually dead. In *Pseudodoxia Epidemica, or Vulgar Errors* (1646), Browne aimed to debunk the myth of autochthony as part of a more general indictment of unverifiable knowledge-claims concerning the "indeterminable" beginning of the world and its "inscrutable" end.[111] Pagan histories, including accounts by Epicurus and Aristotle, afforded Browne "slender satisfaction," but he was "sufficiently satisfied" with the account of Genesis related by Moses, from which he concluded that "there was…never any Autochthon, or man arising from the earth but Adam, for the woman being formed out of the rib, was once removed from earth."[112] Because Eve was born from Adam's rib rather than from the earth, in other words, the offspring of Adam and Eve are also therefore

---

[111] Browne, *Pseudodoxia Epidemica*, 440.

[112] Ibid., 441.

"once removed from earth," and hence not fully autochthonous.

Browne deemed traditional autochthony unacceptable
because it tells history from the wrong direction, as it were,
by emphasizing archeology or the study of beginnings
rather than eschatology or the study of ends. The "conceit"
of autochthony, he writes, which is "applyed unto the originall of man, and the beginning of the world, is more justly
appropriable unto its end; for then indeed men shall rise
out of the earth, the graves shall shoot up their concealed
seeds, and in that great Autumne, men shall spring up, and
awake from their Chaos againe."[113] That Browne shifted
the focus of autochthony to the dead is not surprising,
since it was already a central trope in fifth-century Athenian funeral orations, in which mourners, upon interring
their dead, reasserted that they themselves were born from
the earth.[114] But Browne Christianized the pagan tradition
by revising autochthony as an image of the Resurrection.

The resulting distinction, between Christian autochthones resurrected from the earth and pagan autochthones merely born from it, informed early modern English
concepts of race, which scholars including Loomba and
Burton have shown to be a vastly complex and amorphous
category in the period, when "the quasi-biological notion
that physical characteristics denoted distinct types of

---

[113] Ibid., 441-442.

[114] See Detienne, "The Metamorphoses of Autochthony in the Days
of National Identity," 87.

human beings and distinct moral and social features…had not yet come into being."[115] With potentially lethal consequences, early modern autochthony discourse intersects the concept of race with decisions about what is human and what is nonhuman, about what lives and what is dead. Browne went as far as to separate the earth-resurrected race of Christian autochthones from "the generation of the Giants," with a mass-extinction event that annihilates the latter before the former arrives. Browne thus exemplifies what seems to have been a common view: that non-Christian races claiming to be autochthonous are (or at least should) already be dead, having perished in Noah's Flood.

Later seventeenth-century authors also articulated racial difference through the vernacular of autochthony. In the speculative cosmogony *Telluris Theoria Sacra, or Sacred Theory of the Earth* (1684), for instance, English theologian Thomas Burnet imagined that in the next millennium, following another mass annihilation event on the scale of the biblical Flood and Fire, a new earth will emerge, one free of war, sickness, and the "perpetual Drudgery for the necessaries of a Mortal Life." Burnet supposed that this "Future Earth" will host two races, radically distinct from one another in temper, disposition, and origin: "The one born from Heaven, Sons of God, and of the Resurrection: who are the true Saints and heirs of the Millennium. The

---

[115] Ania Loomba and Jonathan Burton, eds., *Race in Early Modern England* (New York: Palgrave Macmillan, 2007), 2.

others born of the Earth, Sons of the Earth, generated from the slime of the ground, and the heat of the Sun, as brute Creatures were at first."[116] I show below that Spenser described autochthonous giants in similar terms, as creatures born of Mother Earth's "natiue slime."[117] Burnet concluded from his reading of Genesis that the antediluvian earth, like the future earth, also seems to have had "two or three orders or races" including giants, humans created by God, and humans procreated by themselves. "This mixture of these two Races," he writes, "whatsoever they were, gave, it seems, so great offence to God, that he destroy'd that World upon it, in a Deluge of Water."[118] Such speculations had traction through the end of the seventeenth century, and Sir Isaac Newton was among the many admirers of Burnet's theories.

Browne's Christianization of pagan autochthony, then, represented for contemporaries more than an ideological shift or revision of an antiquated idea. It signaled rather a pervasive anxiety about the coexistence of distinct races, a fear that not all autochthones were extinct but rather still intermixed among the living. His eschatological reading of autochthony had precedent in ancient Greek versions of the myth, which according to Loraux, are "prepared

---

[116] Thomas Burnet, *The Theory of the Earth containing an account of the original of the earth, and of all the general changes which it hath already undergone, or is to undergo till the consummation of all things* (London, 1697), 146; 149.

[117] Spenser, *The Faerie Queene*, II.x.9.

[118] Burnet, *The Theory of the Earth*, 150.

to annihilate a first human race in order to give humanity a new start: the flood removes men from the face of the earth, but Deucalion and Pyrrha, by throwing stones onto the ground, produce a new human race."[119] The concern of Browne's English contemporaries, however, was the possibility that humanity's new start was not absolutely new, that the new race had begun before the former had been annihilated. This preoccupation, originally grounded in myth and religion but easily translated to political and colonial contexts, explains Browne's repeated efforts to link autochthones with the dead.

Over a decade following his disavowal of autochthony in *Pseudodoxia*, Browne reprised the theme in *Hydriotaphia, Urn Burial, or a Discourse of the Sepulchral Urns lately found in Norfolk* (1658), his contribution to the antiquarian genre of historiography through which English landowners reasserted their elite genealogy and territorial claims in the wake of widespread destruction of property (including graves) and social upheaval during the Civil Wars.[120] In *The Antiquities of Warwickshire* (1656), for instance, William Dugdale reiterated Walter Raleigh's view that history "hath given us life in our understanding since the World it self had life and beginning…having made us acquainted with our dead Ancestors, and out of the depth and darknesse of the

---

[119] Loraux, *Born of the Earth*, 3.

[120] Marjorie Swann, *Curiosities and Texts: The Culture of Collecting in Early Modern England* (Philadelphia: University of Pennsylvania Press, 2001), 123.

Earth delivered us their memorie and fame."[121] Browne, by contrast, writing on behalf of his patron Thomas Le Gros, inverted the genre's logic by stressing that urns unearthed from Le Gros' land do not contain the remains of his ancestors: "We are farre from erecting your worth upon the pillars of your Fore-fathers, whose merits you illustrate."[122] Le Gros was a living embodiment of the merits of his ancestors, making it unnecessary to dig up their memory or their physical remains as evidence. Browne regarded his landed patron "as a Gemme of the Old Rock," including a proverb in the margin: "Adamas de rupe veteri praestant-issimus" ("The most outstanding diamond comes from ancient rock").[123] This alludes, simultaneously and ambigu-ously, both to Le Gros' particularly outstanding family lin-eage to which Browne stands subordinate, as well as to Browne and Le Gros' common descent from Adam, cap-tured in the Latin pun on Adamas.[124] Browne thus exploits autochthony discourse to level an egalitarian challenge to the social superiority of an elite benefactor who is also his "Friend," while at the same time deferring to the estab-lished hierarchy that makes the landed Le Gros his better.

The unearthed urns are not only unrelated to Le Gros,

---

[121] William Dugdale, *The Antiquities of Warwickshire* (1656), preface. See Raleigh, *The History of the World* (1614).

[122] Thomas Browne, *The Works of Sir Thomas Browne*, vol. 4., ed. Geoffrey Keynes (New York: William Edwin Rudge, 1929), 3.

[123] Ibid., 5.

[124] Swann, *Curiosities and Texts: The Culture of Collecting in Early Modern England*, 128.

Browne suggests, but also unrelated to any living English person. "When the bones of King Arthur were digged up, the old Race might think, they beheld therein some Originals of themselves; Unto these of our Urnes none here can pretend relation."[125] Browne depicts the urns as doubly autochthonous: first, in that they appear to have sprung from the earth itself (although in reality they were discovered by laborers working the field), and second, because they possibly contain the remains of Britain's first inhabitants. These autochthones pose no threat, however, for the simple fact that they are dead and cannot, therefore, lay claim to anything: "The commerce of the living is not to be transferred unto the dead: It is no injustice to take that which none complains to lose, and no man is wronged where no man is possessor."[126] In other words, while the living can claim the possessions of the dead, the inverse is not true, and the silent claims of the dead do nothing to unsettle the landed English inhabitants of Norfolk.[127]

---

[125] Thomas Browne, *Hydriotaphia, Urn-Burial, or, A Discourse of the Sepulchral Urns Lately Found in Norfolk for Thomas Le Gros of Crostwick or Crostwight*, in *The Works of Sir Thomas Browne*, ed. Geoffrey Keynes (London: Farber and Farber, 1964), 132.

[126] Ibid., 153.

[127] The claims of these autochthones would be no more legitimate were they living, however. See Christopher Brooks, *Law, Politics, and Society in Early Modern England* (Cambridge: Cambridge University Press, 2008), 324-35. Brooks has observed that in early modern England "it was nearly impossible to achieve property in land," because "according to the common-law mind, land was held, seised, not owned outright."

In his capacities as physician and antiquarian, Browne arrogates the originally theological-political sovereignty over life and death, such that he imagines it to be within his power to foster the life of the living (through medicine) and to revive the dead (through historiography): "to preserve the living, and make the dead to live, to keep men out of their Urnes, and discourse of humane fragments in them, is not impertinent unto our profession; whose study is life and death," he tells Le Gros.[128]

Browne compares the discovery of the urns from Norfolk soil to the discovery of the New World, thus implicitly linking indigenous populations to the land of the dead. The passage of time, he writes, "makes new discoveries in earth, and even earth it self a discovery. That great Antiquity America lay buried for a thousand years; and a large part of the earth is still in the Urne unto us."[129] What appears at first glance to be an innocuous double entendre accrues chilling significance in light of Browne's insistence that the unearthed urns, despite being autochthonous, cannot make claims on Le Gros' land because they are safely dead, "silently expressing old mortality, the ruins of forgotten times, and can only speak with life," insofar as the living speak on their behalf.[130]

Showing that they are dead, however, is not enough for Browne to silence the potential claims of the Norfolk

---

[128] Browne, *Urn Burial* (Keynes 1964), 132.

[129] Browne, *Urn Burial* (Keynes 1929), 7.

[130] Ibid., 3.

autochthones and, by extension, their indigenous American analogues. He goes further, arguing that their burial practices, exhibiting no belief in resurrection, therefore disqualify them from claiming true autochthonous status: "if Adam were made out of an extract of the Earth," Browne hypothesizes, then "all parts might challenge a restitution, yet few have returned their bones farre lower then they might receive them; not affecting the graves of Giants, under hilly and heavy coverings."[131] In other words, if it were admitted that Adam was an earth-extracted autochthon, then any people on earth might justifiably lay claim to any part of it, demanding "restitution" from those who neglect to claim autochthony. But since all living humans descend from Adam, as Browne posits in *Pseudodoxia*, it follows that no living people can claim to be more or less autochthonous than any other. Browne ultimately secures Le Gros' claim to the land, neutralizing the potential threat of egalitarianism inherent in autochthony by subordinating it to the Christian Right of Conquest. In the case that there are no living autochthones, possession is relinquished to the current tenant, while if all people are deemed autochthonous, then the legitimate (i.e., Christian) autochthones distinguish themselves from illegitimate autochthones by burying themselves in shallow graves and so testifying to their belief in Resurrection, since those who "hope to rise again, would not be content…to place their reliques as to

---

[131] Ibid., 7.

lie beyond discovery," he writes.[132]

For Browne, "the graves of Giants" emblematize the illegitimate, pagan brand of autochthony, because unlike the relatively shallow graves of Christians, they are deep underground and thus exhibit no hope of bodily Resurrection. This explains why he writes in *Pseudodoxia* that autochthony "is a conceit answerable unto the generation of the Giants, not admittable in Philosophy, much lesse in Divinity, which distinctly informeth wee are all the seed of Adam, that the whole world perished unto eight persons before the Flood, and was after peopled by the Colonies of the sonnes of Noah; there was therefore never any Autochthon, or man arising from the earth but Adam."[133]

Browne likely derives his opinion that autochthony pertains to giants from Raphael Holinshed's famous *Chronicles* (1587), which reports that the gigantic first inhabitants of the British Isles "tooke their name of the soile where they were borne: for Gigantes signifieth the sons of the earth: the Aborigines, or (as Cesar calleth them) Indigenae[,] that is, borne and bred out of the earth w[h]ere they inhabited." This etymological genealogy, Holinshed observes, has led many common people to believe that autochthonous aboriginals not descended from Adam continue to live on the face of the earth, "but verelie...their opinion is not to be allowed in any condition," he declares.[134] Like

---

[132] Ibid.

[133] Browne, *Pseudodoxia Epidemica*, 441.

[134] Raphael Holinshed, *The first and second volumes of Chronicles* (London,

Holinshed, for whom autochthony "is not to be allowed" and like Browne, for whom it is "not admittable" (and like both, who link it to giants and indigenous populations), Edmund Spenser repeatedly stages the annihilation of autochthonous giants in *The Faerie Queene* (1596), part of the epic poem's sustained representation of the disavowal of autochthony in early modern English culture at large.

Colonizing the Autochthonous Giant

In contrast to Thomas Browne's world, which he believed was "peopled by the Colonies" of Noah's offspring, the real and poetically imagined worlds inhabited by Spenser were not fully colonized by "the seed of Adam," but rather still peopled by autochthonous races with radically other genealogies. Scholars have remarked Spenser's implication in colonialism at least since C.S. Lewis' claim in 1936 that the poet "was the instrument of a detestable policy in Ireland."[135] Just over two decades ago, literary critic Edward Said argued that Spenserians had failed to link *The Faerie Queene* with the poet's "bloodthirsty plans for Ireland, where he imagined a British army virtually exterminating the native inhabitants."[136]

Notwithstanding the rich scholarship on Spenser and

1587), 1.3.

[135] C.S. Lewis, *The Allegory of Love: A Study in Medieval Tradition* (Oxford: The Clarendon Press, 1936), 349.

[136] Edward Said, *Culture and Imperialism* (New York: Vintage, 1993), 7.

Ireland in the years following Said's observation,[137] scholars have largely overlooked how Spenser frames his allegorical representation of the colonized Irish through the
discourse of autochthony. Drawing this link activates new
readings of *The Faerie Queene*; at the same time, Spenser's
poem sheds light on early modern autochthony discourse.

According to Spenser's chronicle of Briton kings in
book 2, the land's first inhabitants were "a saluage nation"
of "hideous Giaunts, and halfe beastly men," whose huge
stature "amazed" the "sonnes of men" to behold.[138] "They
held this land, and with their filthinesse/Polluted this same
gentle soyle long time" until eventually the earth—although
they were "borne of her owne natiue slime"—begins to
"abhorre" the giants.[139] The Giants' misuse of the land,
described in strikingly ecological terms, outweighs and
negates their right of possession as autochthones. Their
pollution of the soil denotes both spiritual desecration
and physical contamination. While Spenser could not have
imagined the catastrophic consequences of pollution in
the terms we understand today, he nevertheless describes a

---

[137] See, for example, Andrew Hadfield, *Spenser's Irish Experience:
Wilde Fruit and Salvage Soyl* (Oxford: Oxford University Press, 1997).
See also *Salvaging Spenser: Colonialism, Culture and Identity* (London:
Macmillan Press; New York: St. Martin's Press, 1997), where Willy
Maley has worked to salvage Spenser's reputation by arguing that
the author has become a scapegoat for anxieties about English
colonization of Ireland.
[138] Spenser, *The Faerie Queene*, II.x.7.
[139] Ibid., II.x.9.

compelling *lex terrae*, or law of the land, whereby territorial sovereignty belongs to the more ecologically responsible inhabitants.

Eventually Brutus, who is "anciently deriu'd/From roiall stocke of old Assaracs line," arrives to dispossess the giants of their "vniust possession" of English soil. Spenser admits elsewhere that the myth of Brutus founding Britain—which he likely borrows from Geoffrey of Monmouth's twelfth-century *Historia Regum Britanniae*—is "impossible to prove."[140] His account of the removal of autochthones from British soil therefore hinges on the acceptance of another equally unverifiable myth, much as Browne in *Pseudodoxia* declares the inscrutability of all origin stories before asserting the authority of Genesis over pagan autochthony narratives.

The opening sentence of a 1659 survey of Newcastle by William Gray strikingly replicates Spenser's either/or decision between, on the one hand, accepting British autochthony, and on the other hand, allowing that the English are descendants of Brutus. Unlike Spenser, however, Gray decided on the former view. "Britains were Autochthenes," Gray writes, "natives of this Island, for more ancient inhabitants we finde none....Their originall from the Trojans, by Brute, is altogether fabulous; there being no Greek or Latine Authors, or any Monument in this

---

[140] Ibid., 249n. "A cancelled passage in *View* 197 notes that the tale of Brutus conquering and inhabiting this land is 'impossible to prove.'"

Island, which makes mention hereof."[141] But for Spenser, the historical fiction that Brutus repossessed English soil from autochthonous giants—which Holinshed, to be sure, presented as historical truth—functioned as a kind of noble lie, establishing Britain as the torchbearer of ancient imperialism while at the same time severing its bond to autochthony.

Book 2's chronicle of Briton kings, like Artegal's battle with the Giant in book 5, implies that English territorial sovereignty rests not on autochthony but rather on its supplantation, whether by an alternative origin/destination story, by right of conquest, or by sheer force. "The land, which warlike Britons now possesse,/And therein haue their mighty empire raysd,/In antique times was saluage wildernesse,/Vnpeopled, vnmannurd," the chronicle states, hinting obliquely toward but also obscuring the British empire's ongoing struggle to (un)people and (un)manure the "saluage wildernesse" of Ireland.[142] That England was unpeopled in antiquity does not mean that it was uninhabited, because the chronicle acknowledges the native, "hideous Giaunts," and because in early modern parlance to "people" also signified settling down "as inhabitants or colonists."[143] In other words, despite the

---

[141] "THE FIRST NATIVES OF THIS ISLAND," *Chorographia, or, A survey of Newcastle upon Tine the estate of this country under the Romans* (London, 1649).

[142] Spenser, *The Faerie Queene*, II.x.5.

[143] "People," v. 3, *Oxford English Dictionary*.

autochthonous people inhabiting it, English soil remained unpeopled before it was colonized by foreign settlers. Establishing that ancient England was unpeopled may have allowed Spenser to bury an uncomfortable reality—that colonization entails not just conquering but also eradicating natives—beneath the more benign suggestion that the land was already unpopulated prior to the arrival of the settlers.

Nevertheless, arguably by definition early modern colonization involved the extermination of earlier inhabitants. Thomas Hobbes, for instance, describes colonies as groups "sent out from the commonwealth…to inhabit a foreign country, either formerly void of inhabitants, or made void then by war."[144] The discourse of autochthony, then, with its traditional representations of annihilation and generation, depopulation followed by repopulation, serves to undergird the task of colonization, as Spenser demonstrates with the notion of an originally "Vnpeopled" England in book 2, as well as in Artegal's battle with the Giant in book 5, and again in the fictional but more concretely historical dialogue, *A View of The State of Ireland* (1596; published 1633). According to the logic of autochthony and of colonization, moreover, the depopulation must be absolute, "in order to give humanity a new start" (Loraux) and to avoid what Burnet called the "mixture" of races—that is, cohabitation and miscegenation between "Sons of

---

[144] Hobbes, *Leviathan*, 168.

Earth" and "Sons of Resurrection," between heaven-born humans and giants born from the "slime" of the ground.

Spenser's chronicle maintains that England's indigenous giants were already annihilated by their pollution of the soil by the time Brutus arrives. This was not the case for potential early modern English colonies in lands still peopled by earlier inhabitants. When the ancient notion of autochthony resurfaces in the context of colonialism, it is therefore as a liability to be claimed only in peril of one's life. Thus, in Richard Hakluyt's *The Principal Navigations* (1589-1600), a widely-read collaboration that contributed to the settlement of North America, Arngrimus Ionas vehemently denies that his Icelandic compatriots "were autochthones, that is, earth-bred, or bred out of their owne soile like vnto trees and herbs," even as he proudly declares "the in-bred affection" he bears for his country. Ionas casts off Icelandic autochthony as a rumor spread by "some strangers" intending "to deface" Iceland's global stature, "making it a by word, and a laughing-stocke to all other nations."[145] It is not immediately clear why at the start of the seventeenth century Ionas regards autochthony as a "reproach" rather than the mark of pride that it was in antiquity; nor is it obvious what strangers have to gain by characterizing Icelanders as autochthones, nor what Ionas stands to lose by not refuting the charge. He has reason to assume, however, that allowing the charge of autochthony

---

[145] Arngrimus Ionas, "A Briefe Commentarie of Island," in *Principall Navigations* (London, 1599), 553.

to stick, beyond making Iceland a global laughingstock, also potentially exposes the lives of its people to colonial violence.

Ionas' motives for rejecting Icelanders' autochthony come into clearer focus alongside the opening dialogue of Spenser's *View*, which dwells on Ireland's "commodious soyl" and posits the removal of "unwholesome" people from "good" land as a central task of colonization. When the stock Englishman Eudoxus asks the colonist Irenius how to reform Ireland "if not by laws and ordinances," the latter's response shows the danger of identifying or being identified as autochthonous in a colonized land. "Even by the sword; for all these evils must first be cut away by a strong hand, before any good can bee planted, like as the corrupt braunches and unwholesome boughs are first to bee pruned, and the foule mosse cleansed and scraped away, before the tree can bring forth any good fruite."[146] In the context of colonialism, the dehumanization of autochthonous lives justifies their eradication: supposedly born in the same manner as trees and herbs, their deaths are similarly naturalized, such that Spenser/ Irenius can describe them euphemistically, as "pruned," or "cleansed and scraped away," rather than systematically starved and murdered.

Significantly, Irenius' weapon and tool of choice for

---

[146] Edmund Spenser, *A View of the State of Ireland*, ed. Andrew Hadfield and Willy Maley (Oxford and Malden: Blackwell Publishers, 1997), 93.

taming Ireland is the sword. As Foucault has observed, one of the characteristic prerogatives of premodern sovereignty "was formulated as the 'power of life and death' [and] was in reality the right to take life or let live. Its symbol, after all, was the sword."[147] Again, Foucault posits that beginning in the seventeenth century this ancient sovereign right "was replaced by a power to foster life or disallow it to the point of death."[148] The extermination of autochthonous populations, as represented in *A View of The State of Ireland* and *The Faerie Queene*, marshals both the ancient sovereign prerogative to take life by the sword as well as the modern sovereign right to disallow life, for example, through systematic starvation.

One early modern method for disallowing the life of autochthonous populations was the prevention of "manurance," or the cultivation and occupation of land, as Spenser depicts in book 2's chronicle by describing ancient Britain as unpeopled as well as "vnmannurd," and again in the contemporary context of View. In the latter text, Eudoxus is skeptical that Ireland might be subdued quickly with so few colonists, but Irenius assures him of a speedy conclusion to the violence based on his testimony of the infamous Munster famine, which followed in the wake of the Desmond Rebellions (1569-1573 and 1579-1583) and which Spenser himself had witnessed.

By garrisoning themselves while un-manuring the sur-

---

[147] Foucault, "Right of Death and Power over Life," 259.
[148] Ibid., 261.

rounding land with a kind of scorched earth policy, English colonists successfully annihilated the Munster population in less than a year and a half, "that in short space there were none almost left, and a most populous and plentifull country suddainely left voyde of man and beast," according to Irenius. Munster, which "was a most rich and plentifull country, full of corne and cattle," became a wasteland teeming with dead and dying natives: "Out of every corner of the woods and glynnes they came creeping forth upon their hands...they looked like anatomies of death, they spake like ghosts crying out of their graves; they did eat the dead carrions," even digging up graves to eat the flesh of the dead.[149] Far from considering this a tragedy or war crime, Irenius recommends extrapolating future policy from the famine: All natives would need to submit themselves to English garrisons for identification. The remaining "loose people" would either be killed "by the sword," or otherwise "kept from manurance, and their cattle from running abroad...would quickly consume themselves, and devoure one another."[150] Elsewhere, Irenius condemns

---

[149] Spenser, *A View of the State of Ireland*, 101-102.

[150] Ibid., 50 and 101-2. Cf. Hakluyt, *The Principal Nauigations*, I.491. The Samoyed people or "Samoit hath his name...of eating himselfe: as if in in times past, they liued as the Cannibals, eating one another." He attributes this etymology to the Russians, however, under whom the Samoit are "at this time" subject. "But as the Samoits themselues will say, they were called Samoie, that is, of themselues, as though they were Indigene, or people bred vpon that very soyle, that neuer changed their seate from one place to another, as most nations haue done."

the Irish as primitive and hence worthy of extermination because of their "custome of boolying," or wandering with herds of cattle. He appears to find this way of life especially problematic because it sustains "out-lawes, or loose people," who otherwise would starve or be forced to seek refuge in the towns, where "they would soone be caught."[151] Where Irenius imagines autochthones, rooted to the land like plants and as easily extirpable, the "loose people" by contrast threaten to undermine the absolute depopulation of Ireland.

English colonists may not have believed that the native Irish were literally rooted to the soil; indeed, the nomadic cattle-herders were living proof of the contrary. However, colonial policies aimed at rooting earlier inhabitants to the land—including what Greenblatt has described as "vast projects undertaken to fix and enclose the native populations in the mines, in encomiendas, in fortified hamlets, and ultimately, in mass graves"[152]—reveal a practical attempt to make indigenous people autochthonous on English terms.

There are distinctions to be made between autochthones that are already dead—such as Spenser's giants and Browne's Norfolk urns, "silently expressing old mortality" and unable to "speak with life"[153]—and the soon-to-be-dead native Irish whom Spenser describes as "anatomies

---

[151] Spenser, *A View of the State of Ireland*, 55.

[152] Stephen Greenblatt, *Renaissance Self-Fashioning from More to Shakespeare* (Chicago: University of Chicago Press, 2005), 183.

[153] Browne, *Urn Burial* (Keynes 1929), 3.

of death," and who speak like ghosts risen from the grave. However, the pervasive cultural link between autochthones and extinct, nonhuman races provided an ideological justification for colonial violence, insofar as it constitutes, in Browne's words, "no injustice to take" land or life from those who are already dead.

There is also a difference, to be sure, between the "vnmannurd" British soil depicted in *The Faerie Queene*, inhabited by indigenous giants who pollute rather than cultivate it,[154] and the colonized Irish soil, whose inhabitants are "kept from manurance," that is, prevented by the English from cultivating their own land. But the difference may have been blurred in English colonial ideology, which was ingrained with cultural representations of autochthones as incapable and unworthy of possessing their own land. As early as the mid-sixteenth-century, English soldiers deliberately decimated Irish corn fields, even as they subscribed, ironically, to characterizations of the native Irish as unwilling to work the land.[155]

Such convenient stereotypes persisted into the seventeenth-century. Gerard Boate and Samuel Hartlib report in *Irelands naturall history* (1657), for example, that the Irish, "being one of the most barbarous Nations of the whole earth have at all times been so far from" discovering mines, "that even in these last years, and since the Eng-

---

[154] Spenser, *The Faerie Queene*, II.x.9.
[155] See John Patrick Montano, *The Roots of English Colonialism in Ireland* (Cambridge: Cambridge University Press, 2011), 10.

lish have begun to discover some," no Irish person "hath applyed himself to that business, or in the least manner furthered it." The English thus literally undermine potential claims of Irish autochthones by industriously digging the land that the latter, in their view, inhabit only superficially. Strikingly, the authors link earlier English colonists "from the time of the first Conquest, untill the beginning of Queen Elizabeths Reign" with the native Irish, in that both fail to unearth precious minerals. While the Irish have no excuse not to mine but their barbarity, however, Boate and Hartlib absolve the English settlers of their negligence because they were too embroiled in war to "ever find the opportunity of seeking for Mines, and searching out the Metals hidden in the bowels of the Earth."[156] Nevertheless, the link betrays an anxiety among later English colonists about the impossibility of distinguishing autochthones from non-autochthones.

As Elizabeth Fowler has observed, "putative ancient originals had been so altered by innumerable invasions, migrations, miscegenations, and internal wars that they were in fact unknowable and impracticable. Significant numbers of English colonists had lived there since the twelfth century and now often resisted Elizabethan policy more than did the so-called 'wild' Irish."[157] Exacerbat-

---

[156] Gerard Boate and Samuel Hartlib, *Irelands Naturall History* (London, 1657), 123-4.

[157] Elizabeth Fowler, "The Failure of Moral Philosophy in the Work of Edmund Spenser," *Representations* 51 (1995): 47-76; 60-61.

ing the practical confusion of natives and colonists was the ideological confusion between, on the one hand, the dead autochthones of the mythological past as well as of the theological future, and on the other hand, the living autochthones of the early modern present.

The English fear of becoming (or being confused for) autochthonous is manifest in Spenser's reactionary fidelity to the myth of Trojan origins; in Burnet's theory that the racial "mixture" of giants and humans led God to destroy the world in the Flood; and in English colonial policies aimed at eradicating entire native populations. The threat of autochthony is especially prevalent in book 5 of *The Faerie Queene*, the "Legend of Justice," which begins with a reversal of Ovid's pagan account of a world-annihilating deluge followed by repopulation. As history devolves from the Golden Age to a Stone Age, the proem narrates, humankind simultaneously departs from its autochthonous origin and arrives at its autochthonous destination. Human life, originally generated in the earth, degenerates at last into inanimate stone.

> For from the golden age, that first was named,
> It's now at earst become a stonie one; And men
> themselues, the which at first were framed Of
> earthly mould, and form'd of flesh and bone,
> Are now transformed into hardest stone: Such
> as behind their backs (so backward bred) Were
> throwne by Pyrrha and Deucalione:

> And if then those any worse may be red, They
> into that ere long will be degendered.[158]

The stones into which Spenser's humans degenerate form a chiasmus with the stones thrown by Ovid's
Pyrrha and Deucalion, which instead evolve over time into
humans. Like Browne's conditional acceptance of autochthony—that is, provided that it apply to eschatology rather
than to archeology—Spenser allows the idea only as a kind
of palinode. Hence the pun on the "backward" breeding
of Pyrrha and Deucalion's stony offspring, which signals
the degeneracy of present-day autochthones as well as the
preposterousness of pagan origin myths.[159] While human
history is the subject of Spenser's stanza, the third person
pronoun "they" sufficiently others the race of "men" such
that the reader need not identify with their autochthony.
Furthermore, although the proem describes a successful case of autochthonous repopulation with Pyrrha and
Deucalion, the rest of book 5 shows a series of abortive
attempts at stone-throwing, where the stones, no longer
seeds for repopulation, are reduced to mere weapons,
inanimate objects with no potential for life.

In canto 2, Pollente's daughter Munera begs in vain for
mercy as Talus besieges her castle, since "neither force of

---

[158] Spenser, *The Faerie Queene*, V.Proem.2.

[159] See Cohen, *Stone: An Ecology of the Inhuman*, 201. "As material
metaphor, stone is often deployed to immobilize a people, to
condemn them to surpassed history and exclude them from
coexistence, the conveyor of a racializing trope."

stones which they did throw,/Nor powr of charms, which she against him wrought,/Might otherwise preuaile, or make him cease for ought."[160] But "no pitty would" make Talus "change the course/Of Iustice," and while Munera submissively kneels before him, he chops off "her suppliant hands," as well as her feet, nailing them "on high, that all might them behold."[161] Talus goes further still, destroying the stones of Munera's castle to make the defeat absolute: "And lastly all that Castle quite he raced,/Euen from the sole of his foundation,/And all the hewen stones thereof defaced,/That there mote be no hope of reparation,/Nor memory thereof to any nation."[162]

Artegal's Talionic justice efficiently removes bad people from the land they wrongfully inhabit—Munera and Pollente are murderous thieves, although one might protest that this does not unconditionally justify their execution. As iterant colonists, however, Artegal and Talus neglect to govern the lands they depopulate, moving on to the next conflict with no regard for the power vacuums they create along the way. The final stanza of book 5 culminates with more fruitless stone-throwing, as the Blatant Beast scolds Artegal, "And stones did cast, yet he for nought would swerue/From his right course,"[163] proceeding unscathed to "Faery Court," leaving an unpeopled land in his wake.

---

[160] Spenser, *The Faerie Queene*, V.ii.22.

[161] Ibid., V.ii.26.

[162] Ibid., V.ii.28.

[163] Ibid., V.xii.43.

As with the proem's reversal of the myth of Pyrrha and Deucalion, the episode of the Giant in book 5, canto 2 raises the specter of autochthony in order to defeat it. Just as readers are free not to identify with the "stonie" race of autochthones in the proem, we may also align ourselves with the Giant in his battle against Artegal. Early modern readers generally did not do so, however, with the exception of egalitarian radicals such as the Levellers. Spenser never names the Giant, but readers traditionally refer to him as the Egalitarian Giant, the Giant with the Scales, or the Levelling Giant. In the 1640s Royalist supporters of King Charles I regarded the Giant's plan to redistribute wealth and reduce all things "unto equality"[164] as a "lively representation of our times," finding themselves vindicated in the triumph of Artegal's defense of divine hierarchy and status quo.[165]

For modern critics such as A.C. Hamilton, the Giant symbolizes "the dangers of early communism,"[166] a reading supported by the Giant's proposal to reallocate "all the wealth of rich men to the poore."[167] Graham Hough has posited that Spenser's "contemporary target" was the Anabaptists, who "attracted unfavorable attention in Enland in

---

[164] Ibid., V.ii.32.

[165] John N. King, "The Faerie Leveller: A 1648 Royalist Reading of *The Faerie Queene*, V.ii.29-54," *Huntington Library Quarterly*, vol. 48, no. 3 (Summer 1985), 297-308; 297.

[166] Spenser, *The Faerie Queene*, 520n.

[167] Ibid., V.ii.32-38.

1575."[168] Michael O'Connell concurs that the Giant stands for Anabaptist socialism, which was regarded as "the dominant philosophical threat" to Elizabethan society,[169] and T.K. Dunseath agrees that it "is highly probable" that "the episode of the reforming giant" represents Spenser's indictment of the Anabaptists.[170]

This compelling consensus overlooks what hides in plain sight: that the allegorical Giant represents himself and the people gathering around him as much as he stands for any abstract ideology or historical analogue. Early modern readers were more likely to register the Giant's reiterative claims of autochthony. To read the Giant primarily as an Anabaptist is to Christianize him, but the egalitarianism he seeks as an autochthone is pagan and therefore levelled on behalf of those living in this world, not those resurrected in the next.

We first approach the Giant from the perspective of Artegal and Talus, who are travelling by sea when they spy him on the coast.

---

[168] Graham Hough, *A Preface to The Faerie Queene* (London: Gerald Duckworth, 1962), 194.

[169] Albert Charles Hamilton, *The Spenser Encyclopedia* (Toronto: University of Toronto Press, 1990), 281.

[170] T.K. Dunseath, *Spenser's Allegory of Justice* (Princeton: Princeton University Press, 1968), 96-97.

> They saw before them, far as they could vew,
> Full many people gathered in a crew:
> Whose great assembly they did much admire,
> For neuer there the like resort they knew.
> So towardes them they coasted, to enquire
> What thing so many nations met, did there
> desire.[171]

Artegal and Talus "admire" what appears to be a kind of republic or international community of "many nations" and "many people gathered" around a "thing" that has not yet come into view. Then they behold this "mighty Gyant stand/Vpon a rocke, and holding forth on hie/An huge great paire of ballance in his hand," a conspicuous challenge to the "righteous balance" of Astraea, who teaches Artegal "to weigh both right and wrong/In equall ballance with due recompence," before she leaves her kingdom on earth for heaven.[172] The Giant's form of justice, his way of measuring right and wrong, emerges from his autochthony, which clarifies why it is incompatible with Artegal's worldview.

Artegal aims to unpeople the Giant's land by preventing its inhabitants from organizing as people. To that end, he revises the once admirable "great assembly" as "the vulgar" who no longer gather but now "flocke,/And cluster thicke" around the Giant, "Like foolish flies about an hony crocke,/In hope by him great benefite to gaine,/And

---

[171] Spenser, *The Faerie Queene*, V.ii.29.
[172] Ibid., V.i.5-11.

vncontrolled freedome to obtaine."[173] Among the "many people" who gather around the Giant are "fooles, women, and boys"[174] whom Artegal disregards contemptuously as evidence of the Giant's illegitimacy, yet who also constitute the typically disenfranchised groups that are denied equality, freedom, and justice under the status quo that Artegal defends.

Dismissing the Giant as a populist demagogue, Artegal betrays another reason why autochthony was "not allowable" for early modern English subjects under monarchical rule—namely, because it revived the threat of democracy. The Giant's call for sociopolitical equality harkens back to Socrates' argument in the Platonic dialogue *Menexenus*, that unlike other states inhabited by "a heterogeneous collection of all sorts of people, so that their polities also are heterogeneous...our people, on the contrary, being all born of one mother, claim to be neither the slaves of one another nor the masters; rather does our natural birthequality drive us to seek lawfully legal equality."[175] But Artegal fails or refuses to recognize the democratic potential of the people gathering around the Giant; instead, he views them much like the "loose people" targeted by Irenius in his description of the Munster famine.

An exchange from Spenser's *A View of The State of*

---

[173] Ibid., V.ii.33.

[174] Ibid., V.ii.30.

[175] Plato, *Menexenus*, quoted in and trans. Geschiere, *The Perils of Belonging: Autochthony, Citizenship, and Exclusion in Africa and Europe*, 10.

Ireland confirms the allegorical link between the native Irish and the "great assembly" of people surrounding the Giant. "There is a great use among the Irish to make great assemblies together upon a rath or hill," Irenius observes, whereupon "commonly resort all the scum of loose people, where they may freely meet and confer" on whatever matters they wish.[176] Irenius attributes the construction of "these mounts and great stones" to the Saxons and Danes, which satisfies Eudoxus as an alternative to the common misconception that the assembly places are "old Giants trivets," prehistoric stone structures "that "would not else be brought into order or reared up without the strength of Giants."[177]

Eudoxus may find the latter narrative unallowable and even repugnant because it consolidates native populations around a symbol of indigenous strength. But if in *A View of The State of Ireland* the Giants are safely dead, inanimate stones the only remnants of their extinct race, in *The Faerie Queene*, by contrast, the Giant stands "Vpon a rocke" as a living representative of autochthony. Spenser's poem therefore confronts readers with the question that Browne, for instance, circumvents in *Urn Burial*, where the unearthed urns cannot claim autochthony because they

---

[176] Spenser, *A View of the State of Ireland*, 77.

[177] Ibid., 77. See Cohen, *Stone: An Ecology of the Inhuman*, 201. "Autochthonous British presence often materializes within English narrative as lithic intrusion: mounds, ruins, cities wrought of gold or gems, sudden subterranean spaces."

are dead: if an autochthon were able to "speak with life," what would s/he say?

First, Spenser's Giant proposes to take up "all the earth" and divide it from sea, air, and fire in order to re-weigh the world and "restore" the "surplus" of each element to its original dispensation.[178]

> For why, he sayd they all vnequall were,
> And had encroched vppon others share,
> Like as the sea (which plaine he shewed there)
> Had worne the earth, so did the fire the aire;
> So all the rest did others parts empaire.
> And so were realmes and nations run awry.
> All which he vndertooke for to repaire,
> In sort as they were formed aunciently;
> And all things would reduce vnto equality.[179]

Intending to redress both inequality in nature as well as human inequality, the Giant aims to level geopolitical hierarchy by leveling geography, flattening the "mountains hie" that tower over "the lowly plaine" while taking down "Tyrants" and "Lordings" that tower over the common people. The Giant's plan to "repaire" all things "as they were formed" anciently—in other words, of the earth, as both the proem and Artegal concur—levels a challenge at colonialist empires that "empaire" lands inhabited by others just as the sea encroaches upon the earth through

---

[178] Spenser, *The Faerie Queene*, V.ii.31.

[179] Ibid., V.ii.32.

natural erosion.[180]

But Artegal accuses the Giant of presuming "to weigh the world anew," without first knowing, as Artegal presumably does, how things were weighed in the past.[181] He censures the Giant for showing "great wrong" instead of showing "right," which is to say not only that the Giant's claim of autochthony is wrong, but also that it fails by emphasizing the wrongs or injustices suffered by autochthonous peoples rather than positing their right. Nevertheless, Artegal shows himself to be wrong about the world as the proem describes it, when he tells the Giant that "no change hath yet beene found" in the geocentric cosmos observed by Ptolemy, and that "heauenly iustice" has kept everything as it was in the beginning, when "not a dram was missing of their right" and everyone knew "their certaine bound," unlike the Giant who refuses to be put in his place.[182]

However, Artegal's claim that the Giant shows wrong instead of right rather shows the Giant to be right about the world, where according to the proem, "Right now is wrong, and wrong that was is right,/As all things else in time are chaunged quight./Ne wonder; for the heauens reuolution/Is wandred farre from where it first was

---

[180] See Fowler, "The Failure of Moral Philosophy in the Work of Edmund Spenser," 60-61. "[T]he orthographic merging of 'empire' with 'impair' epitomizes the anticolonial argument."

[181] Spenser, *The Faerie Queene*, V.ii.34.

[182] Ibid., V.ii.35-36.

pight,"[183] an observation the Giant reiterates for Artegal:

> Thou foolishe Elfe (said then the Gyant wroth)
> Seest not, how badly all things present bee,
> And each estate quite out of order go'th?
> The sea it selfe doest thou not plainely see
> Encroch vppon the land there vnder thee;
> And th'earth it selfe how daily its increast,
> By all that dying to it turned be?
> Were it not good that wrong were then surceast,
> And from the most, that some were giuen to the
> least?[184]

The Giant views it as "wrong" that Artegal and the sea that is "vnder" him have infringed on the land, while "all that dying" have overburdened it. The unnamed resource he proposes to redistribute "from the most...to the least" therefore includes not only wealth and sovereignty, but also life itself, which requires living space. The Giant's invocation of autochthony in "th'earth it selfe"—autos ("it selfe") and chthōn ("th'earth")—is not lost on Artegal, who swiftly seeks to reappropriate and neutralize the discourse. "[T]he earth is not augmented more," he corrects the Giant,

> By all that dying into it doe fade.
> For of the earth they formed were of yore;
> How euer gay their blossome or their blade

_____

[183] Ibid., V.Proem.4.
[184] Ibid., V.ii.37. Emphasis mine.

101

Doe flourish now, they into dust shall vade.
What wrong then is it, if that when they die,
They turne to that, whereof they first were
made?[185]

Sterilizing the Giant's political claim of autochthony by subsuming it under theological and universalizing tropes, Artegal's response resembles the language of *The Book of Common Prayer*: "we are mortal, formed of the earth, and unto earth shall we return."[186] However, where this statement owns its autochthony, as it were, with the first-person plural "we," Artegal's riposte to the Giant, by contrast, distances autochthones with the third-person pronouns "they" and "their" a total of seven times. On the one hand, the Christian revision absorbs the Giant's naturalistic autochthony such that the latter has no force as a territorial claim: if all humans, no less than giants, are born of the earth, then everybody and therefore nobody has a more original right to possess land. Instead, might makes right, and might, in this case, belongs overwhelmingly to Artegal and Talus.

On the other hand, the grammatical shift from "we" in *The Book of Common Prayer* to "they" in Artegal's response serves to other autochthones and to project mortality onto them, linking them with the dead and dying. Unlike Christian *memento mori* and *vanitas* tropes, which imply a kind of levelling egalitarianism in death, this reading preserves

---

[185] Ibid., V.ii.39-40.
[186] Church of England, *The Book of Common Prayer*, 482.

hierarchy by identifying only specific populations or races as earth-born in order to justify the potential "wrong" of their annihilation.

Artegal thus insinuates that "all that dying" observed by the Giant has no weight: first, in the literal sense that the accumulating corpses of autochthones do not enlarge the earth, having been born from it in the first place; second, in the metaphorical sense that their deaths are insignificant because their lives did not matter to begin with. "They liue, they die, like as he doth ordaine,/Ne euer any asketh reason why."[187] Artegal's reasoning here, I suggest, less resembles a pious Providentialism that levels all lives as equally autochthonous—born from and returned to the same earth—than it resembles a colonial disregard for indigenous lives regarded as expendable because they are autochthonous in a worldly rather than in a Christian sense.

Indeed, it is difficult not to hear Artegal's response to the Giant echoed in Frantz Fanon's bleak observation over three and half centuries later in *The Wretched of the Earth* (1961): "The town belonging to the colonized people…is a place of ill fame, peopled by men of evil repute. They are born there, it matters little where or how; they die there, it matters little where, nor how."[188] While it is critical to evaluate the relative merits of the Giant's claims and Artegal's

---

[187] Spenser, *The Faerie Queene*, V.ii.41.

[188] Frantz Fanon, *Wretched of the Earth*, trans. C. Farrington (New York: Grove Weidenfeld, 1991), 37-39.

counterarguments, dwelling too heavily on these risks eliding the most flagrant and overarching injustice of the episode—namely, that Artegal and Talus "admire" something
on the coast and within a matter of twenty-four stanzas
they have left in their wake a dead Giant and an unpeopled
"field forsooke" of its former inhabitants.[189]

In the final analysis, Artegal's "right" (which the Giant
sees only as "wrong") is the power of life and death over
the autochthonous population. Artegal and Talus actively
exercise the premodern sovereign prerogative to take life
when they kill the Giant, over whose people they then pas-
sively exercise the modern sovereign prerogative either to
foster or disallow life. They decide on the latter by default
as they proceed on their journey without redressing the
life-threatening injustice and inequality that gave rise to
the Giant in the first place. To prove his sovereignty, Artegal challenges the Giant to "take the right" and weigh it
against "so much wrong." Artegal then places "the right"
in one scale while the Giant "fill[s] the other scale with
so much wrong./But all the wrongs that he therein could
lay," fail to outweigh Artegal's right, so that "all the wrongs
could not a litle right downe way."[190] Artegal explains that
the Giant's balance can merely "right or wrong betoken"—
that is, indicate what is wrong and what is right—whereas
"the doome of right" or its judgment must be "in the mind"
and therefore, as Artegal posited earlier of the thoughts

---

[189] Spenser, *The Faerie Queene*, V.ii.54.
[190] Ibid., V.ii.46.

that "flow" from the human mind, it cannot be weighed. It is in Artegal's interest to construe right and wrong as intangible, abstract principles, because it allows for his flexible morality based on the "equity" and "conscience" he learned from Astraea, according to which Artegal's internal justification for his actions—his righteousness—weighs more than the justice of their external consequences.[191] If the Giant is right that "wrongs" have weight, then he is also right that "all that dying" in fact does augment the earth and that "so much wrong" would successfully "counterpeise" or outweigh Artegal's right to take or disallow the life of autochthonous peoples.

Ultimately, "the right" outweighs "the truth," and when Artegal instructs the Giant to balance the two, Artegal's "right [sits] in the middest of the beame alone."[192] It is reasonable that the Giant rejects "the right" that is divorced from truth, and yet with this forfeiture he appears to authorize his own death warrant. This suggests that "the right" claimed by Artegal is the power over life and death.

> But he [the Giant] the right from thence did thrust
> away, For it was not the right, which he did seeke...
> Whom when so lewdly minded Talus found,
> Approching nigh vnto him cheeke by cheeke,
> He shouldered him from off the higher ground,
> And down the rock him throwing, in the sea him
> dround.

---

[191] Ibid., V.i.7.
[192] Ibid., V.ii.48.

Even in death, the Giant stands for autochthony: as when Artegal and Talus first approach him standing "Vpon a rocke," now he resembles "a ship, whom cruell tempest driues/Vpon a rocke with horrible dismay,/Her shattered ribs in thousand peeces" like "His timbered bones all broken."[193] The cross-gendering metaphor, turning the male giant into a female ship, echoes the proem's fear that humankind will be "degendered" into something worse than the stones thrown by Pyrrha and Deucalion. At the same time, the Giant's downfall aligns him with the Old Testament giants thought to have perished in the Flood, as Dunseath argues,[194] while the shipwreck serves as a dismal contrast to humankind's successful repopulation of the earth by "the Colonies" aboard Noah's ship, as Browne calls them.

Notwithstanding the suggestion of annihilation, however, the ship's "shattered ribs" also evoke the autochthone Adam's rib from which Eve is born, while the Giant's "timbered bones" conjure the Old Testament book of *Ezekiel*, in which God promises to bring "my people…out of [their] graves, and…into the land of Israel" after breathing life into bones, which then "lived, and stood up upon their feet, an exceeding great army."[195] Finally, the context of book 5—which insists that things carried by the sea from one territory to another rightfully belong to the

---

[193] Ibid., V.ii.50.

[194] Dunseath, *Spenser's Allegory of Justice*, 107-108.

[195] *The book of Ezekiel*, 37:10.

latter—raises the question of where the Giant's bones and ribs will wash up next, thus exposing Talus' giganticide as a myopic and temporary solution to the colonization of unpeopled lands.

More immediately, the giganticide creates a power vacuum which Artegal, as a knight errant en route to Faerie Court, is not prepared to fill; it unpeoples the land by preventing them from gathering as people, democratically or otherwise, and by transforming the entire population into enemy combatants who can now be killed indiscriminately, with still more impunity than when they were merely regarded as autochthones: "[W]hen the people," who once gathered in "great assembly" around the Giant, "saw his sudden desolation,/They...gather in tumultuous rout," and "they rose in armes, and all in battell order stood."[196] These soldiers—whose spontaneous militarization recalls the army of dead bones narrated by Ezekiel, as well as the dragon's teeth sown by Cadmus—are no longer people but a "lawlesse multitude" that shows the limits of Artegal's justice. Artegal wants neither to kill the autochthones, lest their blood stain "his noble hands," nor allow them to live, for fear that "they with shame would" pursue him. "He much was troubled," and, paralyzed by indecision, he sends Talus "t'inquire/The cause of their array, and truce for to desire."[197]

First allowing the Giant to be killed and then question-

---

[196] Spenser, *The Faerie Queene*,, V.ii.51.
[197] Ibid., V.ii.52.

ing the "cause" of his people's mobilization, Artegal not only adds insult to injury but also implicates himself in the accusation he had levelled at the Giant earlier, namely, that "of things subiect to thy daily vew/Thou doest not know the causes, nor their courses dew."[198] That he sends Talus to negotiate a truce confirms Artegal's poor judgment if not his injustice, given that the "yron man" has just arrogated and arbitrarily exercised the power to take life. When Talus approaches the gathering, they attack first, justifiably but with futility, "all their weapons" failing to make a dent in his disproportionate strength. Artegal does not recall him, and Talus proceeds to overthrow the gathering "like a swarme of flyes" until they disperse and hide away.[199] Thus, although Talus does not directly kill any of the Giant's people, he nevertheless exposes the population to death like a "a Faulcon" flying "at a flush of Ducks," terrorizing them "with dreadfull sight/Of death, the which them almost ouertooke."[200] Now hidden "in holes and bushes" and "almost" overtaken by death, the once "great assembly" is further reduced to resemble the "loose people" in Irenius' account of the Munster Famine, whom war and starvation scatter and decimate, and who at last come "creeping forth" from "every corner" of the wilderness like the living dead.[201]

---

[198] Ibid., V.ii.42.

[199] Ibid., V.ii.53.

[200] Ibid., V.ii.54.

[201] Spenser, *A View of the State of Ireland*, 101-102.

Remarkably, mid-seventeenth-century English authors welcomed the brand of justice meted out by Talus, and not only to be exercised on foreign populations but also at home. John Milton, for example, writes in *Eikonoklastes* (October 1649), his iconoclastic justification for the regicide of Charles I, that "[i]f there were a man of iron, such as Talus, by our Poet Spencer, is fain'd to be the page of Justice, who with his iron flaile could doe all this, and expeditiously, without those deceitful forms and circumstances of Law, worse th[a]n ceremonies in Religion; I say God send it do[w]n, whether by one Talus, or by a thousand."[202] Not surprisingly, twenty-first-century readers are more reticent than Milton in admiring Talus' ability to thresh out falsehood from truth and right from wrong, without red tape but also without due process, like an unaccountable police force that is itself judge, jury, and executioner.

It is significant that Talus is the one who kills the autochthonous Giant, because the former represents a new kind of earthly sovereignty emergent in the early modern period, according to which those capable of unearthing precious material have the right to the lands of others who are imagined to have sprung from the earth naturally through no industry or technological innovation of their own. Talus has been read as an aggregation of several characters from pagan and Christian myth. His role as a law-enforcer links him to Talos, the "brazen" man

---

[202] John Milton, *Eikonoklastes* (London, 1650), 35.

given to Minos by Zeus in a dialogue attributed to Plato.[203] Angus Fletcher, alternatively, has remarked Talus' resemblance to the giant made of gold, silver, bronze, iron, and clay in Nebuchadnezzar's dream in the book of *Daniel*.[204] His name also alludes to the "retaliation" of Talionic justice, from the Latin *talio*, "Recompensation or requitynge of an hurte or offence wyth a lyke hurte or offence, as an eye for an eye."[205] It has gone largely unnoticed, however, that the iron man's name echoes Tellus, the Roman Goddess of the Earth, although early moderns were familiar with Isidore of Seville's etymology, that "Earth is called tellus because we gather, tollimus, its fruit."[206] Spenser's Talus—read as fruit of the earth that is not yielded naturally but rather crafted using metals that might well have been ripped from Irish mines—harbingers a new world order in which the life of privileged populations derives from the depredation of the earth and the eradication of

---

[203] See Edmund Spenser, *The Works of Edmund Spenser: A Variorum Edition, Faerie Queene Book Five*, ed. Edwin Greenlaw, Charles Grosvenor Osgood, and Frederick Morgan Padelford (Baltimore: Johns Hopkins University Press, 2001), 166.

[204] Angus Fletcher, *The Prophetic Moment: An Essay on Spenser* (Chicago: University of Chicago Press, 1971), 141. Cf. the book of *Daniel*, 2.32-35.

[205] Richard Huloet, *Abecedarium Anglico Latinum* (London, 1552).

[206] Isidore of Seville, *Etymologies*, trans. Priscilla Throop (Charlotte, Vermont: MedievalMS, 2005), XIV.1.1. See also Pliny's *History of the World* (trans. 1601), which includes a brief alphabetized catalogue of "words of Art" and their explanations. The first entry under "T" is "TEllus," defined tersely as "the Earth."

races seen to be rooted to it.

Talus embodies a unique way of supplanting earth-born life, but Spenser's representation of giganticide in *The Faerie Queene* and genocide in *A View of The State of Ireland* are entirely typical of his culture; both arguably emerge from the early modern English discourse of autochthony. It is through this discourse that Spenser's contemporaries figured the separation of races as a separation of species, an ideological process manifested in renderings of autochthonous lives as nonhuman: for example, Ingelo's intelligent mushrooms, Ionas' trees and herbs, Spenser's flies and ducks, and the giants of Browne and Spenser. This way of thinking betrays itself, moreover, in the early modern anxiety about miscegenation and the "mixture" of races. Insofar as the biological category of species defines the largest group of organisms capable of interbreeding, then preventing colonized races from peopling their land is tantamount to their dehumanization.

The early modern discourse of autochthony facilitates the intersection of racial difference with the categories of living and dead, thus prefiguring Foucault's observation of biopolitical racism beginning in the nineteenth century, which, he argues, constitutes "the condition for the acceptability of putting to death."[207] Again, Browne promulgates this ideology by linking the discovery of dead autochthones on Norfolk soil to the discovery of the New

---

[207] Achille Mbembe, "Necropolitics," *Public Culture* 15(1) (Duke University Press, 2003): 11-40; 17.

World, although the latter, he conveniently omits, was still peopled by living inhabitants. Spenser's Artegal likewise delegitimizes the Giant's complaint that his people are dying en masse, because, Artegal reasons, the people are autochthones—"of the earth they formed were"—and therefore always already akin to the dead.

Peopling the Isle With Calibans

The preceding pages have responded to the question raised at the start of this chapter: why does Shakespeare's Prospero address Caliban, who is native to the island on which the former has settled, as "earth"? I have worked to show that being born "of the earth" means something quite different in the contexts of ancient Athenian autochthony, orthodox Anglican theology, and early modern English colonial ideology. In colonial contexts, some humans came to be seen as earthlier than others, a status that served to justify the dispossession of their land and even of their right to life. In stark contrast to Spenser's Giant, who stands "Vpon a rock" in life as in death, Caliban protests to Prospero, "here you sty me in this hard rock, whiles you do keep from me the rest o' the island" (1.2.344-347).

The prepositional difference between the Giant standing upon a rock and Caliban confined in a rock represents the difference between unallowable and allowable forms of autochthony in the early modern English worldview. Prospero accuses Caliban of being a "most lying slave," whom he treated "with human care" until Caliban attempted "to violate" Prospero's child, Miranda. Caliban does not refute the allegation: "O ho, O ho! Would't had been done! Thou didst prevent me; I had peopled else this isle with Calibans" (1.2.348-354).[208] While Prospero is rightly concerned to protect Miranda, Caliban indicates a more insidious motive for confining him in the rock, namely, to prevent him from peopling his own island.[209]

For Prospero, the rape attempt justifies his enslavement and abuse of Caliban, but—if we were to reframe this dynamic in the terms established by Artegal and the Giant in *The Faerie Queene*—does Caliban's "wrong" outweigh his "right" to people his homeland? What right does Prospero have to prevent him from doing so, beyond the right to protect Miranda? On a closer reading, Prospero appears motivated to stop Caliban from reproducing by any means, no less than he is motivated to protect Miranda: "Abhorrèd slave," he tells Caliban, "thy vile race…had that in't which good natures/Could not abide to be with; therefore wast thou/Deservedly confined into this rock" (1.2.354-

---

[208] See Lupton, "Creature Caliban," 20. She has remarked that "people" here not only implies "humanity taken as a whole… but also a people, an ethnos, gens, or nation of Calibans that would take its place among other ethne."

[209] See Philip Mason, forward to *Prospero and Caliban*, 12. "[A]fter reading Mannoni, one is inclined to wonder whether Prospero did not, by projecting his own desire on to Caliban, first put the thought into his head."

364). The race Prospero has in mind, it is reasonable to assume, is the earth-born race of autochthones. It little matters that Caliban is merely native to the island and not technically autochthonous, as Prospero acknowledges, just as it little matters to Spenser's Irenius that the native Irish are not literally born from the earth. What matters is that the discourse of autochthony and its attendant tropes— including nonhuman earth-born races, annihilation, and repopulation—are ready at hand in the early modern English imaginary. Merely addressing Caliban as "earth" brings this discourse to the fore, unearthing, as it were, a bio-political racism that calls into question Caliban's humanity and his status as a living person.

When King Alonso's drunken jester Trinculo stumbles upon Caliban, who is fetching wood as Prospero's slave, Trinculo wonders whether the native is "a man or a fish? Dead or alive?" and speculates how much Caliban would be worth in England, where the people "will not give a doit [i.e., half of an English farthing] to relieve a lame beggar, [yet] they will lay out ten to see a dead Indian" (2.2.23-31). In other words, the shipwrecked European cares whether Caliban is alive or dead primarily for economic reasons; the implication is that the life of a beggar living in England, whether native or stranger, is worth less than the spectacle of an exotic dead body. For Prospero, by contrast, at least so long as he remains on the island, Caliban is worth more alive than he is dead, as he reminds Miranda: "We cannot miss him: he does make our fire,/Fetch in our wood and serves in offices/That profit us" (1.2.314-317). Prospero's sovereignty, then, consists not only in allowing Caliban to live but also making him live, a reiteration of the power exercised over Caliban's mother Sycorax in Algiers, who despite her capital crimes, she did "one thing" for which "they would not take her life" (1.2.268-269).

To be sure, Caliban is not alone subject to Prospero's power of life and death. For instance, Ariel prevents Antonio and Sebastian from murdering the sleeping Alonso and Gonzalo, lest, Ariel explains, Prospero's "project dies—to keep them living" (2.1.295). Likewise, seeking Prospero's blessing to marry Miranda, Ferdinand vows to "hope for quiet days, fair issue, and long life" (4.1.23-24), an oath which pleases Prospero because it aligns with the paradigm of biopower underlying his "project." Prospero's biopower extends even to the dead: "graves at my command have waked their sleepers, oped, and let 'em forth by my so potent art" (5.1.48-50). Prospero does not exercise biopower exclusively over Caliban, then, but the latter's isolated and foregrounded earthliness makes his bare life exceptionally vulnerable.

Prospero allows Caliban to live but prevents him from peopling the island, and Prospero might disallow Caliban's life to the point of death without constituting a wrong, according to the colonial logic captured by the question Artegal asks of earth-born autochthones: "What wrong then is it, if that when they die,/They turne to that, whereof they first were made?"[210] Again, Artegal's third-person "they" implies that not all races are earth-born and that it would be wrong if "all that dying" pertained rather to non-autochthonous humans. Likewise, by singling out Caliban as "earth," Prospero conditions the acceptability of his death. Whether Caliban lives or dies depends on the command of Prospero, who would likely agree with Artegal's admonition to the Giant concerning the lives and deaths of autochthones, that is, never to ask the "reason why."[211] Caliban is subject to an extreme but not special case of Prospero's power of life and death, however, and it will be useful to investigate how such biopower was exerted over European lives, particularly over early-seventeenth-century English lives, including readers of *The Faerie Queene* and audiences of *The Tempest*.

English culture arguably defined acceptable forms of human life against the unsanctioned, dehumanized, bare life of autochthones. The isolation of autochthonous life served to justify annihilating entire populations, either by the direct violence of the sword, or by disallowing life and exposing to death through colonial projects such as the earth-scorching prevention of manurance. Unlike autochthonous lives, English lives were seen to matter—whereas the former are disallowed, the latter are fostered. English subjects increasingly imagined themselves as living and

---

[210] Spenser, *The Faerie Queene*, V.ii.39-40.
[211] Ibid., V.ii..41.

dying not (only) "as he doth ordaine,"[212] where he is Providence or the king, but also as they themselves ordained. In other words, English people began taking interest in and control over their own earthly life, which is to say life that is embodied, biological, secular, and political, but which is decidedly not to say life that is born from the earth.

Prospero's "project" to keep those under his control alive is not an isolated endeavor on the island of Shakespeare's play, but rather one instance of a larger project of life-prolongation in seventeenth-century England, which brings power over life and death—or at least the illusion of it—into the hands of everyday English people. This project is exemplified in Francis Bacon's *History of Life and Death* (1623; Englished, 1638), to which the following chapter turns.

---

[212] Ibid.

The New Science of Life Prolongation

In Shakespeare's *As You Like It* (1599), the melancholy Jaques calls all the world a stage and then narrates the life of man in seven parts, each a performance of behavioral norms, sartorial fashions, and subjective attitudes that are characteristic of a particular stage of life.

> At first the infant, mewling and puking in the nurse's arms. Then the whining schoolboy with his satchel and shining morning face, creeping like snail unwillingly to school. And then the lover, sighing like furnace, with a woeful ballad made to his mistress' eyebrow. Then, a soldier, full of strange oaths, and bearded like the pard, jealous in honour, sudden, and quick in quarrel, seeking the bubble reputation even in the cannon's mouth. And then the justice, in fair round belly with good capon lined, with eyes severe and beard of formal cut, full of wise saws and modern instances; and so he plays his part. The sixth age shifts into the lean and slippered pantaloon, with spectacles on nose and pouch on side, his youthful hose, well saved, a world too wide for his shrunk shank, and his big, manly voice, turning again toward childish treble, pipes and whistles in his sound.

> Last scene of all, that ends this strange, eventful
> history, is second childishness and mere
> oblivion, sans teeth, sans eyes, sans taste, sans
> everything (2.7.138-165).

Strikingly absent from Jaques' qualitative rubric is any quantitative evaluation of life. He says nothing about the duration of each stage, about how many years it takes to progress through all seven ages, or about the numerical age at which infants become schoolboys, lovers become soldiers, the young become old, and so on. Although the account features body parts (arms, face, belly, eyes, nose, and shank) and embodied actions (puking, sighing, and quarreling), Jaques does not describe the body's biological or physiological development across the stages of life—nor could he have in a play written just before the emergence of such new scientific discourses.

Jaques' account affords an instructive comparison with the "Scale or Ladder of Mans life" in Francis Bacon's *History Naturall And Experimentall, of Life and Death. Or of the Prolongation of Life* (1623; 1638), a text, I argue, that represents an unprecedented event in the histories of medicine and politics, and more generally, in the history of Western ideas about life and death. Bacon would have agreed with Jaques' description of life as an "eventful history," but unlike Jaques, Bacon included numerical age in his account and articulated biological rather than social markers of development: "Quickening...Birth, Sucking, feeding on

Pap, and Spoon-meat in Infancy, of teeth at two yeares old, secret haire at twelve or foureteene...hayre...under the armeholes, a budding Beard...full strength and agility, Graynesse, Baldnesse...inclining to a creature with three feete, Death."[213] Where Jaques' account is circular, figuring old age and death as returns to "childishness and mere oblivion," Bacon's "Scale or Ladder" is a linear lifeline that ends in death. Such linear perspective, I will show, comports with Bacon's wish to prolong the length of life, to slow its progress toward death, and to reverse the course of senescence back toward rejuvenation.

Bacon excluded the subjective, socio-symbolic identities that characterize human life in Jaques' account.[214] The goal of *The History of Life and Death* is to prolong "Mans life," but Bacon's omission of subjectivity makes his account more or less applicable to the biological development of other nonhuman, mammalian creatures. Notwithstanding his quantitative, biologized, and unliterary representation of life, however, Bacon did not fully depart from symbolic language; for example, in the poetic description of old age as a creature with three feet—that is, a biped with a cane.

---

[213] Francis Bacon, *The Historie of Life and Death. With Observations Naturall and Experimentall for the Prolonging of Life* (London: printed by John Okes for Humphrey Mosely, 1638), 275.

[214] See Margaret Morganroth Gullette, *Aged by Culture* (Chicago and London: The University of Chicago Press, 2004), 7. "If we mean by ideology a system that socializes us into certain beliefs and ways of speaking about what it means to be 'human,' while suppressing alternatives, it is useful to [discuss] 'age ideology.'"

Such residual poeticism in a new scientific context reflects my claim that even as accounts of life became increasingly quantitative in the seventeenth century, they never completely transcended earlier, qualitative modes of evaluating life that still pervaded theological, ethical, and cultural discourses of the period.

Bacon's use of the term "creature" further underscores his interest in forms of life that humans share with nonhumans.[215] He explicitly remarked the creaturely life only of the elderly, however, those who are nearest to death on his "Scale or Ladder," if not according to the ethical axiom whereby all mortal creatures are always equidistant to death. Without fully denuding the old of their sociosymbolic significance, Bacon's apparent parapraxis nevertheless associates elderly life in particular with creaturely life. In an account of "Mans life" that is already potentially de-humanizing, this invites questions that preoccupied seventeenth-century conversations surrounding longevity: is human life commensurable with nonhuman life? When and where should accounts of life begin and end? Specifically, while evaluating longevity in national populations, should the lives of unborn or prerational infants, inmates of Bethlem Royal Hospital insane asylum, incarcerated

---

[215] Recall from the previous chapter Julia Reinhard Lupton's reading of "creature Caliban" as a form of "'bare life,' pure vitality denuded of its symbolic significance and political capacity and then sequestered within the domain of civilization as its disavowed core" ("Creature Caliban," 2).

criminals, the elderly, and others declared to be *non compos mentis* be taken into account?

Such questions about what counts as life were motivated by moral, theological, and empirical concerns in the seventeenth century. They were not yet, and not inevitably, instrumentalized by state biopower in decisions about which lives are worth living and prolonging and which are unworthy of life, but they already elicited the anthropogenesis by which sovereignty institutes sociopolitical order, as I argue throughout this book by way of Agamben. Chapter 1 showed that English colonial identity defined itself in part against autochthony, which Anglicans depicted as a creaturely or vegetative lifeform comparable to the life of animals, insects, plants, and even the earth itself; which is to say, a lifeform that is not state-sanctioned and therefore liable to be killed with impunity. Differentiating autochthonous lives from human lives was one way authors delineated the boundaries of English power: the extent of its duty to control, protect, foster, or intervene in the life of governed populations. Chapter 3 argues that early modern English sovereignty, informed by an orthodox Christian tradition of anthropogenesis, depended upon a popular belief that an immortal, disembodied, and rational soul makes human life incommensurable with the life of mortal creatures. The Leveller Richard Overton challenged this tradition by representing human life as wholly embodied and absolutely mortal. The present chapter argues that Bacon likewise enabled the reorganization of sociopolitical structures by reconceiving life as an embodied thing in the world that is subject to myriad influences including history, the environment, nationality, individual lifestyle, and medical technology.

The two most frequent words in *The History of Life and Death* are "living" and "bodies." Bacon's unprecedented interest in nutritive, embodied life, I suggest, facilitated the reordering of political sovereignty around the biological life of national populations, reflecting a nascent discourse of biopower that it also enabled. In the centuries following Bacon, this discourse increasingly aligned nutritive life "with the biological heritage of the nation," according to Foucault,[216] as sovereignty was exercised "at the level of life itself…[which] gave power its access even to the body."[217] My critical intervention is two-fold: first, to elucidate and revise Bacon's place in intellectual history by taking into account the theoretical paradigm of biopower; second, to interrogate the history of biopower through early modern primary sources that both corroborate and problematize the theses of Foucault and Agamben.

It is a critical commonplace that Bacon linked knowledge to power and that the guiding motive of his new sci-

---

[216] Giorgio Agamben, *The Open: Man and Animal*, 15. See also Hobbes, *Leviathan*, 163. "The nutrition of a commonwealth consisteth, in the plenty, and distribution of materials conducing to life: in concoction, or preparation; and (when concocted) in the conveyance of it, by convenient conduits, to the public use."

[217] Foucault, "Right of Death and Power over Life," 265.

ence was to increase human power over nature.[218] Extant scholarship has overlooked and underestimated Bacon's interest in life-prolongation, however, which preoccupied him throughout his career before culminating in *The History of Life and Death*. Against the traditional consensus that Bacon's concern with life-prolongation was subordinate to his larger goal of advancing knowledge, I propose that Bacon's wish to prolong life was concomitant with if not prior to his articulation of a new scientific ethos.

The few critical treatments of *The History of Life and Death* are descriptive but not analytical,[219] and they resemble "most cultural and social histories of old age," which according to Helen Small, have relegated philosophy to history and science, placing "Bacon as a late transitional figure to modern science."[220] Georges Minois has suggested, for instance, that because Bacon was "a philosopher, a scientist and a politician of the first rank, his interest in old age encompassed all three points of view."[221] Minois did

---

[218] See George Williamson, "Mutability, Decay, and seventeenth-century Melancholy," *ELH*, vol. 2, no. 2 (September 1935), 121-150; 133. Williamson has observed that "Bacon alone seems to have risen to the clear conception of progress as power acquired of nature."
[219] See, for example, Pat Thane, *Old Age in English History: Past Experiences, Present Issues* (New York: Oxford University Press, 2000), 59-61. See also, Thomas R. Cole, *The Journey of Life: A Cultural History of Aging in America* (Cambridge: Cambridge University Press, 1992), 30.
[220] Helen Small, *The Long Life* (Oxford: Oxford University Press, 2007), 7.
[221] Georges Minois, *History of Old Age: From Antiquity to the Renaissance*,

not elaborate on what specifically resulted from the convergence of these three points of view, beyond remarking that Bacon "considered the principal fault of aged politicians to be indecision."[222] I aim more precisely to parse and analyze the interaction between Bacon's theological, philosophical, scientific, and political investments as they unfold in *The History of Life and Death*.

I read Bacon not just as a transitional figure—from early modern to modern, from theology to history, or from philosophy to science—but also as an embodiment of imperfect and yet unrealized transitions. Stephen Gaukroger has argued that "Bacon's was the first systematic, comprehensive attempt to transform the early modern philosopher from someone whose primary concern is with how to live morally into someone whose primary concern is with the understanding of and reshaping of natural processes."[223] Without disputing this claim, I shift focus to the ways that moral philosophy and the reshaping of natural processes were for Bacon not only mutually conflicting but also mutually constitutive.[224]

---

trans. Sarah Hanbury Tenison (Chicago: The University of Chicago Press, 1987), 269.

[222] Ibid.

[223] Stephen Gaukroger, *Francis Bacon and the Transformation of Early-Modern Philosophy* (Cambridge, Cambridge University Press, 2001), 5.

[224] I aim to extrapolate from early modern sources an interdisciplinary perspective on aging to address a philosophical impoverishment in the fields of age studies. See Small, *The Long Life*, 7. "Geriatric medicine and gerontology have, since the late nineteenth century and the late 1940s respectively, claimed an expertise in the subject

The new science of prolonging embodied life contradicted tenets of Christian orthodoxy such as its ethical orientation toward postmortem reward and punishment, and its dualistic ascription of life to the soul and mortality to the body. Stephen A. McKnight has remarked that "prevailing scholarship often ignores Bacon's religious ideas or dismisses them as part of the cultural iconography that Bacon manipulates to conceal or disguise his modern, secular, materialistic, rationalist views."[225] McKnight, John C. Brigs, and Perez Zagorin have argued, however, that Bacon's theological rhetoric "is a genuine reflection of his belief, not a cynical manipulation of prevailing religious sentiment."[226] There was indeed conflict between Bacon's theological and scientific commitments. Zagorin has remarked that Bacon's "very hopeful outlook on human regeneration was at odds with the religion of the age and his own Calvinistic heritage."[227] I concur with the view that

that has helped to push philosophy away from the forefront of the debate. It is more surprisingly the case also in the relatively new and self-consciously interdisciplinary fields of 'age studies' (the study of ageing across the life course) and 'critical gerontology' (that strand within gerontology which has especially advocated stronger ties to the humanities)."

[225] Stephen A. McKnight, *Religious Foundations of Francis Bacon's Thought* (Columbia: University of Missouri Press, 2006), 2.

[226] Ibid. See also John C. Briggs, "Bacon's Science and Religion," in *Cambridge Companion to Bacon*, ed. Markku Peltonen (Cambridge: Cambridge University Press, 1996), 172-99.

[227] Perez Zagorin, *Francis Bacon* (Princeton: Princeton University Press, 1998), 45-46.

Bacon genuinely sought to reconcile these conflicts and contradictions, to which I would add Agamben's observation that "secularization can also be understood…as a specific performance of Christian faith."[228] Bacon is often regarded as a defender of the separation between science and religion, a pioneer of the secularization that paved the way for the Scientific Revolution and the Enlightenment. His work on life-prolongation shows, however, that such secularization was not absolute and that it involved a careful incorporation of competing values and worldviews.

Bacon agreed with his contemporaries that life is only worth prolonging if it is useful and purposeful. He valued "the Offices and Duties of Life" over life itself and prescribed nothing that would interrupt or hinder "common duties and businesses."[229] But where in his early work Bacon considered the means to prolong *rational* life—for example, through epistemological shortcuts that expedited the transmission of knowledge and so theoretically left more time for living—his intention for *The History of Life and Death* was rather to prolong *nutritive* life, which required "a two-fold search…considering mans body as livelesse and unnourished; and as living, and nourished."[230]

---

[228] Giorgio Agamben, *The Signature of all Things: On Method* (Zone Books, 2009), 100. See also Giorgio Agamben, *The Kingdom and the Glory: For a Theological Genealogy of Economy and Government (Homo Sacer II, 2)* (Stanford: Stanford University Press, 2011), 48; 50-1; 108-9; 130.

[229] Ibid., 139.

[230] Francis Bacon, "The Access," *The historie of life and death. With observations naturall and experimentall for the prolonging of life* (printed by

This decisive articulation of the difference between the living and the lifeless constitutes an act of anthropogenesis, which, like Bacon's "Scale or Ladder of Mans life," generalizes the bare, nutritive, biological component of human lives almost to the point of de-humanizing them. Another version of the text, published the same year and for the same Humphrey Mosley but by a different printer, rendered the same passage in subtly but substantially different terms: "our Inquisition shall be double; First we will consider the Bodie of Man, as Inanimate, and not Repaired by Nourishment; Secondly, as Animate, and Repaired by Nourishment."[231] This may suggest that "living" and "animate" were interchangeable synonyms in English discourse in 1638, but it also reflects two distinct editorial decisions: one defining the subjects of Bacon's life-prolongation as "living" or "livelesse" human bodies, the other seeming to imply that Bacon's focus on bodies has levelled human life beyond the rank of creatures and plants to the status of (in)animate things.

Whatever motivated these editorial discrepancies, the version printed by John Haviland, who also published the original Latin version of Bacon's *Historia Vitae & Mortis* in 1623, preserved with English cognates the original vocabulary of (in)animacy: "*Primò contemplando Corpus humanum,*

John Okes for Humphrey Mosely, London, 1638), 7.

[231] Francis Bacon, "The Preface," *Historie naturall and experimentall, of life and death. Or of the prolongation of life* (printed by John Haviland for William Lee and Humphrey Mosley, London, 1638).

tanquam Inanimatum, & Inalimentatum; deinde tanquam Anima-tum, & Alimentatum."[232] The printer who translated these terms into a distinction between "living" and "livelesse" bodies was John Okes, whose father Nicholas Okes had printed a range of seventeenth-century dramatic texts including Shakespeare's *True Chronicle Historie of the Life and Death of King Lear and His Three Daughters* (1608). Speculations about how the father's work might have informed the son's decision to copywrite and print Bacon's *History* are outside the scope of this chapter, but Shakespeare's play dramatizes key issues circumscribing Bacon's work in life-prolongation, including old age and youth, sovereign biopower, and the political status of nonhuman lifeforms.

On the one hand, Bacon's decision to make nourishment the litmus test for what counts as life aligns with the comprehensive scope of his scientific method, because the nutritive or vegetative life shared by humans, animals, and plants is the most capacious category of life in Aristotle's tripartite division,[233] "the originative power the possession of which leads us to speak of things as *living* at all,"[234] "the most primitive and widely distributed power of soul, being indeed that one in virtue of which all are said to have life."[235] On the other hand, Bacon's project

---

[232] Francis Bacon, *Historia Vitae & Mortis* (London, 1623), 13-14.

[233] Jeffrey Nealon, *Plant Theory: Biopower and Vegetable Life* (Stanford University Press, 2016), 36-37.

[234] Aristotle, *De Anima*, trans. J.A. Smith, *The Basic Works of Aristotle*, ed. Richard McKeon (New York: Random House, 1941), 557.

[235] Ibid., 561.

may appear myopic in light of the subsequent history of human bodies in persistent vegetative states, bodies on the threshold between the living and the lifeless that are often exploited as sites of theological, ethical, legal, and political contestation.[236] Bacon's concept of nutritive life remained imbued with moral, theological, and political values, however, such that it was not inherently dehumanizing despite its now patent potential to be instrumentalized toward that end.

In addition to its alternative mode of anthropogenesis, which instituted a new epistemological (if not yet socio-political) order around nutritive life, *The History of Life and Death* also facilitated the integration of medicine and politics, an essential stage in the development of biopower.[237] Bacon hoped that the "great utility" of his work would inspire others to regard physicians as "Stewards of Divine Omnipotency and Clemency, in prolonging and renew-

---

[236] For Agamben, the nutritive life that Bacon hoped to prolong is "bare life…detached from any brain activity, and so to speak, from any subject." The isolation of nutritive life "constitutes in every sense a fundamental event for Western science, for example, by enabling advances in modern medicine and surgery (*The Open: Man and Animal*, 14-15).

[237] Agamben has identified this integration as "one of the essential characteristics of modern biopolitics," according to which "the sovereign decision on bare life comes to be displaced from strictly political motivations and areas to a more ambiguous terrain in which the physician and the sovereign seem to exchange roles" (*Homo Sacer*, 143).

ing the life of Man."[238] Latent in this medico-theological rhetoric is a claim about the decentralization of political power—namely, that sovereignty, conceived as absolute power or "Omnipotency" over life and death, bypasses the monarch and the state in its direct transfer from divine Providence to physicians. The new science of life-prolongation thus called for a proto-technocratic distribution of sovereignty to physicians and other experts. Where the positive form of this imagined bio-omnipotence is the power to prolong life, its negative form is the clemency to let live and the mercy to allow to die if not to kill directly.

Thomas Browne, himself a physician, remarked that anyone has the power, if not the right, to kill anyone else: the "one comfort left [is] that though it be in the power of the weakest arme to take away life, it is not in the strongest to deprive us of death."[239] Bacon's new science of life-prolongation nowhere called for a forceful deprivation of death, but the yet inarticulate discourse of seventeenth-century biopower already registered a concern that power to prolong life—whether stewarded by physicians, politicians, or by an alliance of state authority and technical expertise—might encroach upon the "one comfort" that still consoled Browne—namely, that nobody has the

---

[238] Bacon, "To the Living and Posterity," *The historie of life and death.*
[239] Browne, *Religio Medici*, 1.44. Cf. Hobbes, *Leviathan*, 82. "For as to the strength of the body, the weakest has strength enough to kill the strongest, either by secret machination, or by confederacy with others, that are in the same danger with himself."

power, let alone the right, to make others live by depriving them of death.

Chapter 4 shows that Shakespeare's *Lear* already dramatized the paradigms of life-prolongation and death-deprivation as two interwoven threads of the same fabric. The dramaturgical decision to let Lear, Cordelia, and others die at the end of the play—which shocked and repulsed audiences for centuries with what many saw as its gratuitously morbid production of corpses—arguably represents an act of clemency that counteracts the unbridled but ultimately impotent will to biopower driving the play.

The life-prolonging power of seventeenth-century physicians was checked by epistemological and technological limits from becoming power to deprive of death, but Bacon's work established the methodological and ideological conditions for this development in the future. His focus on nutritive life did not devalue human lives but rather instituted new criteria for evaluating them.[240] The new paradigm of longevity theoretically enabled a revaluation of all values whereby the forms and ways of life deemed to be good come to align with those deemed to be good *for long life*, and whereby life worth living becomes tantamount to life worth prolonging. *The History* explicitly valued longer life over shorter life; tacitly, it also ranked

---

[240] The fundamental biopolitical structure of modernity," according to Agamben (*Homo Sacer*, 136-137), is sovereignty's "decision on the value (or nonvalue) of life as such." This sovereign decision first emerged in European law during the early twentieth century.

human, creaturely, and vegetative lives not according to traditional ontotheological hierarchies but according to their relative length. In particular, Bacon evaluated human bodies, national populations, and ways of life not (directly) according to socioeconomic, moral, or political values but according to their conduciveness to long life.

The predominant voices in early modern English culture stressed the eternity of the incorporeal soul, while they described the prolongation of embodied life as an accumulation of more misery, debility, and sin, as well as an irreligious and unethical act of cowardice.[241] Bacon acknowledged but strategically revised such pejorative views of longevity. "For long Life [is] an increasing heape of sinnes and sorrowes lightly esteemed of Christians

---

[241] It is telling that the earliest occurrence of "longevity" cited in the *Oxford English Dictionary* contrasts the term against "eternity," because an entire discourse concerning life's length flourished in the space between early modern English culture's shifting attention from eternity, or everlastingness, to diuturnity, or long-lastingness. The citation comes from *Staffords Heavenly Dogge: or the Life and Death of Diogenes* (London, 1615), where Anthony Stafford contrasts the noble death of the eponymous ancient Greek philosopher against the allegedly more contemptible deaths of Alexander the Great and King Louis XI of France. In contrast to King Louis—who in his final days paid his physician an exorbitant amount of money "to prolong his too well beloued life"—Diogenes welcomed death as the only physician that could cure him, believing in "the longeuity of the soule, and not the eternity" (104-106). Typically of seventeenth-century English culture, Stafford holds up Diogenes' belief in longevity as a paragon to emulate not because the philosopher strove to prolong life, but on the contrary, because unlike Alexander and King Louis, he had the wisdom to know when to make a good end.

aspiring to Heaven," he admitted; nevertheless, long life "should not be dispised, because it affoords longer opportunity of doing good Workes."[242] Bacon's contemporaries generally devalued and indeed despised prolonged life, because they presupposed that the quality of life declines irreversibly as the senescent body decays inevitably. In stark contrast, Bacon posited that life's quality could improve and appreciate in value the longer it lasted. Addressing the belief promulgated throughout English culture that longer life makes it harder to reach heaven, the appeal to "good Workes" captured a major doctrinal dispute within Christianity; at the same time, it reconciled, in part by eliding, the conflicts between the new science of life-prolongation, orthodox Anglican theology, and conventional morality.

Unlike early modern Catholics, who regarded the performance of good works as a means toward salvation, Protestants professed sola fides ("faith alone") and rejected the salvific power of good works. The prospect of "longer opportunity" to perform good works would not then have motivated or justified Anglicans to prolong life. Even supposing that Bacon referred to secular and humanitarian rather than theological good works, his apology for life-prolongation clashes with the seventeenth-century English ethical paradigm inherited from the ancient Roman Stoic philosopher and playwright Seneca, according to which life lived purposefully is sufficiently long to accomplish good

---

[242] Bacon, *The historie of life and death*, 1-2.

works. Bacon's new science eventually prevailed, I suggest, because it assimilated and accommodated earlier traditions rather than rejecting them. The form of Bacon's proposal that "good Workes" justify longer life, for instance, pre-figured what sociologist Max Weber has identified as the "Protestant work ethic," the notion that the secularization of a religious morality based on self-discipline, hard work, and organization of one's life laid the groundwork for the formation of capitalism.

On the one hand, the same Calvinist predestinarian-ism that rejected the salvific power of good works also led Bacon's contemporaries to refute human power to pro-long life. On the other hand, Weber argued that Calvinists continued to value good works as signs of, if no longer as means toward, salvation. As Nikolas Rose has succinctly remarked, Weber "found an elective affinity between the Protestant ethic and the spirit of early capitalism, generat-ing the forms of life that made foresight, prudence, cal-culation, and accumulation not just legitimate but poten-tial indicators of salvation (Weber 1930)."[243] Analogously, I suggest that Bacon elected affinities between Anglican theology, proto-biology, and the spirit of biopower when he predicted that it will be a sign of salvation to live long in good health. "For while Christians aspire and labour to come to the Land of Promise; it will be a signe of Divine favour, if our shoos and the garments of our frail

---

[243] Rose, *The Politics of Life Itself*, 8.

bodies, be here little worne in our journey in the worlds wildernesse."[244] This is decidedly not to say that life's journey should be short, ending before the body starts to wear and decay, but rather that it should be possible to prevent and reverse the degeneration associated with age. Without challenging the Christian orientation toward the afterlife, Bacon immanentized theological values traditionally ascribed to eternal life within a new scientific paradigm of longevity.

Revising Weber's thesis that "an ascetic morality" contributed to the birth of capitalism, Foucault has argued that an even more consequential development unfolded in in the West during the eighteenth century: "this was nothing less than the entry of life into history…that is, the entry of phenomena peculiar to the life of the human species into the order of knowledge and power, into the sphere of political techniques."[245] I suggest what may be self-evident: that the ongoing entry of life into history was already underway in *The History of Life and Death*. Again, Bacon's new science was not explicitly political, and to my knowledge there is no evidence that the early modern English state enacted Bacon's research on the level of official policy to supervise, regulate, or otherwise intervene in English lives. But because Bacon linked knowledge to power, his epistemological innovations were inherently political, which is not to say that they aligned with any one

---

[244] Bacon, "To the Living and Posterity," *The historie of life and death*.

[245] Michel Foucault, "Right of Death and Power over Life," 264-265.

political ideology.[246]

As Gaukroger has observed, "Bacon's aim is to shape political power around political understanding [that] ultimately take[s] into account broader forms of knowledge, especially scientific knowledge. His point is not to redefine epistemology but to underpin the responsible use of power."[247] Bacon indeed appears to have conceived the new science of life-prolongation not cynically, as a tool to control the English population, but in good faith that its progress would "redound to the good of many."[248] He did not prescribe uniform rules and remedies for prolonging the lives of his readers but instead advised each individual to trust her or his own "discretion" in deciding which rules to follow and which to ignore.[249]

Bacon thus addressed readers not with the paternalism that might be expected from a so-called father of modern science and medicine, but rather with communal "Intentions" intended to optimize, by prolonging, the collective life of individuals.[250] To be sure, Bacon's imagined com-

---

[246] See Bronwen Price, *Francis Bacon's "The New Atlantis" : New Interdisciplinary Essays* (Manchester: Manchester University Press, 2003), 28. Price paraphrases, "Pérez-Ramos notes that royalist historians, like Thomas Sprat, were keen to disguise the achievements of Republican Baconianism 'so that experimental science could be made politically unobjectionable.'"

[247] Gaukroger, *Francis Bacon and the Transformation of Early-Modern Philosophy*, 18.

[248] Bacon, "To the Living and Posterity," *The historie of life and death.*

[249] Ibid., 141.

[250] This accords with Gaukroger's claim that Bacon's "was the first

munity of physicians, patients, and populations organized around a paradigm of longevity remained unrealized for at least a century following his death, for his contemporaries were generally ambivalent about and even hostile toward the pursuit of long life.

What Good is Short Life?

Even if Bacon persuaded some contemporaries that life's length was within their power to determine, many had reasons not to desire longer life, including Seneca's paradoxical assertion that striving to prolong life is the surest way to shorten it: "Do you want to know, finally, how it is they do not live long? See how they desire to live long! Worn-out old men pray like street-beggars for the addition of a few years."[251] The idea that long life is good, or at least better than short life, was less self-evident for seventeenth-century English people than it is for most Westerners today. Early moderns encountered panegyrics to short life in popular drama, poetry, holy scripture, and in learned philosophical, theological, and scientific treatises. The ubiquitous encomia of short life may be read as

systematic, comprehensive attempt to transform the epistemological activity of the philosopher from something essentially individual to something essentially communal" (*Francis Bacon and the Transformation of Early-Modern Philosophy*, 5).

[251] Seneca, "On the Shortness of Life," in *Dialogues and Essays*, trans. John Davie (Oxford and New York: Oxford University Press, 2007), 150.

instances of stoic *amor fati*, or as cultural mechanisms to cope with the seemingly inexorable fact that early modern life *was* short, especially in comparison to the great longevity of the ancients reported in the Bible, as seventeenth-century authors frequently remarked.

The average life expectancy at birth for male English aristocrats between the years 1575-1674 was thirty-two years, and barely thirty-five years for female nobility. One fifth of all children, on average, did not survive their first year of life, while only a third of all children survived beyond their tenth year.[252] The high mortality rate of young children skewed the average life expectancy downward, but even so, one was fortunate to survive into one's forties—that is, if one desired to live longer than one's peers. Bacon's contemporaries generally did not admit such desire, and many expressed repugnance at the idea of prolonging life in a state of sin, disease, and decrepitude. They concurred with the ancient Roman philosopher Cicero, who marveled that people wish to survive into old age, "because (as I thinke) if they might liue l[on]ger, their life could be no pleasanter, then it hath bene."[253] Bacon was the exception among his early modern peers for proposing that longer life might be qualitatively better than

---

[252] Henry Kamen, *Early Modern European Society* (New York: Routledge, 2000), 18.

[253] Marcus Tullius Cicero, *Those fyue questions, which Marke Tullye Cicero, disputed in his manor of Tusculanum*, trans. John Doman (London, 1561), I.

shorter life.

In a poem featured in Tottel's widely read miscellany *Songes and Sonettes* (1557), the English aristocrat Henry Howard sang that "lenger life" means only the accumulation of more sin on one's spiritual ledger: "The lesse account, the soner made:/The count soone made, the merrier mind:/The merrier minde doth thought euade,/ Short life in truth this thing doth trie./Wherefore come death, and let me dye."[254] For better or worse, the Earl of Surrey did not live longer than thirty years, but this death-driven conceit survived well into the next century.

Following the execution of Charles I and the end of the Civil Wars, former Royal Physician Walter Charleton granted "that Vivacity [i.e., longevity][255] in this transitory World…is a Benediction of God…a Document of Divine Grace, or an Evidence of Gods singular love," but he stipulated that it is "infinitely" better to die young and attain "early delivery…from this calamitous prison of Mortality," also known as life.[256] "For this life is no Mansion," Charleton surmised, "but a narrow and incommodious Inne, standing in the way to a better, whose Term is Eternity: and therefore…thrice happy he, who arrives at his journies end, before he is weary of travell."[257] The poet John Taylor

---

[254] Henry Howard, "Vpon consideration of the state of this life he wisheth death," in *Songes and Sonettes; Tottel's Miscellany* (London, 1557).
[255] "Vivacity," n. 3.a., *Oxford English Dictionary*.
[256] Walter Charleton, *The Darknes of Atheism Dispelled by the Light of Nature: a physico-theologicall treatise* (London, 1652),235.
[257] Ibid., 234.

echoed Charleton's conceit in an epigram comparing long and short life: "If life be long, 'tis troublesome and weary,/ Their Miseries are most that longest tarry:/We make the bad world worse, he travells best/That soonest ends his journey, and at rest."[258] Thomas Browne also concurred with this view: "Now for my life, it is a miracle of thirty years...for the World, I count it not an Inn, but an Hospital; and a place not to live, but to dye in."[259] Browne's case is especially interesting, because while as a physician he recognized his professional obligation "to preserve the living,"[260] he was also indifferent and even hostile to the pursuit of longer life.

Browne's epistle to the reader of *Religio Medici* (1643), for example, begins by censuring those who wish to out-live everyone around them and to survive even the end of the world: "Certainly that man were greedy of life, who should desire to live when all the world were at an end,"[261] he opined, conveying an apocalyptic millenarianism that was widespread during the English Civil Wars. Elsewhere in the text, Browne looked back to "those long living times" when old people could barely remember their youth, when they could live for seven or eight centuries

---

[258] John Taylor, "On long and short life," in *Epigrammes Written on Purpose to be Read* (London, 1651), 9.

[259] *Religio Medici*, 2.11.

[260] *Urn Burial*, 5.

[261] *Religio Medici*, "To the Reader." Montaigne makes a similar claim in "That to Philosophize is to Learn how to Die."

before worrying about "apoplexies" or "palsies,"[262] and "when living was so lasting that homicide might admit of distinctive qualifications from the age of the person, & it might seeme a lesser offense to kill a man at 8 hundred then at fortie, and when life was so well worth the living that few or none would kill themselves."[263] Browne supposed, in other words, that if the present limits of human life were scaled out long enough, then different quantities of age ("8 hundred" and "fortie") would yield "distinctive qualifications," such that the life of an eight-hundred-year-old person might be less legally sanctioned, less worth living and preserving, than the life of a forty-year-old, which is twenty times shorter.[264] While Browne relegated great longevity to an irrecoverable past, he also anticipated potential challenges of the future of long life envisioned by Bacon.

The causality or correlation between long life and

---

[262] Before the development of physiology, apoplexy widely signified internal bleeding, stroke, heart attack, sudden loss of consciousness, and/or sudden death. Palsy referred to various types of paralysis.

[263] Thomas Browne, "A Passage from a Manuscript," *Religio Medici and Urne-Buriall*, ed. Greenblatt and Targoff (New York: New York Review Books, 2012), 141.

[264] Browne's hypothetical "might" leaves room for alternative ways of qualifying the quantitative measurements of age, however, and conversely it might be a graver transgression to kill an older person insofar as a greater quantity of life is taken, where "life" stands for accumulated experience, wisdom, or knowledge rather than an increasing heap of sins and sorrows or a multiplying mass of miseries.

life worth living is not immediately clear from Browne's claim that when people lived long, "life was so well worth the living that few or none would kill themselves." One implication is that more than a "few" of Browne's short-lived contemporaries contemplated and committed suicide. Even King Charles publicly reported an occasional "desire to die," which he rejected, however, in favor of Christian patience, striving neither to hanker after earthly life nor rush toward eternity.

> I am not so old, as to be weary of life; nor (I
> hope) so bad, as to be either afraid to die, or
> ashamed to live: true, I am so afflicted, as might
> make Me sometime even desire to die; if I did
> not consider, That it is the greatest glory of a
> Christians life to die daily in conquering by a
> lively faith, and patient hopes of a better life,
> those partiall and quotidian deaths, which kill
> us (as it were) by piece-meales, and make us
> overlive our owne fates; while We are deprived
> of health, honour, liberty, power, credit, safety,
> or estate; and those other comforts of dearest
> relations, which are as the life of our lives.[265]

The king's rhetoric echoes Macbeth's unattainable ideal of "that which should accompany old age," namely, "honour, love, obedience, troops of friends" (5.3.25-26), while also recalling Macbeth's feeling of having "lived

---

[265] King Charles I, *Eikaon basilikae, The pourtraicture of His Sacred Majesitie in his solitudes and sufferings* (London, 1649).

long enough" (5.3.23) that is offset by his rejection of suicide: "Why should I play the Roman fool, and die on mine own sword? Whiles I see lives, the gashes do better upon them" (5.10.1-3). Shakespeare, Browne, and King Charles all articulated the more general predicament facing seventeenth-century Anglicans who had to balance between, on the one hand, staying alive in spite of wanting to die, and, on the other hand, not tarrying too long, overliving their divinely appointed end, or outlasting the point after which life was no longer worth living.[266]

English culture's prohibition of suicide is irreducible to the theological motives cited by Hamlet: "that the Everlasting...fixed His canon 'gainst self-slaughter" (1.2.131-132), and that fear of postmortem dreams in the "sleep of death" compels people to endure the "calamity of so long life" (3.1.71).[267] Because suicides threatened to arrogate

---

[266] Michael MacDonald and Terence R. Murphy, *Sleepless Souls: Suicide in Early Modern England* (Oxford: Clarendon Press, 1990), 2-5. See also Weikart, *Death of Humanity*: "In addition to religious penalties for suicide, such as not being buried in hallowed ground, medieval and early modern European legal codes forbade suicide and even tried to restrain it by threatening confiscation of property from the heirs of those guilty of taking their own lives. The Protestant Reformation only stiffened attitudes against suicide in the sixteenth and early seventeenth centuries" (217). "Studies of suicide in early modern England indicate that secularized attitudes toward human life prompted a growing tide of suicides at the end of the seventeenth century that continued to increase during the first half of the eighteenth century" (219).
[267] See also Donne, *Biathanatos* (1608; 1644); and John Sym, *Lifes Preservative Against Self-Killing* (1637).

the right of God or the sovereign to decide which lives are worth living, the prohibition of self-murder became increasingly imperative with the advent of biopower.[268] Browne maintained that while it is not "unlawful" to strive to live longer than Christ did (thirty-three years), it is nevertheless ill-advised for two reasons. First, because scripture promises eternal youth ("there shall be no grey hairs in heaven"), such that to "outlive...perfections" by growing old in this life is to "run on here but to be retrograde hereafter."[269] Second, because he believed that "age doth not rectify, but incurvate our natures, turning bad dispositions into worser habits, and (like diseases) brings on incurable vices; for every day, as we grow weaker in age, we grow stronger in sin, and the number of our days doth but make our sins innumerable."[270] Perhaps they privately desired long life, but in theory and in public most of Browne's contemporaries agreed that life becomes increasingly worse with age.

In actual practice there were reasons to want to grow

---

[268] Foucault, "Right of Death and Power over Life," 261. Foucault observed that suicide "was one of the first astonishments of a society in which political power had assigned itself the task of administering life" (261).

[269] Browne, *Religio Medici*, 1.42.

[270] Ibid. Browne's view of aging is not only regressive and reactionary; it is also progressive, which is especially evident in Browne's simile, that age is "like diseases" insofar as the effects of aging are like "incurable vices;" contained in this simile is the kernel of the fundamental debate about twenty-first-century longevity, namely whether aging should be treated as a disease.

old in early modern England, including the privilege of governance and political power in a culture that has been described as a gerontocracy.[271] That many (literate) English people wanted to live long is evident in the market for texts such as Tobias Venner's 1620 *Via recta ad vitam longam* ("The straight way toward long life"), which gives advice concerning nourishment, sleep, exercise, and excretion and was re-published in multiple editions over the following four decades; George Starkey's *Natures explication and Helmont's vindication, Or A short and sure way to a long and sound life* (1657), an emphatic defense of life-prolonging chemical medicines; and the Flemish Jesuit Leonard Lessius' *Hygiasticon, Or the right course of preserving life and health unto extream old age* (1634), a treatise on temperance and sobriety. Notwithstanding such texts, the predominant view in English culture still represented old age as an undesirable part of life that is barely worth living.[272]

Georges Minois has remarked the ambivalence of

---

[271] Minois, *History of Old Age*, 294-298; See also Michael Witmore, *Shakespearean Metaphysics* (London: Continuum International Publishing Group, 2008), 69.

[272] Thane has remarked that some early moderns "were optimistic that superlongevity not only could but did exist. This belief was encouraged by the existence of apparently attested cases. That these were generally found among the rural poor was taken as proof that the immoderate life of modern, especially urban society was the chief cause of 'premature' sickness and death. 'Old Par', for example, Thomas Parr, who was allegedly 153 when he died in London in 1635 aroused both elite and popular excitement" (*Old Age in English History*, 60-61).

early moderns who "venerate[d] the old but only in theory and after they were dead."[273] Beginning in the sixteenth century, the upsurge of virulent ideological attacks against the elderly "derived from the impotent rage of a generation which worshipped youth and beauty."[274] As a result of Renaissance cults of youth, "old age and death constituted the greatest of scandals."[275] It can be difficult to parse English culture's theoretical vilification of old age from its practical reverence for the elderly, as a result of overlapping modes of evaluating life. A section from the collec-

---

[273] Minois, *History of Old Age*, 294.

[274] Ibid., 249.

[275] Ibid., 250. Shakespeare dramatizes this theme nowhere so keenly as in *The History of the Life and Death of King Lear*. When Regan suggests that Lear ask Goneril for forgiveness, he imagines apologizing for being old: "'Dear daughter, I confess that I am old…Age is unnecessary: on my knees I beg that you'll vouchsafe me raiment, bed, and food'" (7.306-308). Lear's performative mock apology shows his critical distance from cultural tropes disparaging old age, but it voices practical as well as ideological concerns about the elderly, such as their right and access to life's basic necessities, including clothing, shelter, and food. As Helen Small has observed, "Remarkably little of the vast literature on *King Lear*…says much or anything about old age. Critics have tended to think of that play…as being about more general subjects (the human condition, man's relation with nature) or more specific ones (anger, love, kingship, English history). Similarly, they have often, and not without justification, seen literary depictions of old age as metaphors or symbols for other things: the status of art, the promise or otherwise of immortality. Old age in literature is rarely if ever only about itself—but as far as criticism has been concerned, it has oddly rarely been much about itself at all" (*The Long Life* [Oxford: Oxford University Press, 2007], 5-6).

tion of poems *The Passionate Pilgrim* (1599), for example, appears directly to have informed Bacon's observations on "The Differences of youth and Age" in *The History of Life and Death*. "Youth is full of pleasance," the poem declares, "Age is full of care...Youth is full of sport, Ages breath is short,/Youth is nimble, Age is lame/Youth is hot and bold, Age is weake and cold,/Youth is wild, and Age is tame."[276]

Several decades later, Bacon adopted a strikingly similar rhetorical formula: "Age is hard; youth emulates...age envies; youth is religious, and fervently zealous...youth is liberall, bountifull, and loving, age covetous."[277] Bacon purportedly based this essentializing representation of old age on empirical observation, but he also clearly filched it from entrenched cultural ideology. Bacon nonetheless departed from cultural orthodoxy in daring to propose that life might unfold otherwise, that it should be possible to grow old without aging, possible for the elderly to retain the qualities and capacities traditionally relinquished to the young.

---

[276] William Shakespeare et al., *The Passionate Pilgrime* (London, 1599).

[277] Bacon, *The historie of life and death*, 280.

The Mismeasurement of Longevity

The last known work of Anthony Stafford, a "Gentleman of high birth" who perished "in the time of the civil wars," was *Honour and Vertue Triumphing over the Grave* (1640). It is "a biography of his kinsman Henry, fourteenth Baron Stafford, who had died in 1637 at the age of sixteen," and like Stafford's other works, it strives to identify the qualities of "true Nobility."[278] Stafford maintained that "if we will harken to Reason…she will tell us that brevity of Life is to be preferred before longevity. If we will give beliefe to Seneca, he will assure us that Nature never bestowed a greater Benefit on man than shortnesse of Life, it being so full of Cares, Feares, Dangers, and Miseries, that Death is become the Common wish of all men afflicted."[279] Many did indeed "give beliefe to Seneca," whose work was a bedrock of early modern English culture. In particular, Seneca's epistle "On the Brevity, as Contrasted with the Length of Life" shaped seventeenth-century English conversations about longevity.

Stafford's reductive paraphrase refers to Seneca's argument "that our Life is not short, but that wee make it short, eyther by not vsing it, or by abusing it, or vainely

---

[278] Arnold Hunt, s.v. "Stafford, Anthony (*b*. 1586/7, *d*. in or after 1645)." In *Oxford Dictionary of National Biography*, online, ed. David Cannadine (Oxford: Oxford University Press, 2004-. Accessed April 11, 2017, http://www.oxforddnb.com.turing.library.northwestern. edu/view/article/26200.

[279] Anthony Stafford, *Honour and Vertue Triumphing over the Grave* (London, 1640), 83.

vsing it."[280] Early modern authors routinely reiterated this utilitarian view of life as a thing to be used. Michel de Montaigne wrote, for instance, that "the utility of living consists not in the length of days, but in the use of time; a man may have lived long, and yet lived but a little. Make use of time while it is present with you. It depends upon your will, and not upon the number of days, to have a sufficient length of life."[281] Seneca's ethical evaluation of life, which prioritizes use-value over length, not only yielded to but also conditioned new seventeenth-century modes of measuring life.

Longevity discourse both reflects and complicates the early modern shift from qualitative to quantitative views of reality to which historians of science have attributed the emergence of modern disciplines including astronomy, physics, navigation, music, and medicine.[282] As Michael Witmore has noted, it was during the early seventeenth century that "numerical age became an important measure of one's progress through life, numbers coming to provide precision to a concept of human development that was usually measured with qualified nouns such as infant, child, adolescent, stripling, boy, girl, wench or maid."[283]

According to Minois, practices of compiling statistics

---

[280] Seneca, *The Workees of Lucius Annaeus Seneca, both morall and naturall,* trans. Thomas Lodge et al. (London, 1614), 672.

[281] Montaigne, "To Philosophize is to Learn to Die," 80.

[282] Paula Blank, *Shakespeare and the Mismeasure of Renaissance Man* (Ithaca: Cornell University Press, 2006), 2.

[283] Witmore, *Shakespearean Metaphysics*, 69.

about longevity and calculating average life expectancy were sporadic in medieval Europe but "really took off during the seventeenth century with the advent of the tontines," a plan for raising capital where each investor contributes an initial sum and receives an annuity that increases in value as investors die. "Life assurance took off rather more slowly" Minois added, "because of opposition from the Church, which considered speculation on the life and death of men heinous."[284] The rise of quantitative measurements of life may indicate nascent practical paradigms that were subsequently recolonized by ancient ethical and theological discourses of longevity; alternatively, I argue that these ancient discourses always already inhered in new pragmatic measurements of life.

Galileo's watchword, "to measure what is measurable and to try to render measurable what is not so as yet"[285] may be characteristic of the trajectory of Western thought, but English authors discovered in longevity discourse a place of refuge from and a locus of resistance to the new scientific project of quantifying everything. They heeded Seneca's warning that white hair and wrinkles signify only that one has existed a long time, not necessarily that one has lived long,[286] but this admonition accrued new signifi-

---

[284] Minois, *History of Old Age*, 290.

[285] Quoted in Karel Berka, *Measurement: Its Concepts, Theories, and Problems*, trans. Augustin Riska, *Boston Studies in the Philosophy of Science* 72 (Dordrecht, Holland: D. Reidel, 1983), 9.

[286] Seneca, "On the Shortness of Life," 147.

cance, and caused new confusion, for seventeenth-century poets, physicians, proto-scientists, and politicians deciding how to measure life and which lives to measure.

In *The First Anniversary* (1611), for instance, an elegiac poem that commemorates the death of a fourteen-year-old girl while lamenting the limits and dangers of new scientific knowledge, John Donne supposed that life's shortness makes it impossible to tell time correctly: "Alas, we scarce live long enough to try/Whether a true made clocke run right, or lie./Old Grandsires talke of yesterday with sorrow,/And for our children we reserve to morrow" (129-132).[287] That life is too short to "try" to measure time suggests that life is too short to undertake the quintessentially new scientific activities of testing, probing, and proving through experimental trials.[288] The second line is unequivocally Senecan, however, in its qualitative attribution of life's shortness to lapses in presence of mind, that is, to the anticipatory futurity of the young and the backward-looking regret of the old.

Donne's suggestion that short-lived humans have lost the ability to tell time preemptively delegitimized the perspective from which Robert Boyle, the pioneer of chemistry and early developer of the new scientific method, later compared the accuracy of his watch and clock. In *Occa-*

---

[287] John Donne, "The First Anniversary," in *The Complete Poetry and Selected Prose of John Donne*, ed. Charles M. Coffin (New York: The Modern Library, 2001).

[288] "Try," v. 11a., *Oxford English Dictionary*.

sional Reflections (1665), Boyle considered the circular dial-plate of his clock, which was "many times larger" than the face of his watch. At the time he began observing, "the Index" [i.e., the hand] of the Clock had then past through a far greater quantity of space than that of the Watch." When the time was actually midnight—which Boyle some-how determined off the page and independently of either the watch or the clock—the watch had accurately "arriv'd at the mark of the twelfth hour," while the clock's index still lagged behind at the eleventh.[289] From this Boyle concluded that the smaller watch ran "truer…than the Clock."[290] One might expect the new scientific practitioner to extrapolate from his observation a theory of spatial-ized or instrumentalized temporality; instead, he reflects in a Senecan vein on the mismeasurement of longevity that results from taking mere long lasting for long life.

> Thus in estimating Men's Lives, there is
> something else to be look'd at than the meer
> duration of them: For there are some Men, who
> having Loyter'd and Trifled away very many
> Years in the World, have no other Argument
> of their Age than the Church-books of their
> Gray-hairs; and as little do they indeed Live,
> than waste a number of insignificant Years in
> successive or perpetual Diversions from the
> true business and end of Life. These, and many

---

[289] Robert Boyle, *Occasional Reflections* (London, 1665), 216-17.
[290] Ibid., 217.

> other kinds of Persons, that consume much
> Time to little purpose, may be said rather to
> have Lasted long, than to have Liv'd long.[291]

Although in Boyle's narration the quantitative experiment with time-keeping instruments precedes the qualitative morality lesson, it is also arguable that Boyle's internalization of Senecan ethics preceded and informed his experimental trials. His belief that "estimating" human life—assigning value to it or approximating it without precise numerical measurement—requires accounting for more than its duration led Boyle to divide life into biological lasting and "true" living.

While Boyle offered a clear idea of what it means to last (to loiter and waste time with diversions), he was less explicit about what it means to live, apart from that it entails adhering to "the true business and end of Life." This suggests that humans must live purposefully in order to be counted among the living, but the ambiguity of Boyle's "true business" makes it difficult to decide who, if anyone, ever truly lives. The widespread classical belief that humans should live in accordance with their nature informed seventeenth-century notions of true living. Browne, for instance, asserted that "every man truly lives, so long as he acts his nature, or some way makes good the faculties of himself," whereas those "rushing upon professions and ways of life unequal to their natures, dishonor

---

[291] Ibid., 218.

not only themselves and their functions, but pervert the harmony of the whole world."[292] As Keith Thomas has observed, however, early modern English "lives, like ours, were usually unplanned, and the business of daily living got in the way of the formulation of any longer-term strategy."[293] I suggest that the (dis)aggregation of living and lasting in seventeenth-century English longevity discourse articulated a form of bare, nutritive, creaturely life, which defined a zone within the human being not deemed to be alive in the "true" sense.

Before they could measure longevity, English authors first had to decide which lifeforms counted as living. The theologian Jeremy Taylor, for example, recommended counting only life that is human, rational, self-conscious, and capable of giving an account of itself; the life of "a living man…that life that distinguishes him from a fool or a bird, that which gives him a capacity next to Angels," and that which is often short compared to the duration of biological lasting.[294] Taylor believed that "the account" of life should not begin while we are still "beholding to others to make the account for us: for we know not of a long time, whether we be alive or no, having but some little

---

[292] Browne, *Pseudodoxia*, i.31. Quoted in Keith Thomas, *The Ends of Life: Roads to Fulfilment in Early Modern England* (Oxford and New York: Oxford University Press, 2009), 42.

[293] Thomas, *The Ends of Life*, 3.

[294] Jeremy Taylor, *The Rule and Exercises of Holy Dying* (London, 1651), 33.

approaches and symptoms of a life."[295] Nor does Taylor think the account should begin when humans can first feed themselves or reproduce, because that would make a human "contemporary with a camel, or a cow," [296] while Taylor, like many of his contemporaries, maintained that animal life was incommensurable with human life. Seventeenth-century longevity discourse thus replicated and proliferated the (de)humanizing function of sovereignty that institutes sociopolitical order through declarations of anthropogenesis.

Taylor warned that "we should be loath to have the accounts of our age taken by the measures of a beast: and fools and distracted persons are reckoned as civilly dead, they are no parts of the Common-wealth, not subject to laws, but secured by them in Charity, and kept from violence as a man keeps his Ox."[297] Insofar as rationality became the marker of life that counts as living, then lives that failed to qualify for or exhibit rationality were as good as dead in Taylor's eyes. That charity, not law, protects oxen and irrational people from suffering and doing violence potentially exposes animals and fools, whose lives Taylor did not count as living, to be killed with legal impunity.[298]

---

[295] Ibid., 21.

[296] Ibid.

[297] Ibid.

[298] This form of violence resembles what theorist Judith Butler, reflecting on her personal experience of the "violence of gender norms," has called "the violence of the foreclosed life, the one that does not get named as 'living,' the one whose incarceration implies

If it is not troubling enough that humans can just as law-fully kill oxen as keep them alive, it is yet more unsettling to think that "fools and distracted persons" may be subject to the same terms. It is more problematic still if this category of "persons" includes not only extreme cases of human life reduced to its vegetative, unconscious state, but also boundary cases where potentially rational people have lapsed into what Boyle called "successive or perpetual Diversions from the true business and end of Life." To be sure, Taylor did not go so far as to suggest that irrational or purposeless lives are unworthy of being lived and so justifiably put or exposed to death; indeed, he conceded that all humans spend much of life irrationally, before their faculty of reason develops and after it decays. Nonetheless, Taylor's mode of measuring life, which involved decisions on the (non) value of different lifeforms, aligned with an emergent paradigm of biopower that subsequently instrumentalized such decisions.

Taylor finally proposed a qualitative account of life that begins when humans arrive at "a certain, steddy use of reason…and when that is, all the world of men cannot

---

a suspension of life, or a sustained death sentence" (*Gender Trouble: Feminism and the Subversion of Identity* [New York: Routledge, 1990], xxi). Butler has argued elsewhere, following Foucault, that although the aim of sovereignty is to sustain and augment itself, it becomes instrumentalized in the management of extra-legal populations, which it identifies "as less than human without entitlement to rights, as the humanly unrecognizable" (*Precarious Life: The Powers of Mourning and Violence* [London and New York: Verso, 2004], 98).

tell precisely. Some are called…at fourteen, some at one and twenty, some never; but all men, late enough; for the life of a man comes upon him slowly and insensibly."[299] Several decades before Taylor fixated on rational, human life, Bacon had turned attention to the vegetative or nutritive life that is common to adults, animals, children, plants, fools, and distracted people alike. *The History of Life and Death* accordingly accounts for the "Length and shortnesse of Life in living creatures," including lions, bears, foxes, camels, horses, asses, mules, harts, dogs, oxen, sheep, goats, cats, rabbits, and a variety of birds. Where Taylor is "loath to" measure rational and irrational lifeforms together, Bacon observed that in Bedlam hospital, "in the Suburbs of London, there are found…many Mad Persons, that live to a great Age."[300] In expanding the scope of his inquiry to include nutritive lifeforms, then, Bacon effectively recognized as living the lives that Taylor "reckoned as civilly dead," that is, as extralegal subjects to be kept alive like animals and just as justifiably put to death.

Although Bacon's inclusion of the nutritive life that humans share with other humans, creatures, and plants is potentially egalitarian, his ontological levelling also establishes a common denominator resembling what King Lear calls "base life" (7.365-367), which subsequently enables

---

[299] Taylor, *The Rule and Exercises of Holy Dying*, 22. For alternate rubrics, see Aristotle's *De Anima*, and Augustine's *Confessions* (esp. book 1, chapters 6-8).
[300] Bacon, *Historie naturall and experimentall, of life and death*, 135.

the re-hierarchization of lifeforms according to the paradigm of longevity.[301] "In colde Northerne Countries men commonly live longer than in hotter," Bacon noted, because "their skin[,] being more compact and close," retains moisture better. He observed further that under the equator "the inhabitants live very long as in Peru and Taprobana," that Mediterranean islanders commonly live long, that Russians do not live as long as inhabitants of the Orkney Islands (the archipelago in northern Scotland), and that the Chinese live longer than Africans.[302] Like seventeenth-century autochthony discourse—characterized by its appeal to common humanity born from the same mother earth, as well as by its xenophobia and genocidal dehumanization of colonized peoples—seventeenth-century longevity discourse was also simultaneously localizing and globalizing, egalitarian and hierarchical.

Bacon's inclusion of nutritive life in the accounts (if not yet the calculations) of scientific (if not yet political) authorities made human life commensurable with non-human life such as that of trees. While this potentially yields a view that might grant trees some of the rights and protections afforded to human persons and subjects, I argue rather that it made it possible to reconceive the life of populations as a national resource. The seventeenth-century diarist John Evelyn boasted that English "forests are undoubtedly the greatest magazines of the wealth and

---

[301] See Agamben, *The Open: Man and Animal*, 14.

[302] Bacon, *The historie of life and death*, 112-113.

glory of this nation; and our oaks the truest oracles of its perpetuity and happiness, as being the only support of that navigation which makes us fear'd abroad, and flourish at home."[303]

Where Evelyn elided the labor of shipwrights, colonists, and others, Bacon, by contrast, shifted national attention to the human component of England's wealth and glory. In *The History of Life and Death*, however, he was no longer primarily interested in the rational human life that is capable of knowledge, culture, and subjectivity—as he was in *The Advancement of Learning* (1605)—but rather in the nutritive life that can be measured, modified, prolonged, and extorted. Bacon was not the first of his contemporaries to compare human and arboreal life, but he was perhaps the first since Aristotle to do so scientifically.

The Hope of Long-Lived Trees

Shakespeare already evoked the commensurability of human and arboreal longevity in *As You Like It* (1599). "Though I look old," Adam assures Orlando, "yet I am strong and lusty; for in my youth I never did apply hot and rebellious liquors in my blood, nor did not with unbashful forehead woo the means of weakness and debility; therefore my age is as a lusty winter, frosty, but kindly: let me go with you; I'll do the service of a younger man in all

---

[303] John Evelyn, *Sylva, or a Discourse of Forest Trees*, 2 vols. (London, 1664), 2:157.

your business and necessities" (2.3.48-56). Orlando appreciates the "constant service" of the "good old man," but he reminds Adam that no amount of provident labor can extort from his aged body the utility and value extortionable from younger lives: "poor old man, thou prun'st a rotten tree, that cannot so much as a blossom yield in lieu of all thy pains and husbandry" (2.3.64-66). More than mere metaphor, the description of Adam's old body as a "rotten tree" suggests a burgeoning mode of evaluating human and nonhuman lives according to the same standard—namely, according to the "blossom" they "yield" or the value of their utility.

Seventeenth-century authors generally professed the Senecan view that values rational, human living, however short, over irrational, creaturely lasting, however long. Like Taylor, therefore, many explicitly avoided comparing human longevity with the lifespans of animals, plants, and even things. They were compelled to insist on the incommensurability of human and nonhuman lifeforms, in part because they feared that if ontological differences were (admitted to be) of quantitative degree rather than of qualitative kind, then the relatively negligible length of human life would belie cherished convictions of human exceptionalism.

The Anglican clergyman George Hakewill asserted, for instance, that the "ordinary age of man being compared with the heavens, the stones, the metals, some beasts & trees is very short, but the longest being compared with

God and Eternity is but as a span, a shadow, a dreame of a shadow, nay mere nothing."[304] Montaigne likewise regarded life-prolongation as futile, because "long life and short life are made all one by death. For there is no long or short for things that are no more."[305] Citing Aristotle's observation of ephemeral "little animals" who last only a day, Montaigne asked, "which of us does not laugh to see this moment of duration considered in terms of happiness or unhappiness? The length or shortness of our duration, if we compare it with eternity, or yet with the duration of mountains, rivers, stars, trees, and even of some animals, is no less ridiculous."[306] If it is risible to construe entomological longevity in the ethical terms of happiness and unhappiness, Montaigne wondered, then why should measurements of human life be any different?[307] Bacon,

---

[304] George Hakewill, *An Apologie of the Power and Prouidence of God in the Gouernment of the World* (Oxford, 1627).

[305] Montaigne, "To Philosophize is to Learn to Die," 77.

[306] Ibid. For the French, see *Selections from Montaigne*, C.H. Conrad Wright (Boston, New York, Chicago: D.C. Heath, 1914). *"Qui de nous ne se mocque de veoir mettre en consideration d'heur ou de malheur ce moment de durée?"*

[307] The popular Elizabethan preacher Henry Smith echoed Montaigne's point, proclaiming in a sermon that "it is hard for a man to think of a short life, and think euil; or to think of a long life, and thinke wel." He arrived at this conclusion from a reading of the psalm where Moses asks the Lord to teach us "to number our daies, that wee may applie our hearts to wisdom." In Smith's orthodox reading of the psalm as a memento mori and warning against vanitas, Moses is not soliciting the technical knowledge required to quantify longevity but rather the wisdom to properly recognize that, young

however, did not laugh; instead, motivated by his belief that "the happinesse of long life is naturally desired,"[308] he seriously considered the longevity of nonhuman lifeforms.

Authors who compared human and arboreal longevity before Bacon's intervention generally valued short-term prolificacy over long-term productivity, whereas Bacon prioritized the latter. "We account not those the best trees that have withstood the rage of many Winters," Stafford remarked, for instance, "but those who in the least time have borne the most fruit. Not hee who playes longest, but sweetliest on an Instrument is to bee Commended. Compared with Eternity, the longest and the shortest Life differ not."[309] Ben Jonson concurred that short-term quality is better than greater quantity of life in his poem "To the Immortal Memory and Friendship of that Noble Pair, Sir Lucius Cary and Sir H. Morison" (1640), written just before Jonson's death and soon after he suffered a paralyzing stroke.[310] "It is not growing like a tree/In bulke, doth make man better bee;/Or, standing long an Oake, three hundred yeare,/To fall a logge, at last, dry, bald, and

---

or old, we always remain in the same relation to mortality. Smith enjoins his listeners to "remember…their end" and so learn to desire "the same things liuing and dying" rather than living as if they were immortal only to scramble for reformation at the end of life ("The Godlie Mans Request," in *The sermons of Maister Henrie Smith* [London: 1593], 546-574; 570).

[308] Bacon, *The historie of life and death*, 2-3.

[309] Stafford, *Honour and Vertue Triumphing over the Grave*, 83.

[310] Gerald Hammond, *Fleeting Things: English Poets and Poems, 1616-1660* (Harvard University Press, 1990), 126.

seare."[311] The poem interweaves a celebration of Morison's brief but happy and noble life with advice to Cary, who has survived his friend. "A Lillie of a Day/Is fairer farre, in May,/Although it fall, and die that night;/It was the Plant, and flowre of light./In small proportions, we just beauties see:/And in short measures, life may perfect bee." Despite being smaller, shorter, and more ephemeral, the life of the lily is qualitatively better than that of the long-standing oak, because it is more proportionate and beautiful.

Jonson's consideration of the lily invokes Christ's parable in the gospel of Luke, which recommends abdicating self-preservation and leaving longevity for divine providence to determine: "Consider the lilies how they grow: they toil not, they spin not; and yet I say unto you, that Solomon in all his glory was not arrayed like one of these."[312] Christ's parable, shifting into something of a taunt, appeals to an exceptionalism that makes humans "better than the fowls," but which is lost when humans take "thought for…life, what [w]e shall eate," because "life is more than meat," and when we plan for the future, "for the morrow shall take thought for the things of itself."[313] Jonson's contemporaries gleaned from Christ's parable

---

[311] Ben Jonson, "To the immortall memorie, and friendship of that noble paire, Sir Lvcius Cary, and Sir H. Morison," *The Workes* (London, 1640), 232-235.

[312] *The book of Luke*, 12:22-27.

[313] *The book of Matthew*, 6:34.

that if plants and animals flourish without spinning and toiling, then it debases humans who not only, in Hamlet's words, "grunt and sweat under a weary life" (3.1.71-79), but who toil further to spin life out even longer. Traditionally read as a metaphorical question about adding years to one's lifespan, the tone of Christ's rhetorical probe—"And which of you with taking thought can add to his stature one cubit?"[314]—epitomizes Christianity's opposition to Bacon's new science of life-prolongation.

Beyond invoking Christ's message to trust our lives with divine providence, Jonson's consideration of the lily also suggests that short life can be just as "perfect" as long life and that long life, moreover, is liable to compromise such perfection.

> Goe now, and tell out dayes summ'd up with feares,
> And make them yeares;
> Produce thy masse of miseries on the Stage,
> To swell thine age;
> Repeat of things a throng,
> To shew thou hast beene long,
> Not liv'd; for life doth her great actions spell,
> By what was done and wrought
> In season, and so brought
> To light: her measures are, how well
> Each syllable answer'd, and was form'd, how faire;
> These make the lines of life, and that's her aire.[315]

---

[314] Ibid., 6:27. Cf. *Luke*, 12:25.

[315] Jonson, "To the immortall memorie, and friendship of that noble

Rearticulating the distinction between living and mere being or lasting, the poem recalls Seneca's critique of those who foolishly "take pride in living to advanced old age [since] as with a play, so with life: what matters is not how long it is but how well it is performed."[316] Many of Jonson's contemporaries agreed that in measuring life, the perfection of its proportion and the quality of its performance are what count, not its quantitative magnitude, length, or duration. For others including Donne and Bacon, however, the rub was that the "small proportions" and "short measures" of life appeared disproportionate and inadequate to the "great actions" that they emulated in the long-lived ancients.

In *The First Anniversary*, for instance, Donne looked back to a time "When, if a slow-pac'd starre had stolne away/From the observers marking, he might stay/Two or three hundred yeares to see't againe,/And then make up his observation plaine" (117-120).[317] In other words, humans once lived long enough to observe long-term processes for themselves, whereas seventeenth-century observers had to rely on the textual testimony of their predecessors. "There is not now that mankind, which was then," the poem laments, "When, Stagge, and Raven, and

---

paire, Sir Lvcius Cary, and Sir H. Morison."

[316] Seneca, Epistle 77.20, quoted in Emily R. Wilson, *Mocked with Death: Tragic Overliving from Socrates to Milton* (Baltimore and London: The Johns Hopkins University Press, 2004), 97.

[317] Spenser also describes celestial alterations, the observation of which requires a "few thousand years" (*The Faerie Queene*, V.proem).

the long-liv'd tree,/Compar'd with man, dy'd in minori-
tie" (112-116). These lines register a widespread and deep-
rooted despair in English culture, a sense of fallenness and
irreversible loss that was exacerbated by transhistorical and
cross-ontological comparisons of longevity derived from
Judeo-Christian and pagan sources.[318]

Unlike Donne, Montaigne, and Hakewill (who
remarked the shortness of human life compared to trees);
unlike Stafford (who judged short-lived but fruitful trees
to be qualitatively better than those that survive longer);
and unlike Jonson (who supposed that "growing like a tree"
to be bulky and long-standing would not make humans
"better" than they are), Bacon aimed precisely to improve
the quality of human life by prolonging its quantity. In
doing so, his inclusion of nutritive life made it theoretically
possible to extrapolate the secret of arboreal longevity for
human benefit. While for Jonson old trees emblematized

---

[318] In dismal contrast to former times, Donne regards his
seventeenth-century contemporaries and asks, "Where is that
mankinde now? Who lives to age,/Fit to be made Methusalem
his page?" (127-128). According to Genesis, Noah's antediluvian
grandfather Methuselah lived for nearly a millennium, a fact
frequently cited by Donne's contemporaries, who also derived the
notion that ancient humans outlived ravens, stags, and trees from
Pliny, the Roman natural philosopher and contemporary of Seneca
whose work was translated into English in 1601. Pliny in turn
attributes the idea to the Greek poet Hesiod's "fabulous discourse…
touching the age of man…That a crow liveth 9 times as long as we;
and the harts or stags 4 times as long as the crow; but the ravens
thrice as long as they" (*The historie of the world*, trans. Philemon
Holland [London, 1634]), 180.

the prolongation not of life but of low-quality existence, Bacon observed that the quality of arboreal life improves with age. While Donne complained that humans will never again outlive "the long-liv'd tree," Bacon optimistically sought to learn from (rather than envying) the long lives of plants and animals. And while his contemporaries rehearsed the same tried consolations and apologies for short life—for example, that living well is better than living longer—Bacon instead synthesized qualitative and quantitative modes of measurement such that longer life becomes better than shorter life. In other words, Bacon supposed that if it is possible to live well at all, then it should be better to live well longer.

Taking his cue from Aristotle's "On Length and Shortness of Life,"[319] a comparative analysis of longevity within as well as between genus and species, Bacon considered the longevity of specific kinds of trees relative to others, observing the oak, beech, fig, ash, poplar, olive, linden, willow, sycamore, walnut, apple, pear, plum, pomegranate, orange, cedar, cane, and maple trees, among others. "Great trees are generally long-liv'd," he wrote, while "trees whose leaves doe slowly come forth, and fall off, continue longer than trees more forward in producing Fruite and Leaves: also wild Forrest trees live longer than Orchard trees, and

---

[319] Aristotle, *Complete Works of Aristotle, Vol. 1: The Revised Oxford Translation*, ed. Jonathan Barnes (Princeton: Princeton University Press), 740-744.

sharpe Fruit-trees than sweete Fruite-trees."[320] Grounding his argument on the authority of Aristotle allowed Bacon to bypass and counteract the theological and ethical orthodoxy that deemed human and nonhuman lifeforms incommensurable; his motive for doing so was a conviction that arboreal life is in some ways more exceptional than human life.

Bacon approved of Aristotle's observation that the long life of trees results from the way plants nourish and repair themselves, which is superior to the way other "living creatures" do.

> The body of living creatures is confined within certaine bounds, and comming to a due proportion, is continued and preserved by nourishment: nothing that is new growing forth, except Haire and Nailes, accounted excrements, whereby the vigour and strength of living creatures must necessarily sooner decay and waxe old: but Trees putting forth new boughs, branches, and leaves, those renewed parts being young, greene, and flourishing, doe more strongly and cheerfully attract nourishment than seare dry branches, whereby the body, through which such nourishment passes to the boughes, is with more plentifull nourishment moistened.[321]

---

[320] Bacon, *The historie of life and death*, 23.
[321] Ibid., 24-25.

This is a departure from traditional notions of long life in English culture as captured by Jonson's portrait of old age resembling "dry, bald, and seare" oak trees, by Shakespeare's description of Adam's old body as "a rotten tree," and by Macbeth's sense of "hav[ing] lived long enough" because his "way of life is fall'n into the sere, the yellow leaf" (5.3.23-24). When he discovered in arboreal longevity reason for humans to hope that life's quality might be prolonged along with its length, Bacon challenged the predominant view that old age inevitably degenerates toward life that is no longer worth living.

Bacon cited his own empirical observations to corroborate Aristotle's claim that "woods and Trees, by lopping their boughs and branches, flourish more, and live longer."[322] Wittingly or not, however, Bacon supplemented his reading of Aristotle not only with empirical observation but also with ideology imbued from Judeo-Christian scripture, which (if he intended to) he never fully succeeded in detaching from his scientific inquiry. "The greater Observation" that Bacon extrapolated from his discussion of arboreal life, for instance, derives no more from Aristotle than from the fourteenth chapter of the book of *Job* in the Old Testament, which begins by declaring the shortness of human life: "Man that is born of woman is of few days, and full of trouble." The "certaine bounds" that Bacon, purportedly following Aristotle, found to restrict the

---

[322] Ibid.

growth of living creatures thus also evokes the divinely-fixed "bounds" identified by Job: "Seeing [man's] days are determined, the number of his months are with thee. Thou hast appointed his bounds that he cannot pass." Job continues to make precisely the observation with which Bacon concluded his investigation of arboreal life, namely, that "there is hope of a tree, if it be cut down, that it will sprout again, and that the tender branch thereof will not cease." By contrast, "man dieth, and wasteth away; yea, man giveth up the ghost, and where is he?"[323] The implicit payoff of Bacon's recapitulation of Aristotle, then, which is also a return to holy scripture, is that the "hope of a tree" might be enlarged to include otherwise hopeless human beings.

Providence and the Medicalization of Life

Bacon was fascinated with longevity throughout the course of his life and career. In *The Advancement of Learning* (1605), an encyclopedic essay advocating empiricism, he listed life's shortness as one of the primary impediments to knowledge. That humans do not know "the supreme or summary law of nature... 'the work which God worketh from the beginning to the end', [does] not derogate from the capacity of the mind; but may be referred to the impediments, as of shortness of life, ill conjunction of labours, ill tradition of knowledge over from hand to hand,

---

[323] *The book of Job*, 14:1-10.

and many other inconveniences, whereunto the condition of man is subject."[324] In other words, the potential capacity of the human mind is hindered by life's shortness, inadequate collaboration, and the failure to transmit knowledge across generations. While the desire to overcome the latter impediment traditionally justified long life and old age, Minois has observed that the advent of print culture "was for a while the old man's enemy," because it threatened to make redundant the elderly's experience, memory, and wisdom, which no longer required living messengers for their transmission.[325]

The above impediments to knowledge were concatenated in Bacon's mind, because they hearken back to Hippocrates' first aphorism, which Bacon and his contemporaries cited frequently. As one seventeenth-century translation rendered it,

> Life is short, the art is long, occasion suddain,
> experience dangerous, judgment difficult.
> Neither is it suff[ici]ent that the Physician doe
> his office, unless the Patient, and those which
> are attendants about him do their duty, and that
> outward things be as well ordered, as those that
> are given inwardly.[326]

---

[324] Francis Bacon, *The Major Works*, ed. Brian Vickers (Oxford and New York: Oxford University Press, 2002), 123.

[325] Minois, *History of Old Age*, 305. See also Keith Thomas, "Age and Authority in Early Modern England," *Proceedings of the British Academy* 62 (1976): 205-48.

[326] Hippocrates and Galen, *The Aphorisms of Hippocrates, Prince of*

Elsewhere in *Advancement*, Bacon cited Hippocrates' aphorism to argue that the aim of knowledge is to overcome life's shortness in relation to art's long length: "it is the duty and virtue of all knowledge to abridge the infinity of individual experience, as much as the conception of truth will permit, and to remedy the complaint of *vita brevis, ars longa* [life is short, art is long]; which is performed by uniting the notions and conceptions of sciences."[327] Bacon's "remedy" for what he assumed was Hippocrates' "complaint" called for interdisciplinarity and transhistorical collaboration. This new scientific solution to the ancient medical problem of short life is strikingly redolent of Seneca's assertion that "the one way of prolonging mortality, or rather of turning it into immortality" is to combine "all times into one," which is how the philosopher "makes his life a long one."[328] Where Bacon began his career intending to lengthen rational life relatively by abbreviating "art," he spent the end of his career trying to prolong biological life.

Physitians, ed. Jan Van Heurne (London, 1655).

[327] Bacon, *The Major Works*, 197.

[328] Seneca, "On the Shortness of Life," 157. See Richard Yeo, *Notebooks, English Virtuosi, and Early Modern Science* (Chicago: The University of Chicago Press, 2014), 101; 256. Yeo has observed two predominant responses to *vita brevis, ars longa* after Galen's commentaries on Hippocrates in the second century of the common era. There were attempts to prolong lifespan either biologically, for example, by living temperately, or experientially, for example, by practicing Senecan mindfulness. Alternatively, there were efforts to abbreviate art by finding shortcuts to knowledge along with better ways of recording and transmitting it.

He first articulated this project in the unfinished ("not perfected"[329]) and posthumously published utopian novel *New Atlantis* (1627). Bacon appended to the text a kind of new scientific wish list for humankind, the first five items of which are the following:

> The prolongation of life.
> The restitution of youth in some degree.
> The retardation of age.
> The curing of diseases counted incurable.
> The mitigation of pain.[330]

The History of Life and Death may be read, then, as Bacon's exploration and discovery of a real place for the utopian vision of longer life that he imagined in *New Atlantis*. The introductory "Access" to *The History* reprises once again the *vita brevis, ars longa* trope. "Ancient is the saying and complaint," Bacon recalled, "that Life is short, and Art long. Therefore our labours intending to perfect Arts, should by the assistance of the Author of Truth and Life, consider by what meanes the Life of man may be prolonged."[331] Overturning the cultural contempt for life-

---

[329] Bacon, *New Atlantis*, in *The Major Works*, 488.

[330] Ibid., 488-489.

[331] Bacon, *The historie of life and death*, 1-2. Bacon's revision of Hippocrates recalls Marsilio Ficino's argument in book 2 of *Three Books on Life* (*De vita libri tres*, 1489), promisingly titled *How to Prolong Your Life*. In the book's first chapter—"For the perfecting of our knowledge, a long life is necessary: the care that must be taken"— Ficino "conclude[d] that Hippocrates was right in saying that art is long and that we are unable to pursue it unless we have a long life"

prolongation that had accumulated during the two millennia since Hippocrates lived, Bacon once again framed the shortness of life as a medical concern. While Hippocrates' *vita brevis* is axiomatic, however, Bacon construed short life not as a datum but as a problem to be solved; and where the context of Hippocrates' *vita brevis* is decidedly medical, the context of Bacon's reiteration is not only medical but also new scientific (hence its emphasis on the perfectibility of "Arts," broadly construed as skillful knowledge) and theologico-political (hence its deference to Providence and, tacitly, to the authority of earthly sovereignty.)

Bacon's goal of professionalizing physicians as "Stewards of Divine Omnipotency" required not only the decentralization of absolute biopower from the monarch to experts, but also the adherence of subjects and patients to the paradigm of longevity. In the first century CE, the natural philosopher Pliny suggested that no people had ever been "more desirous of long life" than his contemporaries, nor ever "lesse carefull to entertaine the means of long life."[332] Pliny's primary critique of the Roman society in which he and Seneca lived was that people relinquished self-governance to physicians, thereby trusting "strangers" to take care of their "owne bodies."[333] Where Pliny warned readers not to surrender control over their lives to doctors,

---

(167).

[332] Ibid., 118.

[333] Pliny the Elder, *The historie of the world: commonly called, The naturall historie of C. Plinius Secundus* (London, 1634), 118.

the seventeenth-century Leveller and physician Humphrey Brooke insisted, by contrast, that it is "the Duty of a Physitian" to restore and preserve the health of patients; that physicians, "who have the Charge of Bodies," should take even greater care of this charge given that so many laypeople neglect what is for their own good.[334]

In *Ugieine: or A conservatory of health* (1650), Brooke's disquisition on preventative medicine and life-prolongation, short life is no longer characterized by the "great actions" praised by Jonson, nor by the action-spurring *carpe diem* tropes that pervaded seventeenth-century English poetry.[335] Instead, Brooke conceived short life as an avoidable result of intemperance. Not without righteous paternalism, he addressed "the good Fellow, that regards not what he eats, or how much he drinks, [who] is usually plump and Ruddy, [yet] seldome sick, & though happily they live not so long, yet are their lives more pleasurable, which makes good amends for the shortness. For better is a short life and Happy, then a long and Dolorous."[336] The last claim is not the physician's stance (Brooke aimed at the happiness of long life, not of short), but rather his ventriloquism of the intemperate person who lives "as if he lived to Eat,

---

[334] Humphrey Brooke, *Ugieine: or A conservatory of health…Compiled and published for the prevention of sickness, and prolongation of life* (1650), 1-2.
[335] "Our life is short," wrote Robert Herrick, for example, "and our days run/As fast away as does the sun…Then while time serves, and we are but decaying,/Come, my Corinna, come, let's go a-Maying" ("Corinna's Going A-Maying").
[336] Brooke, *Ugieine: or A conservatory of health*, 5.

and did not eat to Live."[337]

Brooke may have heard such reasoning from intemperate patients, but his caricature also alludes to the voluptuous pagan in the gospel of Luke who accumulates a surplus of wealth and tells his soul to "eate, drinke, and be merry."[338] The gospel portrays him as a fool, having provided for an uncertain earthly life but not for his soul's certain afterlife. The pagan elicits a parable from Jesus (a version of that conjured above in Jonson's poem) to which Brooke adhered in his capacity as a physician. "Take no thought for your life what ye shall eate," Jesus instructs, "neither for the body, what ye shall put on. The life is more than meat, and the body is more than raiment."[339] In other words, life is more than the biological survival of the body. To prioritize the flesh over life itself, Brooke suggested, is to risk not only one's physical health through intemperance, but also to risk the afterlife of one's soul like the pagan in the gospel; and yet Brooke still wanted his patients to take thought for what they consumed and to take care to protect their bodies.

---

[337] Ibid., 6.

[338] *The book of Luke*, 12:19. "Let us eat and drink," Brooke's caricature continues, "and if we die tomorrow, let us have our penny worths out to day; For to what end are all delicious things given us, if not to enjoy? Thus pleads the Intemperate: As if he were born for his Belly, and all the noble Faculties of his Soul, the exquisite operations of his Senses, and other Habiliments of his Body ought to be subservient thereunto" (Ugieine, 6).

[339] The book of Luke, 12:22-23.

As Bacon seized on the same parable to make the case for experimenting with life-prolonging medicines, he revised Christ's injunction as an argument for bodily self-care.

> Some of those Things...have not been tried by us, by way of Experiment; (For our Course of life doth not permit that;)...Neverthelesse, wee have been carefull, and that with all Providence and Circumspection; (Seeing the Scripture saith of the Body of Man; That it is more worth than Raiment;) To propound such Remedies as may at least be safe, if peradventure they be not Fruitfull.[340]

To "have been carefull...with all Providence and Circumspection" betrays Bacon's subtle appropriation and reversal of Christ's argument that humans should not care for their own bodies and lives but instead trust that divine providence will provide as it does for fowl and lilies. The providence Bacon had in mind, rather, is human foresight, anticipation of and preparation for the future, prudent government, and management of resources.[341] He refused to concede, in other words, that Christ's question—"which of you with taking thought can add to his stature one cubit?"—is strictly rhetorical and not intended to elicit an affirmative reply.[342]

---

[340] Bacon, *Historie naturall and experimentall, of life and death*, 178-179.

[341] "Providence," n. 1.a. and b., *Oxford English Dictionary*.

[342] *The book of Luke*, 12:22-27.

While early moderns vacillated as to whether anything could (and should) be done to prolong life, they were negotiating an ambivalence about the efficacy or futility of human agency more generally. In *Three Books on Life* (*De vita libri tres*, 1489), the Italian physician, humanist, and Catholic priest Marsilio Ficino argued that "a long life is not just something the fates promise once and for all from the beginning, but something that is produced by our effort ["*Vitam vero longam non solum ab initio semel fata promittunt, sed nostra etiam diligentia praestat.*"].[343] The rhetorical structure of this reminder suggests that fifteenth-century readers presupposed that life was predetermined by supernatural powers. In a telling inversion of Ficino's logic, Browne recalled in *Religio Medici* (1642) that not only natural but also supernatural causes affect longevity.

> And truely there goes a great deale of
> providence to produce a mans life unto
> threescore; there is more required than an able
> temper for those yeeres; though the radicall
> humour containe in it sufficient oyle for
> seventie, yet I perceive in some it gives no light
> past thirtie; men assigne not all the causes of
> long life that write whole books thereof.[344]

---

[343] Marsilio Ficino, "On a Long Life," *Three Books on Life*, eds. Carol V. Kaske and John R. Clark (Medieval and Renaissance Text and Studies, Vol. 57, Binghamton, New York: The Renaissance Society of America, 1989), 166-167.

[344] Browne, *Religio Medici*, 1.43.

That Browne was compelled to remind seventeenth-century English readers of the metaphysical determinants of longevity indicates that many had come to focus exclusively on physical and human-controlled causes. To live long, Browne argued, it is not enough to live temperately or to possess a large quantity of "the radicall humour" (also known as "the root of Life").[345] These may offer clues in predicting longevity, but they are ultimately unreliable according to Browne.

> There is therefore a secrete glome or bottome of
> our dayes; 'twas his wisedome to determine them,
> but his perpetuall and waking providence that
> fulfils and accomplisheth them....some other
> hand that twines the thread of life than that
> of nature...the line of our dayes is drawne by
> night, and...by a pencill that is invisible; wherein
> though wee confesse our ignorance, I am sure we
> doe not erre, if wee say, it is the hand of God.[346]

Although Ficino and Browne acknowledged that forces beyond human power determine longevity, they both still advocated taking action to preserve healthy life. Others, however, who adhered to the doctrine of predestination more strictly than Browne, moralized about life-prolongation without even trying it.

The natural philosopher and Royal Physician Walter Charleton, for example, believed that because longev-

---

[345] J.B., *A Sermon, or The survey of man* (1638; 1652).
[346] Browne, *Religio Medici*, 1.43.

ity is predetermined by divine providence, it follows that human providence cannot be a cause of long life. In his "physico-theologicall treatise" *The Darkness of Atheism Dispelled* (1652), Charleton interrogated "The Mobility of the Terme of Mans Life," that is, whether negligence, intemperance, and disobedience can alter human lifespan, given that it is "immoveably fixt by the Special Providence of God."[347] Charleton presupposed the truth of predestination, but he still wondered whether it were possible to move God, through "repentance, prayers, and piety" to intervene and alter the original dispensation. He concluded that it is not. Accordingly, "to promise Longevity to morigerous Children, when formerly and without any respect to their prevised obedience, God hath prefixt unto them an Instransible Term of life" is to reduce God to "an Anthropopathical Sophisme, or affected expression in the stammering Dialect of Humanity."[348] To presume to have knowledge of or power to control longevity, in other words, is to wrongfully aspire to godhead and to project emotions onto a power that is indifferent to the human desire for longer life. Remarkably, not Bacon's but Charleton's line of thinking remained the dominant mode of longevity discourse into the late seventeenth century.[349]

Theological arguments against the role of human

---

[347] Charleton, *The Darknes of Atheism Dispelled*, 199.

[348] Ibid., 235.

[349] See, for example, Richard Allestree, *A Discourse Concerning the Period of Human Life: Whether Mutable or Immutable* (1677).

providence in determining longevity had serious political implications. Lawrence Stone has noted that in the years leading up to the English Civil Wars (1642-1651), William Laud, the powerful Archbishop of Canterbury, fueled "a counter-revolution in theology, taking the form of a hostility to the Calvinist predestinarian determinism which had been common to all parties in the Elizabethan Church."[350] Perhaps unintentionally, then, Bacon and other proto-scientists who asserted human power over longevity aligned themselves with Laudian and Arminian opponents of Calvinism, thereby intensifying divisions within English society that later culminated in bloodshed.

Added to the opposition from dogmatic Calvinists, Bacon's project of life-prolongation, like the new science more generally, had to contend with the ideology of decay, which according to Herbert Wesinger was "perhaps the strongest impediment to the immediate acceptance of the idea of the Renaissance and so great was its influence that it needed the full efforts of Bacon and his followers to put an end to its vogue in the philosophical area though it kept alive by becoming a convention in poetry."[351] The ideol-

---

[350] Lawrence Stone, *The Causes of the English Revolution 1529-1642* (New York, NY: Harper & Rowe, 1972), 119.

[351] Herbert Wesinger, "Ideas of History during the Renaissance," *Renaissance Essays*, ed. Paul Oskar Kristeller and Philip P. Wiener (Rochester: University of Rochester Press, 1968), 74-94; 93-94. In *The Elizabethan World Picture* (1942), E.M.W. Tillyard writes, "Men were bitter and thought the world was in decay largely because they expected so much" (20).

ogy is alive indeed in *The First Anniversary* (1611), the telling subtitle of which is *An anatomie of the world. Wherein… the frailtie and the decay of this whole World is represented.* For Donne, "the worlds beauty is decai'd, or gone," (249) and "mankinde decayes so soone,/[that] We'are scarce our Fathers shadowes cast at noone:/Onely death addes t'our length: nor are we growne/In stature to be men, till we are none" (143-146). These lines reflect the conventional belief that human life had shortened over time, each generation shorter-lived than its predecessor, the result of a universal decay in nature since the time of the Flood.[352]

A preliminary challenge to the ideology of decay arrived in Hakewill's *Apologie or Declaration of the Power and Providence of God in the Government of the World…an Examination and Censure of the Common Errour Touching Nature's Perpetual and Universal Decay* (1627), which posits a cyclical view of history that includes decay as well as regeneration. Hakewill blamed his contemporaries' myopia for

---

[352] "So short is life," Donne complained, "And as in lasting, so in length is man/Contracted to an inch, who was a spanne" (133-136). Bacon similarly gathered from a literal reading of scripture that human life "was reduced to a moiety," or by half, immediately after the flood, and that three generations later, it was "was contracted & shortened" to just a quarter of its antediluvian length (*The historie of life and death*, 74). Where Donne's response to short life is ethical and pessimistic, Bacon's is scientific and optimistic, but both remarkably use the same passive verb "contracted," which suggests the possibility that postlapsarian human life has retained its proportion despite losing magnitude, and which obfuscates the subjective agency responsible for diminishing human life after the Flood.

the worldview "that all things decay and goe backward," whereas a cosmopolitan thinker such as himself, able to transcend personal historicity to take "a larger view…as a member of the Vniverse, and a Citizen of the World," could see that divine providence restores all that is lost, "that though some members suffer, yet the whole is no way thereby indammaged at any time."[353] If this optimistic faith in divine providence appears naïve and complacent, Hakewill still successfully imagined an alternative to the deep-seated pessimism of the ideology of decline, and in doing so, he made way for Bacon's new science.

One telling section title of *Apologie* highlights Hakewill's defiance of prevailing orthodoxy: "That if our liues be shortened in regard of our Ancestours, we should rather lay the burden of the fault vpon our intemperance, then vpon a decay in Nature." This perpetuated traditional moralizing about temperance, but it also shifted attention from metaphysical to natural causes of longevity. Within this newly-opened space of inquiry, for instance, Hakewill was able to observe that the Scottish highlanders, "and the wild Irish commonly liue longer then those of softer education," that "nice and tender [upbringing] in the more civill times and countreyes [is] no doubt a great enemy to Longevity," as are other child-rearing practices including "nourishing" infants with milk that is not from their

---

[353] George Hakewill, *An Apologie of the Power and Providence of God in the Government of the World* (Oxford, 1627), 156.

own mothers.[354] Despite such forays into the historical ethnography of longevity, however, Hakewill's work was ultimately an apology for divine providence. Unlike Bacon, then, who wanted human art to reverse the consequences attributed to the Fall, Hakewill's progressive but circular revision of the ideology of decay finally left the task of human regeneration in the hands of God.

Politicizing Biotheology

To observe the correlation between longevity and the "*Ages of the world*,"[355] Bacon went further than Hakewill in demystifying the ideology of decay, concluding that the succession of historical ages has "no whit abated from the Length of Life…Neither hath it declined, (As a man would have thought) by little and little."[356] Indeed, most of Bacon's contemporaries "would have thought" just that, inundated as they were with representations of a world in irreversible decline. Bacon's observation that human life had not shortened over time is remarkable not because it is correct,[357] but because it represented life as a physical

---

[354] Ibid., "Preface."

[355] Bacon, *Historie naturall and experimentall, of life and death*, 5.

[356] Ibid., 137.

[357] In fact, twenty-first century researches have shown that the trend of human life expectancy has slowly but steadily increased over the past millennium. To be sure, greater life expectancy is not the same as increased longevity, and the upward trend reflects saving the young from premature death rather than saving the old by adding years at end of life. See Olshansky, Passaro, et al., "A Potential

thing in the world, un-predetermined, knowable, subject to human power as well as to environmental and historical contingencies.

Life is "longer, for the most part," Bacon reported, "when the times are barbarous, and Men fare lesse deliciously, and are more given to Bodily Exercises: Shorter, when the Times are more Civill, and Men abandon themselves to Luxury and Ease."[358] This empirical observation raises ethical and political questions in the context of *The History of Life and Death*, which ranks lifeforms by the length of their lives and hierarchizes ways of life according to their conduciveness to longevity. Rather than isolate and extrapolate the importance of bodily exercise for longer life, that is, Bacon implied that it is better to live during "barbarous" times than during times of peace, because the former is better for long life. Translating longevity research from a descriptive to a prescriptive science thus required the revaluation of competing and inherently ambivalent values.

In addition to the "Ages of the World," Bacon consid-

Decline in Life Expectancy in the United States in the 21st Century," *New England Journal of Medicine*, 352; 11, March 2005): 1138-1145. See also Gregg Easterbrook, "What Happens When We All Live to 100?" *The Atlantic*, October 2014, https://www.theatlantic.com/magazine/archive/2014/10/what-happens-when-we-all-live-to-100/379338/. "A graph of global life expectancy over time looks like an escalator rising smoothly. The trend holds, in most years, in individual nations rich and poor; the whole world is riding the escalator."
[358] Bacon, *Historie naturall and experimentall, of life and death*, 137.

ered myriad other variables, including "Countries, Climates, places of birth...Complexions, Constitutions, shapes and statures of the Body, measure...and proportion of the Limbes, Dyet, government of Life, exercise...kind of Life, affections of the Soule, and divers accidents [that] shorten and lengthen the life of Man."[359] He classified human lives according to skin type, observing that hard, thick, spongy, close-grained, and smooth skin, along with "great wrinkles in the forehead are better signes [of long life] than a smooth forehead." He categorized hair type, recording that bristly hair "is a better signe of long life than dainty soft locks," that black or red hair and a freckled complexion "are [better] signes of longer life, than a white haire and Complexion" and that early balding "is an indifferent signe," because many are "yet long-liv'd" who go bald early.[360]

Although Bacon rejected theological predetermination, these observations betray a proto-biological determinism that complicates his endorsement of life-prolonging practices, diets, medicines, and ways of life.[361] Bacon did

---

[359] Bacon, *The historie of life and death*, 10-12.

[360] Ibid., 121.

[361] Nikolas Rose has noted "the pessimism of most sociological critics, who suggest that we are seeing the rise of a new biological and genetic determinism. Instead I argue that we are seeing the emergence of a novel somatic ethics, imposing obligations yet imbued with hope, oriented to the future yet demanding action in the present. On the one hand, our vitality has been opened up as never before for economic exploitation and the extraction of biovalue, in a new bioeconomics that alters our very conception of

not indicate how data on bodily signs of longevity might be instrumentalized, but a range of potential uses can be imagined: for example, to determine with distributive justice (or eugenic biopower) who can access a finite resource of life-prolonging medicines; or, more innocuously, to use as a self-diagnostic tool whereby Bacon's readers might strategically plan their lives according to their expectations of either long or short life.

Regarding bodily "proportion," Bacon observed that tall-statured people live longer than those of "low stature," that small waists and long legs "betoken longer life" than short legs and large waists do; also that a proportionately small head, average-sized neck, large nostrils, wide mouth, and fatness in youth but not in age "signifie long life," and so on, in an exhaustive but infinitely expandable taxonomy of human lifeforms. *The History of Life and Death* thus assigns new meaning to the ancient notion that life should be measured not by the quantity of it duration or magnitude but by the quality of its proportion and shape. Where tradition conceived this proportion as a moral or ethical quality—such that short life well lived is more perfect than long life lived without proportionately great purpose—Bacon instead called attention to the physical

---

ourselves in the same moment that it enables us to intervene upon ourselves in new ways, On the other hand, our somatic, corporeal neurochemical individuality has become opened up to choice, prudence, responsibility, to experimentation, to contestation, and so to a politics of life itself (*The Politics of Life Itself*, 8).

proportions of embodied life. This shift from the soul to the body, concomitant with larger transitions from theology and ethics toward science and politics, inaugurated a new paradigm by which to reevaluate existing hierarchies of life.

"A religious holy Life may cause a long life" according to Bacon, not because it pleases divine providence but because its characteristic bodily practices and affections such as "rest...joy, noble hope, wholesome feare, [and] sweet sorrow...doe lengthen the naturall life of a mortified Christian."[362] Orthodox Anglicans believed that the purpose of a religious life was to prepare the soul for eternity, not to prepare the body for longevity. To be sure, Bacon presented long life not as the end but as a collateral benefit of religion. Within the larger argument that longer good-quality life is better than shorter good-quality life, however, the suggestion is that religious life is good primarily because it is good for long life.

Below religious life, Bacon cited "the learned life of Philosophers, Rhetoricians, and Grammarians, living in

---

[362] Bacon, *The historie of life and death*, 127. Jeremy Taylor later agreed that "a strict course of piety is the way to prolong our lives in the natural sense, and to adde good portions to the number of our years; and sin is sometimes by natural causality, very often by the anger of God, and the Divine judgment, a cause of sudden and untimely death" (*The Rule and Exercises of Holy Dying*, 32). In other words, piety prolongs life naturally as an embodied practice characterized by temperance, and supernaturally, by not provoking divine wrath to cut life short.

ease" as exceptionally conducive to longevity, because it involves spending time freely in the company of young people.[363] Next he observed country lives, which, by maintaining "a fresh" diet, "being active," and living without "care and envy…therefore prolong life."[364] Last, Bacon remarked that "Military life is good in youth," because many warriors have been "long liv'd," and because "military affections, raised with the desire and hope of Victory, infuse into the Spirits heate agreeable to long life."[365] On the one hand, these ways of life, ranked according to their favorability for longevity, were predetermined for individuals according to official early modern English social theory.[366] On the other hand, increasing social mobility made it practically viable for Bacon's contemporaries to pursue professions and ways of life advantageous to longevity. The paradigm of longevity potentially yields a biological egalitarianism insofar as people from different social strata have access to professions that are equally "good" because, for different reasons, they are equally good for long life. However, the paradigm also potentially exacerbates social divisions, insofar as at stake is no longer just one's temporary position in this world en route to eternity, but one's life itself, reconceived as inseparable from the body.

Perhaps more telling than the myriad causes and signs

---

[363] Bacon, *The historie of life and death*, 128.

[364] Ibid., 129.

[365] Ibid., 129-130.

[366] Thomas, *The Ends of Life*, 16; 29.

of longevity included in *The History of Life and Death* are those that Bacon excluded. His rejection of astrological influences on lifespan, for instance, is especially character-istic of seventeenth-century English culture. "Astrologicall Observations drawne from the Horoscope or Nativity," Bacon declared, "are not allowable."[367] Bacon could not allow astrology for similar reasons that his contempo-raries could not allow the ideas of English autochthony and (I show in the following chapter) mortalism—that is, not because they were proven to be invalid,[368] but because admitting their validity would contradict other cherished convictions. Bacon did not admit as much but instead dismissed planetary influence on longevity as an irratio-nal fiction derived from "superstitious fables, and strange delusions, by which Reason being besieged, hath miser-ably yeelded up the Fort of beleefe."[369] John Parker has

---

[367] Bacon, *The historie of life and death*, 124.

[368] Indeed, Bacon elsewhere acknowledged that the only noteworthy observations concerning the correlation between nativity and longevity have been astrological "which wee rejected" (*Historie naturall and experimentall, of life and death*, 155).

[369] Ibid., 138. See, by contrast, Ficino's advice that even if "you do not approve of astronomical images," you should at least "not neglect the medicines that have been strengthened with a little planetary help—or you will have neglected life itself" (*The Book of Life* [Spring Publications, 1980], 85). By Ficino's criteria, then, Bacon neglected "life itself" by excluding astrology from his study. Bacon's exclusion of astrology also reflects a general ambivalence toward planetary influence in English culture that is epitomized by Edmund in Shakespeare's Lear, who famously calls it "an admirable evasion of whoremaster man, to lay his goatish disposition to the charge

remarked that "the rejection of astral indicators" is a central pillar of English theology.[370] Accordingly, Bacon's disallowance of astrology, like *The History of Life and Death* generally, reveals not the secularization but rather the residual theologism of the new science of life-prolongation.

Bacon's exclusion of astrology served to shift focus to previously overlooked causes of longevity, including age, level of health, lifestyle, and even the marital status of one's parents during conception.[371] Bacon reported, for example, that the lives of bastards are shorter than the lives of legitimate children; the latter, "begotten in lawfull Wedlock, not in Fornication, and in the morning, their Parents being not too lusty and wanton, doe live long."[372] Although this substitution of humoral theory for astrology

---

of a star!" (1.2.115-116). Edmund mocks the conventional belief that because his parents conceived him beneath "the Dragon's tail" constellation, and because he was born beneath the Big Dipper, "it follows, I am rough and lecherous. Fut, I should have been that I am had the maidenliest star in the firmament twinkled on my bastardizing" (1.2.117-121).

[370] John Parker, "The Catastrophe of the Old Comedy: King Lear, Astrology and Christian Atheism." Unpublished manuscript. Acrobat Reader file. See also Tillyard, *The Elizabethan World Picture*, 53: "when Christianity was young and growing, there was general terror of the stars and a wide practice of astrology. The terror was mainly superstitious, and the only way of mitigating the stars' enmity was through magic. It was one of the Church's main tasks to reduce the license of late pagan astrological superstition to her own discipline. There was no question of cutting it out altogether."

[371] Bacon, *The historie of life and death*, 117-118.

[372] Ibid., 118-119.

represents a shift toward empiricism, Bacon's observation of bastardly lives betrays the moralizing prejudices and ingrained ideologies that informed it. Notwithstanding the exhaustive capaciousness of *The History of Life and Death*, Bacon failed to take into account how, for example, socioeconomic hardship potentially influenced the longevity of bastards no less than the unlawfulness of their birth or the ostensible lust of their parents.

Bacon observed that the mother's diet during pregnancy has "considerable" effects on the child's longevity, but that it is difficult to give "rules for judging of Childrens long life by their begetting, and Birth," for two reasons: first, because life outcomes often contradicted expectations predicted by the data; and second, because prescribing rules for longevity required the hierarchization of traditionally incommensurable and ambivalent values, such as whether it is better for English lives to be qualitatively strong or quantitatively long. "Children begotten with a lively courage, prove strong," Bacon remarked, "but through their spirits sharpe inflammation are not long-liv'd."[373] Rather than decide between improving life's quality and increasing its quantity, however, Bacon envisioned a future where longer life and stronger life would be one and the same.

It would be possible to prolong quality life indefinitely, Bacon believed, were it not for "the unequall repairing of

---

[373] Ibid., 118.

some parts sufficiently, others hardly and badly in Age," which makes human bodies "undergoe Mezentius torment, living in the embraces of the dead untill they dye, and being easily repairable, yet through some particular difficulty in restoring, doe decay."[374] Mezentius is the Etruscan king from Virgil's *Aeneid* who killed people by binding them to dead corpses. The trope was widespread and versatile in Bacon's culture.[375] The following chapter, for instance, will elucidate Overton's suggestion that Christian dualism, by ascribing life to the soul and mortality to the body, reduces God to a necromancer who "put[s] a spirit into a dead body," and who is no better than "the tyrant *Mezentius,* that bound living men to dead bodyes, till the putrefaction and corruption of the stincking corps had kild them."[376] In the context of life-prolongation, Bacon's allusion to Mezentius yields at least three interpretations.

First, Mezentius' victims emblematize old age as a

---

[374] Ibid., 4.

[375] A group of Catholic authors supposed in 1630 that joining "in one selfe-same Societie" the Catholic Church and "all the other hereticall and schismaticall sects" was "like [joining] Mezentius dead bodies with liuing bodies" (Du Perron et al., *The Reply of the Most Illustrious Cardinall of Perron, to the Answeare of the Most Excellent King of Great Britain* [Douay, 1630], 405).

[376] Richard Overton, *Mans Mortallitie, or a treatise wherein 'tis proved, both theologically and philosophically, that whole man (as a rationall creature) is a compound wholy mortall: contrary to the common distinction of soule and body: and that the present going of the soule into Heaven or Hell is a meer fiction: and that at the resurrection is the beginning of our immortallity, and then actuall condemnation, and salvation, and not before...* (London, 1643), 44.

living death wherein some body parts continue to repair while other parts decay. Second, the trope refers to Bacon's "two-fold search…considering mans body as livelesse and unnourished; and as living, and nourished."[377] This split conception of the aging individual body as *two* bodies bound together, one living and one dead, aligns with Agamben's claim that the "division of life into vegetal and relational, organic and animal, animal and human… passes first of all as a mobile border within living man, and without this intimate caesura the very decision of what is human and what is not would probably not be possible."[378] By isolating within human beings an organic, vegetal form of life capable of prolongation, Bacon overturned traditional criteria and authority for making anthropogenic decisions, thereby disrupting English orthodoxy and altering the subsequent scientific, social, and political history of life and death.

The allusion to Mezentius finally takes on a life of its own to betray Bacon's potential misgivings about the new science of life-prolongation. English readers knew that Aeneas mortally wounds Mezentius in battle and that the latter's son, Lausus, gives his own life to prevent Aeneas from finishing the kill. Surrounded by the dead and dying, Mezentius survives a short while longer to mourn his son, tragically epitomizing the disproportionately great cost of modest, even negligible, gains in life-prolongation.

---

[377] Bacon, *The historie of life and death*, 7.

[378] Agamben, *The Open: Man and Animal*, 15.

The consensus among seventeenth-century physicians (still current today) that decay and senescence are
inevitable and irreversible is "ignorant and vaine," Bacon
claimed, because "young living creatures being all over
and wholly repaired, do by their increasing in quantity, and
growing better in quality, shew that if the measure and
manner of repairing decayed not, the matter of repairing
might be eternall."[379] The idea that nutritive, embodied life

[379] Ibid., 1-2. Bacon's suggestion that human bodies might be eternal
articulates in a new scientific context the notion mythologized
by Spenser in his account of the Gardin of Adonis, where "[a]
ll things" come into being by "borrow[ing] matter, whereof they
are made," matter that "[b]ecomes a body, and doth then inuade/
The state of life, out of the griesly shade./That substaunce is
eterne," remaining even after "the life decayes, and forme does
fade," perpetually assuming new forms of life (*FQ*, III.vi.37). But
whereas Spenser's eternal substance survives the individual lives of
which it is a substrate, Bacon hopes to secure the identity of human
bodies upon an eternal foundation. The idea of eternal matter was
not new for early moderns, tracing back at least to the Roman poet
Lucretius, who writes in *On Nature of Things* that "[a]ll objects would
be destroyed by a single cause/If there were not eternal matter to
hold them together" and that "[m]atter…[c]an be eternal, though
everything made of it dies" (*De Rerum Natura*, trans. C.H. Sisson
[New York: Routledge, 2003], 21; 28. Cf. Gregg Easterbrook
reiterates a version of Bacon's hypothesis in a recent article in
The Atlantic recently ("What Happens When We All Live to 100?").
"Drugs that lengthen health span are becoming to medical researchers
what vaccines and antibiotics were to previous generations in the lab:
their grail. If health-span research is successful, pharmaceuticals as
remarkable as those earlier generations of drugs may result. In the
process, society might learn the answer to an ancient mystery: Given
that every cell in a mammal's body contains the DNA blueprint of a
healthy young version of itself, why do we age at all?"

"might be eternall" reflects, again, not Bacon's secularization of life but rather the immanentization of theological values within the sphere of biology.[380] The following chapter shows how seventeenth-century English mortalism enacted an analogous convergence of the life of the soul and that of the body, which compelled Richard Overton to inquire, if humans are said to have "endlesse soul[s]…why have we not endlesse bodyes?"[381] Overton could politicize biotheology during the civil wars only because Bacon had already biologized theology in *The History of Life and Death*.

---

[380] Investigating modern medicine's preoccupation with life-prolongation, Michael Mack has argued that "the promise of eternal life has turned immanent in the medical ideal of the long life" such that "the term 'longevity' bears what Giorgio Agamben [calls] the theological 'signature' of eternal life" (*Philosophy and Literature: Challenging Our Infatuation with Numbers* [New York: Bloomsbury, 2014], 11).

[381] Overton, *Mans Mortalitie*, 53.

To Die, To Sleep

S hakespeare's *Measure for Measure* (1604) dramatizes life as it is intersected by competing theological, ethical, and political discourses. Claudio sits in jail, condemned to be executed, or as the prison provost euphemistically puts it, to "be made immortal" (4.2.54), for impregnating Juliet out of wedlock. "Be absolute for death," Duke Vincentio, disguised as a friar, enjoins Claudio, "either death or life shall thereby be the sweeter" (3.1.5-6). Belying his religious disguise, the duke offers Claudio a conspicuously un-Christian consolation that emphasizes not eternal life but earthly life, which is "death's fool," no better than "an after-dinner's sleep," something not to be valued or preserved. "Reason thus with life. If I do lose thee, I do lose a thing that none but fools would keep" (3.1.6-8).

Such contempt for life differs from the Christian trope of *contemptus mundi*, because rather than subordinate this life to the afterlife, the duke commends Claudio only to death. The duke's consolation has ethical value insofar as accepting mortality is necessary for living and dying well; but the duke also compels Claudio to turn absolutely toward death because, as the play shows, sovereignty in Vienna is exercised as biopower, as the power to kill (or make "immortal"), to let or make live by determining the conditions of reproduction as well as of capital punishment. Such biopower requires subjects who identify with being mortal.[382]

As the counterpoint to Claudio, another prisoner on death row named Barnardine frustrates the authorities because he is not directed toward mortality, much less "absolute for death." The provost observes that Barnardine "apprehends death no more dreadfully but as a drunken sleep; careless, reckless, and fearless of what's past, present, or to come; insensible of mortality and desperately mortal" (4.2.132-135). Because he does not fear death, Barnardine poses a problem for those who wish to exercise power over his life, which explains the sadistic mock executions to which the state regularly subjects him. "We have very oft awaked him as if to carry him to execution, and showed him a seeming warrant for it," the provost marvels, but "it hath not moved him at all" (4.2.139-141). The state's power over Barnardine's life requires his fear of death as well as of the afterlife.

When his jailors try to control the narrative about Barnardine's life after death, however, they implicate themselves in the heresy of mortalism, the belief that the soul dies or "sleeps" with the body until both are resurrected together as one at Judgment Day. Barnardine says he is too

---

[382] See Giorgio Agamben, *Homo Sacer: Sovereign Power and Bare Life*, trans. Daniel Heller-Roazen (Stanford: Stanford University Press, 1995), 88-89. "[T]he first foundation of political life is a life that may be killed, which is politicized through its very capacity to be killed." "Not simple natural life, but life exposed to death (bare life or sacred life) is the original political element."

"sleepy" to rise for his execution, but the pimp Pompey, assisting Abhorson the executioner, orders Barnardine to "awake till you are executed, and sleep afterwards" (4.3.25-28). Insofar as "sleep" here serves not only as a metaphor for death but also as a literal description of the state of the soul after the body's death, and insofar as mortalism in Shakespeare's Vienna represents as grave a crime as it came to represent in mid-seventeenth-century England, then what the duke says of Claudio may hold true for Barnardine: that his life is "no greater forfeit to the law than [those] who hath sentenced him" (4.2.145-147).

Contrasting Barnardine's attachment to the bodily pleasures of earthly life against the authorities' alacrity to make him immortal, the scene's comedic effect lies in the culturally overdetermined equivalence between sleep and death. Donne's "Holy Sonnet X," for instance, tells death to "be not proud," because pleasure comes with "rest and sleepe," which are "pictures" of death, and so death must be even more pleasurable. The sonnet's final lines—"One short sleepe past, wee wake eternally,/And death shall be no more"[383]—are unmistakably mortalist, and they conjure Luther's reading of the book of *Ecclesiastes* in *An Exposition of Salomons Booke* (trans. 1573): "the dead lye there acompting neyther dayes nor yeares, but when they are awaked,

---

[383] John Donne, "Holy Sonnet X," *The Complete Poetry and Selected Prose of John Donne*, ed. Charles M. Coffin (New York: The Modern Library, 2001), 262-263.

they shall seeme to have slept scarce one minute."[384] At the start of the Reformation, Luther professed mortalism to circumvent abuses of church power stemming from intercessionary prayer, indulgences, and the notion of purgatory, all of which hang on the belief that the soul survives the death of the body.[385]

While Donne joined many contemporaries in categorically disavowing the heresy, intimations of mortalism were ubiquitous, albeit inconspicuous, in English culture. "We are such stuff as dreams are made on," Prospero says, "and our little life is rounded with a sleep" (*The Tempest*, 4.1.156-158). These lines reverberate the seventh-century *Ecclesiastical History of England*, where the Anglo-Saxon monk Bede the Venerable observed that "the life of men appears for an instant, but whatever follows it, and whatever went before—of that we have no idea at all."[386] Hamlet, too, entertains the heresy while contemplating suicide, in an

---

[384] Martin Luther, *An Exposition of Salomons Booke called Ecclesiastes or the preacher. Seene and allowed* (London: 1573), 151.

[385] Mark Johnston, *Surviving Death* (Princeton and Oxford: Princeton University Press, 2010), 23. "Luther himself favored a doctrine of soul-sleeping or 'Psychopannychism' as it came to be called after Calvin attacked it, the doctrine that the soul is in a state of sleep or suspended mental life in the interregnum between death and the final judgment. Psychopannychism appears explicitly in Luther's *Exposition of Salomon's Book*, a commentary on Qoheleth Luther wrote in 1532, and which appeared in English forty years later."

[386] Bede the Venerable, *Ecclesiastical History of England*, quoted in Peter Heinegg, *Mortalism: Readings on the Meaning of Life* (Amherst, New York: Prometheus Books, 2003), 61.

obvious but overlooked seventeenth-century invocation of mortalism.

Not comforted by Luther's promise that the soul's sleep will be short and quick, Hamlet fears the anguishing dreams of postmortem consciousness: "To die, to sleep. To sleep, perchance to dream. Ay, there's the rub," he worries, since oppression, "the law's delay," and insolent bureaucrats will be tolerated in this life as long as people dread what may come in the afterlife (*Hamlet*, 3.1.66-84). This quasi-mortalist position resembles Luther's *psychopannychism*, which holds that the soul stays awake for an "overnight vigil" in the interim between bodily death and the Resurrection. Hamlet here represents the many seventeenth-century English people for whom immortality was a threat no less than a promise, a privation no less than a prerogative.[387] Apparently immune to this threat, engrossed in bodily pleasures unadulterated by fear of the

---

[387] In pausing to consider whether and what kind of dreams are possible without a body or "mortal coil," Hamlet anticipates later seventeenth-century debates surrounding the soul. In *Immortality of the Soul* (1659), the Platonist philosopher Henry More pursued a similar line of thought. While himself a staunch defender of the soul's immortality, More granted that "it is easy for the Psychopannychites to support their opinion of the Sleep of the Soule. For the Soule being utterly rescinded from all that is corporeal, and having no vital union therewith at all, they will be very prone to infer, that it is impossible she should know anything ad extra, if she can so much as dream. For even that power also may seem incomp[a]tible to her in such a state, she having such an essential aptitude for vital union with Matter" (6).

afterlife, Barnardine tells the duke that he "will not consent to die this day" (4.3.48-49), an assertion of his right to life that the duke tacitly honors by thwarting the execution. Shakespeare does not spell out the connection, but this stay of execution is of a piece with the mortalist confusion of death and sleep that vexes the sovereign power to make him "immortal" by killing him.

Known also as *thnetopsychism* (soul death), *psychopannychism* (the soul's overnight vigil), and *hypnopsychism* (soul sleep), mortalism refers to the heterogeneous collection of traditions—ancient and early modern, pagan and Christian, theological and philosophical—that posit the mortality of the soul. The strain of mortalism emergent in seventeenth-century England was a decidedly Christian reverberation of the controversy that arose at the start of the Protestant Reformation, and before that, during the early centuries of Christianity. The mortalism entertained by Shakespeare, Donne, and their Christian contemporaries was distinct from the annihilationism that they associated with the epicurean poet Lucretius, who asserted the absolute and permanent death of the soul. Still, orthodox Anglicans often failed to distinguish (or deliberately confounded) Christian and pagan versions of mortalism. They found the resemblance between soul sleep and soul death too close for comfort, and they feared that to question the soul's afterlife was to open a Pandora's box, the contents of which would annihilate traditional sociopolitical alliances, hierarchies, and orthodoxies.

In the early 1640s, embroiled in the English Civil War, a Leveller and obscure pamphleteer by the name of Richard Overton published *Man's Mortalitie* (1643), the first sustained and explicit profession of mortalism in England since William Tyndale, who translated the bible into English, was strangled and burned at the stake in 1536 for professing a number of heresies including mortalism.[388] *Man's Mortalitie* is among the least known but most consequential texts published in the seventeenth century. It subsequently influenced Enlightenment thinkers such as John Locke, whose father's library featured a copy of Overton's mortalist treatise.[389] Overton's defense of the soul's mortality constitutes a defense of humanistic and democratic values such as egalitarianism, freedom of speech and of conscience, religious tolerance, and the inalienable rights of embodied individuals including the right to life. Overton discovered that the individual's right to life is inseparable from the individual's right to death; that withholding death—by prolonging life or by promising (or threatening) immortality, potentially impinged no less upon the right to

---

[388] Burns writes, "In the century after Tyndale attacked the orthodox view of the soul's immortality, no Englishman set down a coherent argument for Christian mortalism until formidable defenses of the heresy were prepared by Overton, Milton, and Hobbes" (*Christian Mortalism from Tyndale to Milton* [Cambridge: Harvard University Press, 1972], 5). See also Bryan W. Ball, *The Soul Sleepers: Christian Mortalism from Wycliffe to Priestley* (Cambridge: James Clarke & Co., 2008), 69; 103.

[389] Roger Woolhouse, *Locke: A Biography* (Cambridge: Cambridge University Press, 2007), 7.

life than capital punishment.

Overton's insistence that humans have just one mortal life incensed orthodox Anglicans, who did not recognize the value of embodied life to the extent that Overton did. Overton did not reject the Judeo-Christian sanctity-of-life ethic as his detractors suggested, but instead unveiled its origins in traditions that were outlandish to Anglican orthodoxy. Like Luther and Tyndale before him, he saw mortalism as a *sine qua non* of Christian faith—specifically, because the soul must die if it is believed to be resurrected.[390] Overton's mortalist challenge to the orthodox Anglican "denial of death" and "culture of life" is in fact life-affirming, but the life that it affirms is that of the mortal body. Where Bacon's *History of Life and Death* registered the shift toward corporeal self-preservation that became foundational to biopower, *Man's Mortalitie* exposed immortalism as a nefarious political fiction instrumentalized by church and state authorities to encroach upon the rights of

---

[390] See Burns, *Christian Mortalism from Tyndale to Milton*, 32. Tyndale followed Luther in defending mortalism as a precondition of the Resurrection and hence a central article of Christian faith. In *An Answere Vnto Sir Thomas Mores Dialoge* (1531), Tyndale reframed immortalism as un-Christian and self-contradictory. Tyndale, and later authors including Browne and Overton, aimed to re-Christianize mortalism the same way Browne sought to Christianize autochthony—namely, by subordinating it to the Resurrection. But More dismissed this maneuver as an insincere ploy by mortalists to exonerate themselves from the full weight of what, in his view, they truly believed: that death is the end.

embodied individuals to self-preservation.[391] What appears to be a theological and philosophical discourse on the soul, then, is primarily, or at the very least additionally, a political argument.

While discussions around autochthony and longevity captured English efforts to isolate vegetative life from sensitive and rational life, the debate surrounding mortalism shows widespread attempts to insulate rational life from other lifeforms, an operation which Aristotle deemed impossible—"in mortal beings at least."[392] By the seventeenth century, orthodox thinkers generally equated rational life with life that is human and worth living. They aligned vegetative and sensitive lifeforms, by contrast, with the body, with mortality, and with subhuman life that has no rights and may be killed with impunity. While the colonialist discourse of autochthony (de)humanized lifeforms according to their degree of removal from the earth, English lives were also identified by their possession of a rational, disembodied, and immortal soul, or rather by their professed belief to have such a soul. To the extent that sociopolitical order is instituted through the anthropogenic differentiation of human life from "bare" life, then

---

[391] Roberto Esposito has observed that "only modernity makes of individual self-preservation the presupposition of all other political categories, from sovereignty to liberty" (Bíos: Biopolitics and Philosophy, trans. Timothy Campbell [Minneapolis and London: University of Minnesota Press, 2008], 9).

[392] Aristotle, On the Soul, trans. J.A. Smith, The Basic Works of Aristotle, ed. Richard McKeon (New York: The Modern Library, 2001), 557.

heterodox definitions of human life, such as that posited by Overton, challenge not only political sovereignty but also theological and philosophical tradition.

Like autochthony, orthodox Anglicans found mortalism "repugnant" to their worldview and belief system, and yet rather than let it be forgotten in history's dustbin, they routinely disavowed it and thereby kept it alive. Early modern English anxieties surrounding mortalism involved the fear of becoming or being identified as mortalist oneself. While orthodox authors took pains to establish that mortalism pertained to outlandish, pagan, and even non-human others, Overton uncovered mortalism's roots in the foundations of Anglican belief. Echoing Tyndale, he remarked:

> Divers[e] conceptions and fancies there be, to
> uphold this ridiculous invention of the Soule,
> traducted from the Heathens, who by the Booke
> of Nature understood an immortality after
> Death; but through their ignorance how, or
> which way, this invention (reported to be Plato's)
> was occasioned, and begot a general beliefe:
> and so they, and after them the Christians, have
> thus strained their wits to such miserable shifts,
> to define what it is; but neither conclude any
> certainty, or give satisfaction therein.[393]

[393] Richard Overton, *Mans Mortallitie, or a treatise wherein 'tis proved, both theologically and philosophically, that whole man (as a rationall creature) is a compound wholy mortall: contrary to the common distinction of soule and body: and that the present going of the soule into Heaven or Hell is a meer*

Overton ascribed immortalism to a "general Doctrine" of pagan philosophers who, frequently observing people "die without either punishment or reward, and being ignorant of any Resurrection, taught thence, that mens Souls (after death) remained alive."[394] Over its long history stretching from Plato to Descartes, immortalism came to justify and require a constellation of related beliefs, including human exceptionalism, the disembodiment of the rational soul, and the (sociopolitical) necessity of postmortem justice. Overton turned this ideological entanglement to his advantage to kill many proverbial birds with the single stone of mortalism, at once to level the ontological hierarchies that rank humans over animals and the correlated sociopolitical hierarchies that set certain humans over fellow humans.

Overton was well-versed in the long history of mortalism, and he situated *Man's Mortalitie* in the ancient legacy of which it was the latest resurgence. Despite its historical roots, however, Overton's articulation of mortalism was unprecedented, not least because of the dangerous politi-

fiction: and that at the resurrection is the beginning of our immortallity, and then actuall condemnation, and salvation, and not before. With all doubtes and objections answered, and resolved, both by scripture and reason ; discovering the multitude of blasphemies, and absurdities that arise from the fancie of the soule... (London, 1643), 4-5.

[394] Richard Overton, "The Postscript," *Man Wholly Mortal, or, A treatise wherein't is proved, both theologically and philosophically, that as whole man sinned, so whole man died ...: also, divers other mysteries, as of heaven, hell, the extent of the resurrection, the new creation, &c. opened and presented to the tryal of better judgements* (London, 1655).

cal climate in which it surfaced. Milton came closest to Overton in explicitly endorsing the heresy, but Milton's brief mention of mortalism in *De Doctrina Christiana* was precursory and tentative. Overton's text was unique not only for its theological and philosophical critique of political sovereignty, but also for its new scientific appeals to observable fact. To litigate his case that all life is embodied and inseparable from the body, Overton remarked both the lack of proof for immortality in scripture as well as the absence of empirical evidence in the human body. "Anatomize Man," he goaded readers, "all his lineaments & Dimensions...all his members & faculties," every part of "the Subject Man is corruptible, and himself but a Bundle of corruption, or curious Mass of vicissitudes."[395]

This anatomical challenge either echoed or inspired Thomas Browne, who made a similar point the same year in *Religio Medici* (1643). Browne admitted that in his experience dissecting human bodies he had failed to discover "any proper Organ or instrument for the rationall soule; for in the Braine, which we terme the seate of Reason," he could find nothing that he had not also found "in the crany of a beast."[396] As an immortalist, Browne construed this as negative proof that the human soul is independent

---

[395] Overton, *Man Wholly Mortal*, 15-16.

[396] Browne, *Religio Medici*, 70. For a discussion of Descartes' solution to this dilemma (locating the soul in the pineal gland of the brain), see Jonathan Sawday, *The Body Emblazoned: Dissection and the Human Body in Renaissance Culture* (London and New York: Routledge, 1995), 156.

of the body: "there is something in us, that can be without us, and will be after us, though it is strange that it hath no history, what it was before us, nor cannot tell how it entered in us."[397] Overton, by contrast, refused to believe that for which he found no evidence, and his mortalism led him to be more rigorously empirical than even physicians and proto-scientists of his time.

Overton's mortalism strengthened his empiricism by establishing the link between bodily organs and life functions previously assigned to a disembodied soul. Anticipating cognitive science, for example, Overton appealed to "experience," which suggested to him that rational thought or cogitation depends on the physical state of the brain.

> If the former Brain-pan be hurt, the Senses
> are hindered, but the Cogitation remaineth
> sound. If onely the Middle-pan be harmed, the
> Cogitation is maimed; but the Seat of Sense
> keepes all the five Senses whole: If any hurt
> befall both to the Former and Middle-pan, both
> Sense and Cogitation decay. If the Hinder-pan
> be disordered onely, the Memorie alone, and
> neither Sense nor Cogitation receive harme.[398]

---

[397] Browne, *Religio Medici*, 71. Browne states unequivocally that "I beleeve that the whole frame of a beaste doth perish, and is left in the same state after death, as before it was materialled unto life; that the soules of men know neither contrary nor corruption, that they subsist beyond the body, and outlive death by the priviledge of their proper natures."

[398] Overton, *Man Wholly Mortal*, 8-9.

Overton concluded that the human faculties "of Reason, Consideration, [and] Science" do not transcend the material world, because they "are augmented by Learning, Education, &c. lessened by negligence, idleness, &c. and quite nullified by madness."[399] Among the political payoffs of Overton's empiricist mortalism is its revision of rational thought as embodied and therefore subject to bio-physico-socio-political processes as well as to mortality.

Overton thus disrupted the orthodox modes of anthropogenesis by which English authorities sanctioned rational lifeforms while exposing "bare" lifeforms to death. In an early articulation of reproductive politics, he demonstrated the pitfalls of sovereign acts of anthropogenesis informed by dualistic immortalism.

> If the soule be infused…at the conception, then
> every abortive conception hath an immortall
> spirit in it, and must rise againe… [T]he soule
> is made the vegetative as well as the motive,
> sensitive or rationall part…and so Infants that
> dye in the wombe, or in the birth are lit[t]le
> better then trees, and worse then beasts.[400]

Overton did not dispute that the institution of sociopolitical order demands a sovereign decision about which lifeforms to include and preserve as human. He contended,

---

[399] Ibid., 6.
[400] Overton, *Mans Mortalitie*, 43.

however, that such decisions are not universally valid but historically contingent and subject to contestation.

Unlike Browne, who concluded that the soul "hath no history," Overton historicized the soul, tracing the ancient origins of immortalism through the seventeenth-century contexts in which it played out. Appended to the first edition of *Man's Mortalitie* is a list of thirteen "Occurrences" in English politics between Friday, January 12th, 1644 and the following Friday. Having finished *Man's Mortalitie*, for instance, readers learned that William Brereton, a commander in the Parliamentary army, was "in great distress" under the Royalist siege of Nantwich, Parliament's final stronghold in Cheshire, but that "our Forces" have thwarted "the Enemy valiantly," rescuing "four Peeces of Ordinance, from five thousand English and Irish, under bloudy [John] Bryon."[401] While no explicit link was drawn between Overton's text and these current events, their adjacent publication suggests that Overton expected certain kinds of political association from his readers, including their support of the Parliamentary cause.

In lieu of the list of "occurrences" appended to the 1644 edition of *Man's Mortalitie*, Overton included a postscript to the 1655 version of *Man Wholly Mortal*, which again dislocated mortalism from its seventeenth-century English contexts. The postscript ascribed the

---

[401] Overton, *Mans Mortalitie*, "OCCURENCES Of Certain Speciall and Remarkable Passages in PARLIAMENT, and the affaires of the Kingdome, for fuller Satisfaction," January, 19 1643 [i.e., 1644].

"opinion" of immortalism to the reward-and-punishment morality of pagan philosophers, as well as to "some ancient Chronicles of England," which reported that King Druis, in order "to encourage his Subjects without dread of death to fight his battles, taught them that their Souls were immortal, not subject to death."[402] This historicism might have been more timely a decade earlier while the Civil War was still raging, but it merely brought into greater relief the message already implicit in the original *Man's Mortalitie*—namely, that immortality serves as a political fiction whereby sovereigns exercise power over the bodies of their subjects; more specifically, that Royalists dying en masse on behalf of King Charles, and sectarian Christians slaughtering themselves over "minor" theological nuances, might have inclined more toward peace had they acknowledged the mortality of their souls as well as of their bodies.

---

[402] Overton, *Man Wholly Mortal*, "The Postscript."

Mortalism's Modern Critics

In his review of Norman T. Burns' now classic study, *Christian Mortalism from Tyndale to Milton* (1972), literary critic C.A. Patrides asked tongue-in-cheek whether "Mr. Burns in devoting an entire book to this unpromising subject [had] transformed a minor creek into a mighty torrent, for want of anything better to do."[403] This is a striking echo of the Reformer John Calvin's observation, four and a half centuries prior, that his mortalist opponents had accused him of "stirring up fierce contests about nothing, and making trifling differences the source of violent dissensions."[404] This echo captures the ambivalence, expressed by early moderns and modern critics alike, regarding the extent to which mortalism matters. Because of such ambivalence, mortalism's importance has been underestimated as often as it has been exaggerated.

Few scholars have seriously engaged seventeenth-century mortalism since Burns' intervention over three decades ago.[405] This lapse in the conversation typifies the

---

[403] Norman T. Burns, *Christian Mortalism from Tyndale to Milton* (Cambridge: Harvard University Press, 1972). Review by C.A. Patrides, *Renaissance Quarterly*, vol. 27, no. 3 (1974): 375-376.

[404] John Calvin, *Psychopannychia*, in *Tracts and Treatises in Defense of the Reformed Faith*, trans. Henry Beveridge, volume 3 (Grand Rapids: Wm. B. Eerdmans Publ. Co., 1958), 418.

[405] For some exceptions, see Robert Watson, *The Rest is Silence: Death as Annihilation in the English Renaissance* (Berkeley: University of California Press, 1994); Catherine Wilson, *Epicureanism at the Origins of Modernity* (Oxford: Clarendon Press, 2008); Bryan W. Ball, *The Soul Sleepers: Christian Mortalism from Wycliffe to Priestley* (Cambridge: James

long critical history of mortalism. Himself swept up by the "minor creek" turned "mighty torrent," Patrides admitted elsewhere that mortalism was "a minor but vital current of thought [that] was far more widely disseminated than we have been led to believe."[406] Bryan W. Ball has joined the chorus proclaiming mortalism's minority status.

> In the first place mortalism…was always
> a minority view. The majority of English
> Christians from the very earliest days of the
> Reformation subscribed to the traditional and
> deeply cherished belief in the separate identity
> and inherent immortality of the soul, its release
> from the body at death to immediate heavenly
> felicity, and its ultimate re-unification with the
> body at the general resurrection of the dead at
> the last day.[407]

It is, however, ultimately difficult to establish just how minor an idea early modern mortalism was, because alongside the Christian dualism described by Ball was a rich tradition of English monism that maintained the indivisibility

---

Clarke & Co., 2008); and Richard Sugg, *The Smoke of the Soul: Medicine, Physiology and Religion in Early Modern England* (New York: Palgrave, 2013).

[406] C.A. Patrides, "Psychopannychism in Renaissance Europe," *Studies in Philology*, vol. 60, no. 2, part 1 (April., 1963), 227-229. Although the heresy "may be only a minute portion of the seething cauldron that was the Renaissance," Patrides suggests, "sometimes the fervency of the whole can be appreciated by the intensity of the part."

[407] Ball, *The Soul Sleepers*, 10.

of souls and bodies. The dearth of textual evidence indicates not that the heresy was contained to a small group of adherents, but rather, as Burns has noted, that most mortalists were poor and illiterate, therefore necessarily receiving and promulgating the heresy orally without leaving a written trace.[408] It is reasonable to assume, moreover, that many literate mortalists did not dare to profess the heresy in print. Even Overton, who championed free speech and vociferously challenged authority, was obliged to publish the first editions of *Man's Mortalitie* using only his initials, "R.O."

Modern critics have mirrored early moderns in their uncertainty about mortalism's urgency, but the criticism has diverged from its sources in a way that warrants correction. Critics have tended to dwell on classifying early modern mortalism as either a philosophical or theological discourse.[409] That seventeenth-century English mortal-

---

[408] Burns, *Christian Mortalism*, 2-3. See also Ball, *The Soul Sleepers*, 209-210.

[409] In a 1935 study of Milton's mortalism, the critic George Williamson announces, "It is time that we recognized in this controversy one of the chief intellectual and religious problems of the mid-seventeenth century" ("Milton and the Mortalist Heresy," *Studies in Philology*, XXXII [1935]), 553-579; 566. Despite identifying mortalism as a religious problem, however, Williamson insists on situating Milton's version in a philosophical tradition that includes Epicurus, Pomponazzi, Browne, and Hobbes. Sixteen years later in the same journal, Nathaniel H. Henry challenges Williamson's approach, arguing instead that "Milton's 'mortalism' is best explained in terms of dogmatic theology, even in the commonplaces of theology, rather than in terms of philosophy, or in terms such

ism incorporated both theology and philosophy is already evident, however, in the extended title of *Man's Mortalitie, or a treatise wherein 'tis proved, both Theologically and Phylosophically,"* that humans are "*wholy mortall, contrary to that common distinction of Soule and Body…*" Ceasing to homogenize the interdiscursivity of seventeenth-century mortalism opens attention to the many discourses—including not only theology and philosophy but also science and politics—that informed and were transformed by the idea.

Roughly a century after the resurgence of mortalism during the English Civil War, the priest Francis Blackburne penned *A Short Historical View of the Controversy Concerning an Intermediate State and the Separate Existence of the Soul Between Death and the General Resurrection* (1765), where he remarked that mid-seventeenth-century English thinkers had paid little attention to the debates on the soul that were erupting elsewhere on the continent. Blackburne attributed this negligence to "the confusion of the times," and—demonstrating the methodological pitfalls of neatly

---

as 'mortalism,' a popular coinage in a partisan pamphlet war of 1646" ("Milton and Hobbes: Mortalism and the Intermediate State," *Studies in Philology*, XLVIII [1951], 234-249; 235). More recently, Ball has insisted that we read the development of mortalism from the sixteenth through the eighteenth century "more as a legacy of Reformation theology than as an outcome of the influence of philosophy or rationalism on the theology of the day" (*The Soul Sleepers*, 12). Sugg, by contrast, has resituated mortalism in the context of early modern medicine and physiology as well as theology, remarking the "proto-scientific attitudes of its most famous English adherents" (*The Smoke of the Soul*, 206).

partitioning mortalism into isolated discourses—to the fact that the continental debates were largely philosophical, where in England "the theological controversy turned, in those days, on church power."[410] His discursively rigid view of mortalism led Blackburne to overlook large swaths of the seventeenth-century English debate over the soul. Still, he acknowledged that "one particular writer who distinguished himself by the initials R.O. took occasion in the year 1644, to publish a tract intituled, *Man's mortalitie*."[411] Knowing that mortalism involved both philosophical and theological debates, and that Overton was not alone in the conversation, it is now possible to ask why seventeenth-century English authors were, in fact, preoccupied with debates on the nature of the soul during a time when they had so much else to preoccupy them, not least of all fighting for their lives.

Like a Nightmare on the Brains of the Living

By the seventeenth century, both Catholics and Anglicans regarded the immortality of the human soul as an original pillar of Christian faith. Overton tried to disabuse his contemporaries of this error by recalling that the ideology of immortality has a history that was appropriated by

---

[410] Francis Blackburne, *A Short Historical View of the Controversy Concerning an Intermediate State and the Separate Existence of the Soul Between Death and the General Resurrection* (London: 1765), 48.
[411] Ibid.

but not intrinsic to Christianity. A topical survey of this history will provide context for the conventions and traditions challenged by *Man's Mortalitie*. It is first worth remarking, as Overton and others including Donne and Milton remarked, that Judeo-Christian scripture nowhere explicitly posits the immortality of the soul. On the contrary, the Old Testament book of *Ecclesiastes*, which is among Overton's primary sources, unequivocally rejects the idea that the soul survives the body to enjoy or suffer an afterlife.

Live life joyfully and to the fullest, the book enjoins, "for there is no work, nor device, nor knowledge, nor wisdom, in the grave, whither thou goest."[412] As with Overton's mortalism, what appears in *Ecclesiastes* to be a desperately bleak orientation toward death turns out to be an affirmation of earthly life. Its denial of the afterlife reinvigorates rather than evacuates the meaning of this life. Overton remarked how *Ecclesiastes* "doth shew, that the living suffer oppression, but to the dead is none," because the dead *"know not anything; for a living Dog is better th[a]n a dead Lion."*[413] The suggestion that a living dog is better than a dead lion— which presumes that if both were living, the lion would be better—displays the ethical purchase of mortalism, which by privileging life over particular lifeforms, counteracts traditional ontological and social hierarchies.

Against the orthodox Anglican view that human immortality makes human life exceptional, Overton cited

---

[412] *The book of Ecclesiastes*, 9.9-10.

[413] Overton, *Man's Mortalitie*, 57. See *Ecclesiastes*, 4.1-3; 9.4-5.

the claim of *Ecclesiastes* that humans are no less mortal than animals: "even one thing befalleth them all: as the one dieth, so dieth the other; yea, they have all one breath: so that Man hath no pre-eminence above a Beast: for all is vanity."[414] Overton perceived that immortalist claims of human preeminence over animals were of a piece with certain prerogatives that humans claimed to have over each other. Ecclesiastes abounds with intimations of mortalism; that Overton elected this particular *vanitas* trope as the epigraph for the frontispiece of *Man's Mortalitie* indicates the egalitarian political ecology implicit in his mortalism.

The Christian tradition of immortalism, then, derived not from the Old Testament but from pagan sources, as Overton inconveniently testified. The dogma dates back at least to the Platonic dialogue *Phaedo*, where Socrates presented an epistemological defense of the immortal, disembodied soul: "While we are alive we shall, it would seem, come nearest to knowledge if we have as little as possible to do with the body."[415] Because the body's variable sense perception hinders the mind's attainment of invariable truth, Socrates concluded, the key to knowledge is "separating so far as may be the soul from the body, and habituating it to…dwell alone and apart, so far as possible, both

---

[414] *Ecclesiastes*, 3:19, quoted in Overton, *Mans Mortalitie* (London: 1643), frontispiece.

[415] David Gallop, *Plato's Phaedo* (Oxford: Clarendon Press, 1975), 67a, quoted in Daniel Sherman, *Soul World, and Idea: An Interpretation of Plato's 'Republic' and 'Phaedo'* (New York: Lexington Books, 2013), 220-221.

in this present life and in the life to come, released from the body's fetters."[416]

Hannah Arendt has traced a line of continuity from Plato's doctrine to seventeenth-century Cartesian dualism, remarking that in both, an epistemological demand for incorporeality precedes the defense of immortality.[417] While there is indeed overlap between these two discourses, they are nevertheless separated by over two millennia, and Plato's concept of an immortal soul accrued new layers of meaning as it percolated through watershed moments such as the birth of Christianity and the Protestant Reformation.

The Platonic dogma became less central with the growing prevalence of Aristotelianism in the thirteenth and fourteenth centuries,[418] which may account for its fervent revival in seventeenth-century England alongside widespread critiques of Aristotle and a renaissance of Neopla-

---

[416] Ibid., 67b-c.

[417] The ecstatic experience of forgetting one's own body while deep in thought, Arendt observed, is what "made Plato ascribe immortality to the soul once it has departed from the body and made Descartes conclude 'that the soul can think without the body except that so long as the soul is attached to the body it may be bothered in its operations by the bad disposition of the body's organs'" (*The Life of the Mind* [San Diego, New York, and London: Harcourt, Inc., 1971]), 85.

[418] Ibid., See also, J. Obi Oguejiofor, "The Arguments for the Immortality of the Soul in the First Half of the Thirteenth Century," *Recherches de Théologie Ancienne et Médiévale*. Supplementa, 5 (Leuven: Peeters Publishers, 1995), xiv-426.

tonism. Aristotle critiqued Plato's division, borrowed from Homer, between "mortals" (humans) and "immortals" (gods), because it is neither mutually exclusive nor exhaustive, given that there are nonhuman mortals and humans that have achieved immortality.[419] Regarding the latter, Aristotle argued not "that the person concerned has taken on another life, but that to this very life that was his own, a mark or modification is added."[420] This crucial insight—that immortal life and mortal life are different degrees of the same life—may have suggested to seventeenth-century English readers of Aristotle that their culture's orthodoxy concerning immortality also implied certain assumptions about and demands on embodied life. Aristotle's notion of immortality as a qualification or degree of mortal life, suggesting a continuum of difference in degree but not in kind, served the egalitarian critique of exceptionalism and prerogative couched in *Man's Mortalitie.*

While Christian doctrine successfully assimilated both Plato and Aristotle (and sufficiently ignored texts such as *Ecclesiastes*), it proved impossible to reconcile with the mortalism of Epicurus, a contemporary of Plato and Aristotle.[421] Indeed, Epicurus became a bugbear in early modern

---

[419] Richard Bodéüs, *Aristotle and the Theology of the Living Immortals,* trans. Jan Edward Garrett (Albany: State University of New York Press, 2000), 114. See Aristotle's *Topics,* iv 5.126b38-39.

[420] Ibid., 115. Cf. Aristotle, *Topics,* iv 5.126b39-127a1.

[421] See epicurean poet Lucretius, *On the Nature of Things: De rerum natura,* ed. Anthony Esolen (Baltimore: The John Hopkins University Press, 1995). "[W]hen our mortal flame shall be disjoined,/The

England. From the Reformation through the seventeenth
century, opponents discredited mortalism for being epicurean; conversely, although epicurean philosophy was
attractive for Anglicans, it proved unallowable because
of its mortalism.[422] Epicureanism appealed to Anglicans
because it offered freedom from fear of eternal reward
and punishment, and as Jonathan Goldberg has observed,
because "it dispenses with religious beliefs that make the
afterlife the only life worth living."[423] Burns has argued

---

lifeless lump uncoupled from the mind,/From sense of grief and
pain we shall be free;/We shall not feel, because we shall not be"
(3.10-12). Death is the end, "For we are only we,/While souls and
bodies in one frame agree./Nay, though our atoms should revolve by
chance,/And matter leap into the former dance;/Though time our
life and motion could restore,/And make our bodies what they were
before;/What gain to us would all this bustle bring?/The new-made
man would be another thing" (3.17-24).

[422] See, for instance, Walter Charleton, *Epicurus's Morals* (London:
1656), to which Charleton appends "An Apologie for Epicurus"
listing three ideas of the ancient philosopher that are unallowable in
English culture. The first is mortalism, "That the Souls of Men are
mortall, & so uncapable of all either happiness or misery after death"
(5). See also, John Evelyn, *An Essay on the First Book of T. Lucretius
Carus De Rerum Natura* (London: 1656), 106-7.

[423] Jonathan Goldberg, *The Seeds of Things: Theorizing Sexuality
and Materiality in Renaissance Representations* (New York: Fordham
University Press, 2009), 34-35. "Whereas in Platonic regimes truth
is always impossible to attain, lying elsewhere, not in the body,
Epicurean pleasure refuses such goals and abjures their social
manifestations in the insatiable desire for such supposed goods as
fame, wealth, and progeny, which are always desires for something
beyond them and which inevitably therefore produce only misery
and frustration."

that Epicurus' "pagan mortalism...did not contribute to the development of Christian mortalism in England [and that] even the ideas of the more philosophical Interregnum Christian mortalists stand well apart from Epicurean mortalism."[424] Christian mortalists were not immune to the epicurean ideas exposed to them, however, and while they routinely disavowed epicurean mortalism, their own positions were often defined by this very disavowal.[425]

The doctrine of immortality did not become standard in Christian theology until the fourth and fifth centuries, following Augustine's defense, which like Plato's argument is primarily epistemological. "If science [*disciplina*, from *discere* (to learn)] exists anywhere," Augustine argued, "and if it can exist only in the realm of that which lives and always is...then that must live forever in which science exists."[426] Augustine presupposed that only the living can learn, because "nothing that does not live learns anything,"

---

[424] Burns, *Christian Mortalism from Tyndale to Milton*, 5.

[425] See Catherine Wilson, *Epicureanism at the Origins of Modernity* (Oxford: Oxford University Press, 2008), 110. Accounting for the sixteenth-century appeal of epicurean mortalism, Wilson notes that ecclesiastical authority hinged on the belief of the soul's immortality, for "if the resurrection and eternal life promised by Christ was not a fact, what reason might anyone have for obedience to priests?" Additionally, "the immediate sense that life as such is a good entails a desire for its prolongation, and the impression that all human life is good was perhaps stronger in a culture" such as that of early modern England, where mortality rates were high and life expectancy low.

[426] Augustine, *The Immortality of the Soul*, trans. Ludwig Schopp (Washington, D.C.: The Catholic University of America Press, 1947), 15.

and also that it is the soul not the body that learns, because the body dies and science pertains to what is immortal.[427]

Remarkably, then, the argument that injected the doctrine of immortality into Christianity is neither primarily Christian nor even theological, but based rather on an epistemological claim of pagan provenance. Christianizing a conceptual palimpsest of Plato's dualism and Aristotle's tripartite division of the soul, Augustine rigidified the differences between vegetative, sensitive, and rational lifeforms. He forged the links, on the one hand, between rational, disembodied, immortal, and human life, and on the other hand, between animal life and mortality. Thus emerged a Christian anthropology that defines the human as "a rational and mortal animal," one "inferior to the angels and superior to the beasts, having in common with the beasts mortality, and with the angels reason."[428] In the millennium following Augustine, the doctrine was "more or less taken for granted by everybody, and…rarely challenged or discussed in detail."[429] On the eve of the Protestant Reformation, however, the ideological fault lines began to slip as immortality became a crux at the heart of Christian faith.

---

[427] Ibid., 16.

[428] Augustine, *De Civitate Dei*, book 9, quoted in Wes Williams, *Monsters and Their Meanings in Early Modern Culture* (New York: Oxford University Press, 2011), 236.

[429] Paul Oskar Kristeller, "The Immortality of the Soul," *Renaissance Thought and its Sources*, ed. M. Mooney (New York: Columbia University Press, 1979), 181-196; 186-7.

The year before Luther nailed his *Ninety-Five Theses* to the door of All Saints' Church in Wittenberg, the Italian Aristotelian Pietro Pomponazzi entertained mortalism in *De immortalitate animae* (1516). He concluded that the human soul is essentially mortal and relatively immortal, partaking of both mortality and immortality, because it is ambiguous (*ancipitis*) and multiple rather than simple.[430] Pomponazzi argued that bodily faculties such as growth, nutrition, and decay, which humans share with animals and plants, make humans mortal. By contrast, in the tradition of Augustine and the thirteenth-century Christian Aristotelian Thomas Aquinas,[431] Pomponazzi posited that humans' rational capacity is disembodied and therefore immortal.

> For in performing the functions of the vegetative and of the sensitive soul, which…cannot be performed without a bodily and perishable

[430] Pietro Pomponazzi, *De immortalitate animae*, in *The Renaissance Philosophy of Man: Petrarca, Valla, Ficino, Pico, Pomponazzi, Vives*, ed. Ernst Cassirer, Paul Oskar Kristeller, and John Herman Randall Jr. (Chicago: University of Chicago Press, 1956), 313.

[431] Aquinas argues in *Summa Theologiae* that the rational human soul is an immaterial substance: "It must necessarily be allowed that the principle of intellectual operation, which we call the soul of man, is a principle both incorporeal and subsistent." It was imperative for Aquinas to allow the incorporality of the soul because "it is clear that by means of the intellect man can know all corporeal things. Now whatever knows certain things cannot have any of them in its own nature, because that which is in it naturally would impede the knowledge of anything else…Therefore it is impossible for the intellectual principle to be a body" (*Basic Writings of Thomas Aquinas*, trans. A.C. Pegis [New York: Random House, 1945], 1:685).

> instrument, man assumes mortality. However,
> in knowing and willing, operations...held to be
> performed without any bodily instrument, since
> they prove separability and immateriality, and
> these in turn prove immortality, [such that] man
> is to be numbered among the immortal things.[432]

This concatenation of mortality and embodiment with vegetative and sensitive lifeforms was not heterodox, and Pomponazzi steered safely clear of mortalism by preserving immortality for rational human souls. Nevertheless, he intimated mortalism by his contempt for morality based on reward and punishment in the afterlife, arguing that "those who claim that the soul is mortal seem better to save the grounds of virtue than those whom claim it to be immortal."[433] Pomponazzi did not commit heresy, then, but what for Augustine may have been mere philosophical speculation had by this point become strict orthodoxy that was no longer so open for debate.

In response to the gathering polemics around Pomponazzi's text, the Fifth Council of the Lateran (1512-1517)—the last Roman Catholic Ecumenical Council to assemble before the Reformation—issued the *Apostolici regiminis*, a decree proclaiming that those who "have dared to assert" the mortality of the "reasonable" or "intellectual" soul "shall be shunned and punished as heretics."[434] Remark-

---

[432] Pomponazzi, *De immortalitate animae*, 282.

[433] Ibid., 375.

[434] Norman P. Tanner, ed., *Decrees of the Ecumenical Councils*

ably, the decree limited its concern to the immortality of rational, human life, and by allowing for the mortality of vegetative and sensitive lifeforms, it further cemented the bond between Christian orthodoxy and human exceptionalism. It is critical to note that this orthodoxy did not merely imply the acceptability of the death of plants and animals, and the unacceptability of the death of humans; it also conditioned the acceptability of the death of the vegetative and sensitive life of human beings. Seventeenth-century authors including Descartes and Walter Charleton were still compelled to defend the immortalist decree of *Apostolici regiminis* over a century after it was pronounced.[435]

The same year that Pomponazzi flirted with mortalism in Italy, the English Catholic humanist Thomas More foregrounded, for the first time, the political implications of mortalism. In his fictional political philosophy *Utopia* (1516), More imagined a utopian commonwealth whose citizens "believe that after this life vices will be punished and virtue rewarded. Anyone who denies this proposition they consider less than a man, since he has degraded the sublimity of his own soul to the base level of a beast's wretched body."[436] The nuance of More's formulation sug-

---

(Washington D.C.: Georgetown University Press, 1990).

[435] See Walter Charleton, *The Darknes of Atheism Dispelled…a physico-theologicall treatise* (London: 1652), 96-97. Charleton praised the Fifth Lateran Council's "Anathematization" of heretics including Epicurus, who "murder the immortality of the Soul (the basis of all religion) and deride the Compensation of good and evil actions after death."

[436] Thomas More, *Utopia*, ed. George M. Logan, trans. Robert M.

gests that Utopians attain full membership as humans in the commonwealth not by verifying their possession of an immortal soul, but rather by *believing* that they possess such a soul, or at least by acquiescing not to deny the "proposition."

While epistemological theories provoked Plato and Augustine to posit a disembodied and immortal soul, More and subsequent authors were preempted by ethical and political motives to defend immortality. Because Pomponazzi regarded humans as capable of virtue for its own sake, he thought that embracing mortalism, and thereby dispensing with the superfluous apparatus of postmortem justice, might make societies more amenable to virtue.[437] Like his Utopians, by contrast, More feared that the ground beneath morality would collapse without the expectation of posthumous reward and punishment.

Although English mortalism thrived at the start of the Protestant Reformation, not all opponents of the heresy were Catholics like More, and the polemic also fueled sectarianism among Protestants. In the 1530s, Calvin joined Luther in discrediting the ideas of purgatory and prayers to saints, but he rejected Luther's mortalist solution, instead positing in *Psychopannychia* (1534) "that the souls of the dead are conscious and alive after leaving their bodies, against the error of those ignorant people who think that

---

Adams (Cambridge: Cambridge University Press, 2016), 100.

[437] Pomponazzi, *De immortalitate animae*, 275; 313.

the souls sleep until Judgment Day."[438] Calvin described the "soul-sleepers" as a "faction" that seemed innocuous before it metastasized "lyke a Cancker."[439] He would have reacted earlier to the fledgling heresy had he not thought that it would be "soone forgotten...or els[e] that a few Cockbrayned and lightheadded fellowes would onely keepe it in hugger mugger." But the idea spread more rapidly than Calvin expected, such that by the 1530s the soulsleepers had "already drawne into their error, I know not how many thowsands of people."[440]

Calvin remarked that "the Arabians were the first authors of this error," that "John, Byshop of Rome defended the same," and that "[n]ow when this error had long tyme...been repressed, the Anabaptists beganne lately to revive the same, and blow abroad certein sparkes thereof: which, sparkling farre and wide, in the end, fell out into hoat fiery flames."[441] The Anabaptists were Protestant sectarians whose radical socialism posed a grave threat to Anglican orthodoxy. Again, early readers of *The Faerie Queene* saw the egalitarian-autochthonous Giant as an allegory of Anabaptism, and that during the 1640s Royal-

---

[438] See *Psychopannychie. Traité par lequel est prouvé que les âmes veillent & vivent après qu'elles sont sorties des corps; contre l'erreur de quelques ignorans qui pensent qu'elles dorment jusque au dernier jugement* (Paris, 1558).

[439] John Calvin, *An excellent treatise of the Immortalytie of the soule*, trans. Thomas Stocker (London: 1581), "The Preface of Iohn Calvin to a very friend of his."

[440] Ibid.

[441] Ibid.

ists read the Giant as a proleptic representation of groups such as the Levellers.[442]

Calvin's concern that radical beliefs might take root beyond the extremist fringes of Protestantism set the tone for mortalism's seventeenth-century reception. While determined to dispute the soul-sleepers verbally, Calvin wished there were "other meane[s]…for the soddayne cutting [out] of this mischief which too much encreaseth."[443] Unlike More, Calvin engaged the heresy in strictly theological terms without making a political argument. However, beyond the truism that early modern theology always inhered in early modern politics and vice-versa, Calvin's bellicose rhetoric also suggests the volatile and polarized political climate through which his anti-mortalist argument spread.

Before entering the fray, for instance, he had to acquaint himself with the "power, weapons, and Ambushes" of his mortalist "adversaries," remaining wary of those "whome if a man should touch but with the typp of the finger, would…cry out and say, that we breake the unitie and quietnes of the Church." It is telling that Calvin likened his attack on mortalism to the mere touch of a fingertip that elicits a disproportionately enormous response. Although the soul's immortality was just one tenet of Christianity—

---

[442] John N. King, "Notes and Documents, The Faerie Leveller: A 1648 Royalist Reading of *The Faerie Queene*, V.ii.29-54," 297.

[443] Calvin, *Immortalytie of the soule*, "The Preface of Iohn Calvin to a very friend of his."

and at that, a mere matter of "controversie and debate," rather than an article of faith—it had nevertheless gradually become so ingrained in Christian orthodoxy that to attack it was indeed tantamount to attacking the unity of the church. The order of Calvin's trope, moreover, where physical touch precedes claims of a schismatic church, indicates the *tactile* or material conditions in which theological controversies over mortalism ignited. Mortalists from Luther to Overton reopened divisions within the Church not only for doctrinal reasons, that is, but also (and perhaps primarily) to counteract the authorities' encroachments upon the rights of embodied life, encroachments that ranged from an unwanted touch of a fingertip to false imprisonment and execution.

In the two decades after Calvin published his treatise, the "faction" of soul-sleepers continued to spread among other Protestant sectaries; so much so in England that King Edward VI ordered Thomas Cranmer, Archbishop of Canterbury, to promulgate the articles of Anglican faith in the *Forty-two Articles of Edward* (1552). King Edward had Protestant leanings, and Archbishop Cranmer had been instrumental in arranging Henry VIII's annulment from Catherine of Aragon, which catalyzed the Church of England's divorce from Rome.[444] While the *Forty-two Articles* standardized Protestant belief, two of the articles sent an

---

[444] F.L. Cross and Elizabeth A. Livingstone, *The Oxford Dictionary of the Christian Church* (New York: Oxford University Press, 1997), 428; 625.

ambiguous message about the state's position on mortalism. Encapsulated within this apparently minor ambiguity were tensions that threatened to rive the unity of the English Church. Article 39—"The Resurrection of the Dead is not yet brought to pass"—evokes the mortalist argument of Luther and Tyndale that the soul must die with the body if it is to be resurrected. However, Article 40—"The soulles of them that depart this life do neither die with the bodie nor sleep idlie"[445]—is conspicuously negative and offers no alternative to fill the void left by what it rejects. If departed souls neither die nor sleep, then what do they do? Are they alive and conscious, either suffering or in bliss, and amenable to the prayers of the living? These two of Edward's *Forty-two Articles* suggest that mortalism was like pitch for Anglicans: too messy to touch, and impossible to throw at others without sullying oneself.

Edward's articles were not enforced during Queen Mary I's short Catholic reign.[446] The following decade, Queen Elizabeth omitted articles 39 and 40 from her *Articles of Religion* (1563). This omission suggests that it was safer for authorities to remain silent on the topic of the soul's afterlife than to take a position and risk political fallout. Elizabeth aimed to manufacture consensus about

---

[445] Church of England, *Forty-two Articles of Edward*, quoted in Nathaniel H. Henry, "Milton and Hobbes: Mortalism and the Intermediate State," *Studies in Philology*, vol. 48, no. 2 (April 1951): 234-249; 238.

[446] Cross and Livingstone, *The Oxford Dictionary of the Christian Church*, 625.

matters of Anglican faith, to establish a "via media" or middle way bridging schisms in the Church of England and appealing even to Catholics.[447] Her hoped-for religious uniformity was not put into law until 1571, however, when the political climate became more polarized against the Papacy.[448] The shifting policies from Edward to Elizabeth reveal the colluded motives of church and state power, showing that what early modern English people were led and allowed to believe changed from one regime to the next.

Throughout the sixteenth and seventeenth centuries, Anglicans regularly depicted mortalism as an epidemic: something spread among (*epi-*) the people (*dēmos*) yet necessary to quarantine, something universal but also historically and regionally specific, something English and Christian but also pagan and nonhuman. In *An excellent treatise of the Immortalytie of the soule* (1581), the English translation of Calvin's *Psychopannychia*, Thomas Stocker observed the proliferation of mortalism in the half century since Calvin wrote the book, during a time when "many [were] grievously infected with this monstrous opinion, That the

---

[447] Ibid.

[448] See Arthur Jay Klein, *Intolerance in the Reign of Elizabeth, Queen of England* (Doctoral Dissertation, Faculty of Political Science, Columbia University, 1917), 93-94. Elizabeth's "government was perhaps not utterly indifferent to religious interest, but primarily fighting for self-preservation; the Church itself was inspired by the same fears as the government and well satisfied with the alliance of the two."

Soules of men dyed together with the bodies. Which foule and hellish error I feare, hath possessed and poysoned at this day, the harts and minds of a great number, here at home within this land."[449] Whereas Calvin identified his "adversaries" as Christian Anabaptists, Stocker characterized mortalists as atheists, Epicures, "and belly Gods."[450] At the same time he rendered mortalism un-Christian and outlandish, however, Stocker's rhetoric of infection charts what had already become an English epidemic.[451] Throughout the next century, kings, queens, lords, bishops, divine assemblies, members of parliament, censors of the press, and others enjoying power were rightfully anxious that mortalism might, or already had, spread among the people.

The English Mortality Crisis

Seventeenth-century orthodox Anglicans generally regarded mortalism as a matter of life and death, that is, as a heresy punishable by death; but some including John

---

[449] Calvin, *Immortalytie of the soule*, 2.

[450] Ibid., "The Epistle Dedicatory."

[451] At the close of the seventeenth century, the poet laureate Nahum Tate also characterized mortalism as poisonous, prefacing his 1697 edition of John Davies' *Nosce Te Ipsum* (1599)—a didactic poem defending the soul's immortality—with a recommendation that contemporaries carry Davies' "Antidote about them against the Poyson they have suck'd in from Lucretius or Hobb[e]s" ("The Preface," *The original, nature, and immortality of the soul; Nosce Teipsum* [London: 1697]).

Milton considered it a matter of indifference or an adiaphoron, an error into which one might lapse without calling one's faith or humanity into question or risking one's life. Many authors discussed mortalism; some entertained it more than others, seeking to make it allowable by Christianizing it. With the exception of R.O., however, nobody professed it. "That the humane soule doth not survive the funerals of the body, but absolutely perish in the instant of death," wrote the Royal Physician Walter Charleton, is an "uncomfortable" belief that is "manifestly repugnant" to Christians.[452]

Charleton's Catholic-leaning and Royalist orthodoxy may account for his serial attacks on mortalism across several texts throughout the 1650s. By so regularly opposing the heresy, however, he furthered its proliferation. It is critical to understand how mortalism was at once repulsive and attractive to authors, because the idea epitomizes seventeenth-century structures of thought around other heterodox notions that, like mortalism, oscillated between what was tolerable and open for (heated) discussion and what was unallowable and even punishable by death.

The seventeenth-century English opposition to mortalism registers the same anxieties that Calvin had about the spread of radical Protestantism. In addition, it registers a failed reactionary attempt to preserve existing sociopolitical hierarchies by obfuscating their material ori-

---

[452] Charleton, *Epicurus's Morals*, 5.

gins beneath the guise of a theological dogma asserting immaterial immortality. The orthodox Anglican rejection of mortalism represents a larger trend in early modern England of what Ernest Becker has called "the denial of death."[453] Orthodox defenses of immortality and renunciations of mortalism were among myriad forms of death denial in English culture. I discussed in previous chapters, for example, Prospero's "project...to keep [Caliban and others] living" (*The Tempest*, 2.1.295), and Francis Bacon's project to prolong life. Chapter 4 hears in *King Lear* the repeated denial of Gloucester's wish, if not his right to die.

Beyond being heretical, the thought that death might be absolute and even permanent was psychologically distressing in an era characterized by staggering rates of mortality, crises in faith, and growing interest in and attachment to earthly, embodied life.[454] The bubonic plague, which had devastated England intermittently at the start of the seventeenth century,[455] returned in full force in the 1640s along with smallpox and malaria, heralding what

---

[453] Ernest Becker, *The Denial of Death* (New York: Simon & Schuster, 1973).

[454] Philippe Aries has observed "that probably at no time has man so loved life as he did at the end of the Middle Ages." Aries discovers this "love of life" expressed in the period's art, which reveals "a passionate attachment to things, an attachment that resisted the annihilation of death and changed our vision of the world and of nature" (*The Hour of Our Death*, trans. Helen Weaver [New York: Alfred A. Knopf, Inc., 1981], 132).

[455] Rebecca Totaro, ed., *The Plague Epic in Early Modern England: Heroic Measures, 1603-1721* (New York: Routledge, 2016), 1.

military historian Peter Gaunt calls "a sharp mortality crisis amongst the whole population," which was intensified by the fighting of the English Civil War (1642-1651).[456] By some contemporary accounts, between 1,000 and 1,200 Londoners were dying of the plague per week by the end of the summer of 1640.[457] Compounding disease and starvation, historians estimate that roughly 200,000 English soldiers and civilians died from the fighting alone.[458] English authors continued to reiterate traditional *memento mori* and *vanitas* tropes throughout the period, insisting on the ethical and spiritual value of meditating on mortality. The culture of death denial, however, led many not to dwell on death but to seek to delay, escape, or overcome it.

Literary historian Robert Watson has attributed "the mortality-crisis of Jacobean England" to declining "assurance about personal salvation" accompanied by increasing "attachment to both the external properties and the internal subjectivities of the human individual."[459] Demand for assurances about the life to come "became so great that the Christian denial of death threatened to become visible as a mere ideology, a manipulative illusion rather than an absolute truth."[460] As Christian promises of immortality

---

[456] Peter Gaunt, *The English Civil War: A Military History* (London: I.B. Tauris, 2014), 234-235.

[457] See David Cressy, *England on Edge: Crisis and Revolution 1640-1642* (New York: Oxford University Press, 2006), 62.

[458] Gaunt, *The English Civil War*, 12-13.

[459] Watson, *The Rest is Silence*, 2.

[460] Ibid., 2.

came into question, English culture had "to find ways to unthink [the] thought" that humans are mortal, "to talk itself out of fear, to quarantine a potentially catastrophic cultural epidemic."[461] Indeed, the epidemiological epithets depicting mortalism as an infection reveal a culture of life in early modern England that sought to immunize itself against death. In his riposte to *Man's Mortalitie*, for instance, the Jesuit Guy Holland aimed to disinfect Christianity, proposing that those "infected" by mortalism "may well be termed wilde Arabians, which kind of people by reason of their rude condition and volatile natures, were ever as ready to be cosened, first by this heresie, and after by the grand Impostour Mahomet."[462] Ignoring the possibility that the storied Arabian mortalists were early Christians, Holland typifies orthodox English attempts to project mortalism onto others.

Holland's suggestion that the Arabians "first" became mortalists and "after" became Muslims indicates a concern, which Thomas More had articulated a century earlier, of becoming mortalist. Holland suggested, on the one hand, that one's nature may predispose one toward mortalism, but on the other hand, that falling into mortalism may change one's nature. The focus here is on Christians turn-

---

[461] Ibid., 29.

[462] Guy Holland, *THE Prerogative of Man: OR, THE IMMORTALITY OF HUMANE SOULES (asserted against the vain cavils of a late worthlesse Pamphlet, ENTITVLED, Mans Mortality, &c. Whereunto is added the said Pamphlet it selfe* (Oxford: 1645), 2.

ing into Muslims, but just as More's Utopians considered mortalists to be less than human, Holland likewise deemed Overton "a sorry Animal...whose soule he himselfe thinkes to be mortall...not elevating Beasts to the degree of reason...but contrariwise reproachfully depressing man even as low as bruite beasts, and ascribing to them both a mortality alike."[463] To deny death in seventeenth-century England, then, was a condition for being recognized as human and therefore included and protected in the political order. To be mortalist, to refuse to deny death, was to risk being quarantined as one "infected," to be excluded from the sociopolitical order, and hence to be exposed inordinately to death.

In 1612, Edward Wightman, who professed mortalism among a range of other heresies, was the last person in England to be burned at the stake.[464] Fifteen years later, it seemed allowable at least to entertain mortalism if not

---

[463] Holland, *The Prerogative of Man*, 1-2. Holland might tolerate if Overton were merely participating in the tradition of Plutarch, the first-century Roman-Greek author who argued that animals possess rationality just as humans do. Other authors, including Michel de Montaigne, had already revived this tradition to counteract early modern "discourses of reason," which defined humanity against irrational, animal others, as Erica Fudge has shown in *Brutal Reasoning: Animals, Rationality, and Humanity in Early Modern England* (Ithaca: Cornell University Press, 2006), 87-88.

[464] See Sugg, *The Smoke of the Soul*, 209; Ball, *The Soul Sleepers: Christian Mortalism from Wycliffe to Priestley*, 69-72; See also Ian Atherton and David Como, "The Burning of Edward Wightman: Puritanism, Prelacy and the Politics of Heresy in Early Modern England," in *The English Historical Review*, vol. 120, issue 489 (2005): 1215-1250.

to profess it. On November 19, 1627, Donne confessed in a public sermon that regarding "the immortality of the soul, there is not an express article of the Creed," and that scripture indicates only "what the soul shall suffer, or what the soul shall enjoy" in the afterlife, not that the soul is immortal. Donne stopped short of admitting mortalism, however, instead attributing the omission in scripture to the fact that "so many evidences of the immortality of the soul [are present] to a natural man's reason, that it required not an article of the Creed, to fix this notion of the immortality of the soul."[465]

Notwithstanding this orthodox apology, Donne "may well have wished that he were a mortalist," according to Ramie Targoff, because "such a belief would have resolved many of his deepest anxieties [including] the horrible period of posthumous separation [between body and soul] that Donne dreaded above all else."[466] Donne ultimately elected to live (at least publicly) with his anxieties about body-soul dualism, but his observation that scripture nowhere explicitly mentions the soul's immortality heralded what Ball has called "a new era for mortalism" in England during the 1640s, the result of a "general rise of political and religious radicalism" concomitant with an upsurge "of literate, often highly educated men advocating

---

[465] John Donne, *John Donne: The Major Works*, ed. John Carey (New York: Oxford University Press, 1990), 382.

[466] Ramie Targoff, *John Donne, Body and Soul* (Chicago: The University of Chicago Press, 2008), 9.

or at least considering the idea."[467] As Ball and other historians including Lawrence Stone, Philip Baker, and David Cressy have remarked, the collapse of the censorship of the press in the 1640s further enabled the proliferation of mortalism among other radical ideas.[468]

The backlash was vehement. Neo-Platonist philosopher Henry More, for instance, condemned mortalism in his poem "Antipsychopannychia" (1642).[469] He continued to defend immortality over the next two decades, not only on theological and philosophical grounds, but also because he recognized its ideological utility, and because the alternative made him uneasy. In *Immortality of the Soul* (1659), More made the case for "her [the soul's] own Immortality, and Independence on this terrestriall body."[470] Belief in immortality, he claimed, makes smooth "the intricacies and perplexities of Providence" and promotes "the management of our lives for our greatest happiness."[471] The belief in question concerns the immortal, extraterrestrial

---

[467] Ball, *The Soul Sleepers: Christian Mortalism from Wycliffe to Priestley*, 209.
[468] Ibid., 72; Lawrence Stone, *The Causes of the English Revolution* (New York, Hagerstown, San Francisco, London: Harper & Row, 1972), 66; Baker, *The English Civil War*, ed. John Adamson (New York: Palgrave Macmillan, 2009), 206; Cressy, *England on Edge: Crisis and Revolution 1640-1642* (New York: Oxford University Press, 2006), 103.
[469] Henry More, "Antipsychopannychia," quoted in Burns, *Christian Mortalism*, 99.
[470] Henry More, *The Immortality of the Soule, so farre forth as it is demonstrable from the knowledge of nature and the light of reason* (London: 1659), 1.
[471] Ibid.

soul, but the "lives" More imagined to be managed by such belief are earthly, mortal, and embodied.

As a Neo-Platonist, More's immortalism may have emerged from his epistemological investment in the soul's disembodiment. And as one who strongly protested his Calvinist upbringing, More rejected mortalism less for doctrinal reasons than because of a visceral aversion to the prospect of earthly life bereft of *belief in* immortality. In *An Explanation of the Grand Mystery of Godliness* (1660), More worried that it undermined religion "to think that in the end of our life we shall be dodged and put off by a long senseless and comfortless Sleep of the Soul."[472] The intermission of "the Functions of Life for so long a time," he feared, will make the soul despair "of ever being awaked," compelling Christians to confine their faith "within the narrow verges of this mortal life."[473] Soul-sleep might have been tolerable or even appealing to More, but that it remained untenable because it was too easily confounded with soul-death.

Like Donne and More, Browne entertained but ultimately disavowed mortalism. In *Religio Medici* (1643), he confessed that his youth was "polluted with two or three" heresies, the first of which was mortalism.

> Now the first of mine was that of the Arabians,
> That the Souls of men perished with their

---

[472] Henry More, *An Explanation of the Grand Mystery of Godliness* (London: 1660), 15.
[473] Ibid., 16.

> Bodies, but should yet be raised again at the
> last day. Not that I did absolutely conceive a
> mortality of the Soul; but if that were…and
> that both entered the grave together, yet I held
> the same conceit thereof that we all do of the
> body, that it should rise again.

Despite Christianizing his mortalism by subordinating it to the Resurrection, the heresy proved indefensible for reasons that Browne did not make explicit. He assured readers that it was not some newfangled belief, "but old and obsolete," and that it posed no threat of being "revived," except by "extravagant and irregular" thinkers such as himself. Belying this placating caveat, however, Browne observed that "indeed Heresies perish not with their Authors, but…though they lose their currents in one place, they rise up again in another."[474] The history of mortalism, like that of autochthony and vitalism, is in part a story about the immortality of ideas that wax, wane, and transform but never die. Holland wishfully remarked that "[t]he old and despicable heresy [mortalism] which this obscure authour [Overton] now labours to resuscitate and to conjure up" was already "extinguished…immediately after its birth."[475] It is platitudinous to say that ideas, unlike the individuals who maintain them, cannot die or be killed, but the history of English mortalism displays the power of old ideas to revive and disrupt the present.

---

[474] Thomas Browne, *Religio Medici* (London: 1642), 11.

[475] Holland, *THE Prerogative of Man*, 2.

The English courtier, diplomat, and philosopher Kenelm Digby was more explicitly pragmatic than Browne about his motives for disallowing mortalism—namely, to endorse the Cartesian worldview, to secure the advantages of rational humans, and to condition the acceptability of the death of non-rational others. In the prefatory epistle of *Two Treatises* (1644), Digby reminded his son that the immortality of human souls "is the most important and the most weighty [subject] for a worthy and a gallant person to employ himselfe about."[476] This advice came from Paris, where Digby, a converted Catholic, was in self-imposed exile, escaping the English Civil War. To his son, who remained "in our distressed country" England, Digby proffered immortality as protection "against the worst" that may happen.

Underpinning this neo-Stoic asceticism was Digby's allegiance to Descartes, who thought that nothing apart from atheism so quickly misleads "weak minds…than to imagine that the soul of beasts has the same nature as ours and, consequently, that we have nothing to fear or hope for, after this life, any more than flies or ants."[477] Immortalism satisfied the criteria of Descartes' mechanistic philosophy—which posits a dualism between lifeless, inert bodies

[476] Kenelm Digby, *Two Treatises in the one of which the nature of bodies, in the other, the nature of mans soule is looked into in a way of discovery of the immortality of reasonable soules* (Paris: 1644), "To My Sonne Kenelme Digby."

[477] Descartes, *Discourse on Method*, trans. Desmond M. Clarke (New York: Penguin, 2003), 42.

and the incorporeal souls that move them—as well as his Catholic faith, specifically, his adherence to the decree punishing mortalists as heretics.[478] Following Descartes, Digby defended human immortality both to account for and to justify "the advantage which man hath over unreasonable creatures."[479] To be immortal, in Digby's view, is to be recognized as reasonable and human.

The human soul *must* be immortal, Digby argued, because it is capable of perceiving mortality in other creatures and things: "Mans soule hath not those groundes in her, which maketh all thinges we see, to be mortall," and therefore "we must be allowed to haue acquitted ourselues of the charge, of prouing her Immortall."[480] This epistemological argument harkens back to Aquinas' claim that the rational soul must be disembodied since it can know embodied things.[481] However, filtered through Cartesian dualism and the Church's prohibition on mortalizing the rational soul, Digby's claim reflects the seventeenth-century English culture of death denial, which, Watson has remarked, encouraged people "to project their unacceptable mortality onto other animals, men to project theirs

---

[478] In the preface to *Meditations*, Descartes announces his intention to defend the injunction of the Fifth Lateran Council. See Catherine Wilson, *Descartes's Meditations: An Introduction* (Cambridge and New York: Cambridge University Press, 2003), 235.

[479] Digby, *Two Treatises*, 418-419.

[480] Ibid., 417.

[481] Thomas Aquinas, *Basic Writings of Thomas Aquinas*, trans. A.C. Pegis (New York: Random House, 1945), 1:685.

onto women, Christians onto pagans, Catholics and Protestants onto each other."[482] It is understandable that people did not readily profess mortalism in such a culture, if doing so was to welcome projections of mortality from others, to forfeit one's humanity and one's claim or right to life. Still, Overton was not alone swept up by mortalism's current, nor did he alone consider that the payoffs of resuscitating the heresy outweighed the risks.

Milton, for one, seriously entertained mortalism in *De Doctrina Christiana*. The text's rhetoric and methodology, based on scriptural analysis and logical argumentation, so closely resembles Overton's treatise that Denis Saurat has wondered whether Milton was the true author of *Man's Mortalitie*.[483] I suggest that this intertextual overlap instead indicates that mortalism was less contained than Saurat and others have acknowledged. Milton inquired whether at death "the whole man, or the body alone...is deprived

---

[482] Watson, *The Rest is Silence*, 30.

[483] For example, Anglo-French scholar Denis Saurat, who proposes in *Milton: Man and Thinker* (1925) that "we come closest of all to Milton's most personal ideas in a group of his immediate contemporaries, the Mortalists" (New York: Lincoln Macveagh, 1925), 310. Saurat dedicates an entire chapter to "The Mortalists, 1643-1655." Fifty years later, by contrast, Merritt Y. Hughes omits the entire chapter in which Milton's mortalism appears (entitled "Of The Death of the Body") from his edition of *On Christian Doctrine* in *Complete Poems and Major Prose*, still a standard critical edition since its publication in 1957. Hughes, it seems, found the treatise to be among Milton's major prose, but he deemed mortalism to be among Milton's minor ideas.

of vitality," a question which "owing to the prejudice of divines [and] their preconceived opinions, has usually been dismissed without examination, instead of being treated with the attention it deserves."[484] He deemed "inadmissible" not mortalism but rather the traditional dualistic notion that death is the soul's separation from the body, the "extinction of life" in the body alone; for, if the soul is the body's life source, Milton supposed, then it is illogical that the body can "be said to die, which never had any life of itself."[485] Where in *De Doctrina Christiana* Milton underscored the logical absurdities and contradictions of scripture that result from disavowing mortalism, in *Paradise Lost* (1667) he represented mortalism's appeal in more affective terms, describing Adam's horror of immortality and his despair at being deprived or denied death.[486]

---

[484] John Milton, *A Posthumous Treatise on the Christian Doctrine*, in *Complete Poems and Major Prose*, ed. Merritt Y. Hughes (Indianapolis and Cambridge: Hackett Publishing Company, Inc., 2003), 903-1020; 980. See also, Gordon Campbell, Thomas N. Corns, John K. Hale, and Fiona J. Tweedie, *Milton and the Manuscript of De Doctrina Christiana* (Oxford: Oxford University Press, 2007), 279.
[485] Ibid.
[486] "Why do I overlive," Adam asks, "how gladly would I meet/ Mortalitie my sentence, and be Earth/Insensible, how glad would lay me down/As in my Mother's lap! There I should rest/And sleep secure." "It was but breath/Of life that sinn'd; what dies but what had life/And sin?/The Bodie properly had neither./All of me then shall die." "Yet one doubt/Pursues me still, least of all I cannot die,/ Lest that pure breath of Life, the Spirit of Man/Which God Inspir'd, cannot together perish/With this Corporeal Clod; then in the Grave,/Or in some other dismal place, who knows/But I shall die a

Just as Donne's attraction to mortalism was of a piece with his monism—or at least with his aversion to the dualism that posited a posthumous separation of body and soul—so too was Milton's mortalism monistic. The characteristic monism of seventeenth-century English mortalism, which constituted an alternative and a challenge to Cartesian dualism, accounts for what I have suggested is mortalism's foundational role in the development of democratic values including the individual's inalienable right to life. For Milton,

> [M]an is a living being, intrinsically and properly
> one and individual, not compound or separable,
> not, according to the common opinion, made up
> and framed of two distinct and different natures,
> as of soul and body,—but that the whole man
> is soul, and the soul man, that is to say, a body,
> or substance individual, animated, sensitive, and
> rational.[487]

This monist-mortalist mode of anthropogenesis reinvests the body with life, counteracting the tradition of immortalism that since Augustine had entrenched and essentialized Aristotle's tripartite division by cordoning off rational human life from embodied mortality. Milton saw mortalism not as heresy, but as "a subject which may be discussed without endangering our faith or devotion."[488]

---

living death? O thought/Horrid, if true! yet why!" (10.775-789).
[487] Milton, *Christian Doctrine* (2003), 980.
[488] Milton, *On Christian Doctrine* (2007), 279.

It is uncertain precisely when he reached this conclusion, since he began work on *De Doctrina Christiana* as early as the 1640s and continued through 1659-1660.[489] However, that it was possible during this interim to admit mortalism "without endangering our faith" does not necessarily mean that it was possible to profess the heresy without endangering oneself, which may explain why Milton never published the text during his lifetime.

In any case, the Westminster Assembly of Divines— a group of theologians and members of parliament appointed by the Long Parliament in 1643 to reform the Church of England—was obliged to declare officially in the *Westminster Confession of Faith* (1646-7) that the "bodies of men, after death, return to dust, and see corruption, but their souls (which neither die nor sleep) having an immortal subsistence, immediately return to God who gave them."[490] This circumscribes questions about the intermediate state of the soul between death and the Resurrection, seeking to extirpate from Anglican faith Catholic vestiges such as purgatory without recourse to Luther's mortalist solution. The pronouncement conjures articles 39 and 40 of the *Forty-two Articles of Edward* (1552), which, again, Elizabeth subsequently had removed. Resurrecting these articles at the height of the English Civil War, the

---

[489] Thomas N. Corns and Gordon Campbell, *John Milton: Life, Work, and Thought* (Oxford: Oxford University Press, 2008), 193-194.
[490] Church of England, *The 1647 Westminster Confession of Faith* (London: 1647).

Westminster Assembly rebranded mortalism once again as heresy, a move that Overton protested as an instance of unacceptable collusion between theologians and politicians.

Indeed, the Assembly of Divines was appointed by Parliament, and their common prohibition of mortalism epitomized the entanglement of their agendas. In May 1648, a conservative majority in Parliament issued an ordinance criminalizing anyone who believed that "the soul of man dieth or sleepeth when the body is dead."[491] For annihilationists, the House prescribed the death penalty.[492] These reactionary measures were ineffectual. Burns has remarked that Parliament's ordinance outlawing blasphemy and heresy "lacked the support of the Army, where sectarian ideas were notoriously popular,"[493] and Christopher Hill has noted that increasing religious toleration made "the death penalty on Mortalists…unenforceable."[494] Orthodox Anglicans successfully outlawed mortalism, then, but they failed to quarantine the epidemic, to compel English culture to unthink ideas already thought, or to

---

[491] Great Britain, "May 1648: An Ordinance for the punishing of Blasphemies and Heresies, with the several penalties therein expressed," *Acts and Ordinances of the Interregnum, 1642-1660*, ed. C.H. Firth and R.S. Rait, 3 vols. (London: His Majesty's Stationery Office, 1911), I.1135.

[492] Ibid., I.1134. See also Burns, *Christian Mortalism*, 16; 79.

[493] Burns, *Christian Mortalism*, 79.

[494] Christopher Hill, *The World Turned Upside Down: Radical Ideas During the English Revolution* (New York: Penguin Books, 1991), 179.

silence R.O., who, several years before Parliament and the Assembly of Divines sought to ratify it, had already exposed the doctrine of immortality as a "meer *Fiction*."[495]

Death is a Great Leveller

In his consolation to Claudio, Duke Vincentio wonders why people fear death, since "death…makes these odds all even" (3.1.40-41). These "odds" refer to the hierarchies, injustices, and inequalities to which all living creatures are subject. "O, death's a great disguiser" (4.2.161), the duke later observes, referring to death's levelling of the idiosyncrasies that individuate living persons. "Death is a Leveller," wrote the mid-seventeenth-century poet Katherine Philips. "Beauty, and Kings,/And Conquerours, and all those glorious things,/Are tumbled to their Graves in one rude heap,/Like common dust as quiet and as cheap" (23-26).[496] By the time Philips reiterated this commonplace trope,[497] the Levellers were no longer a dramatic fiction or metaphorical abstraction, but rather an egalitarian political movement that advocated popular sovereignty, and an organization of living persons to be reckoned with.

There are conflicting accounts of the life of the author of *Man's Mortalitie*. One Richard Overton signed a con-

---

[495] Overton, *Man's Mortalitie*, frontispiece.

[496] Katherine Philips, "A Reverie," *Poems* (London: 1667), 86.

[497] See also James Shirley, "Death the Leveller," and John Fox, *Time and the End of Time* (London, 1670), 412. "Death is the great Leveller that will make all equal."

fession of faith upon converting to General Baptism around 1615, which likely means he was born before 1600. Another Richard Overton matriculated at Queens' College, Cambridge in 1631, placing his birth around 1614. There is some evidence that Overton served as a solider, either in the Bishops' Wars or in the English Civil Wars, and that he was a professional printer.[498] He was affiliated with a congregation of English refugees in Amsterdam, many of whom were linked with the Anabaptists and had fled during Queen Elizabeth's reign, "until the meeting of the Long Parliament [in November 1640] emboldened many of them to return."[499] Among their tenets were freedom of conscience, separation of church and state, pacifism, and tolerance, all of which informed Overton's work.

John Lilburne is often regarded as the leader of the Levellers, but Overton has been credited with theorizing and publishing the movement's philosophical program in roughly 150 pamphlets and journalistic works.[500] In January 1646, Overton attended a debate on mortalism at Thomas Lambe's General Baptist congregation in Bell Alley, Coleman Street, London. Along with other Levellers, Over-

---

[498] B. J. Gibbons, s.v. "Overton, Richard (*fl.* 1640–1663)." In *Oxford Dictionary of National Biography*, online, ed. David Cannadine (Oxford: Oxford University Press, 2004-. Accessed November 2, 2016, http://www.oxforddnb.com.turing.library.northwestern.edu/view/article/20974.

[499] Henry Noel Brailsford, *The Levellers and the English Revolution* (Stanford: Stanford University Press, 1961), 49-50.

[500] Gibbons, s.v. "Overton, Richard (*fl.* 1640–1663)."

ton had been a member of the congregation as early as January 1644, and he recalled routine violent harassment by Presbyterian mobs. Remarkably, when London's Lord Mayor attempted to disperse the congregation's discussion of mortalism, Overton managed to sustain the conversation for another five hours, expanding the original topic to include a debate on the right of authorities to interfere in matters of conscience.[501]

The debate at Lambe's congregation exemplifies Overton's bold civil disobedience and his commitment to values cherished by modern democracies, including freedom of assembly, freedom of the press, and freedom of speech. Belying those who depicted mortalism as an infectious epidemic spread by zealous heretics, Overton presented his case without proselytizing. He welcomed challengers to convince him to renounce his position, inviting readers to take from *Man's Mortalitie* only what served them. "If anything in it be worth thy owning, take it, it is thine as well as mine."[502] Overton was not doctrinaire; on the contrary, he aimed to expose the dangers of uncritical adherence to doctrines such as the immortality of the soul.

Overton's nuanced departures from mortalist tradition reveal peculiar features of the ideological landscape in mid-seventeenth-century England. Roughly thirteen decades after Luther claimed that the soul's sleep would be short and quick, for instance, Overton repeated the

---

[501] Ibid.

[502] Overton, *Man's Mortalitie*, "To the Reader."

assurance but with a difference: "for though there be long time to the Living till the Resurrection, there is none to the Dead…yea, the twinkling of an eye to the living, is more time, then a thousand, yea ten thousand yeares is to the dead."[503] Like Luther, Overton circumscribed the conscious experience of the dead to circumvent the Catholic beliefs and practices of "Purgatorie…Prayers unto dead Saints, to the Virgin Mary, and a World of such-like fancies [that] are grounded upon the Invention of the Soul."[504] But Overton additionally foregrounded the long time remaining to the living before the Resurrection; notwithstanding the catastrophic mortality-crisis of the English Civil War, then, Overton did not think the end of the world was near. In contrast to the apocalyptic millenarianism by which Browne introduced *Religio Medici* ("that man were greedy of life, who should desire to live when all the world were at an end"),[505] Overton's mortalist refusal to deny death corresponded with his "desire to live," and to preserve and protect life for the living as well as for posterity.

Enacting this paradigm of embodied life-preservation required Overton's revision of orthodox modes of anthropogenesis; while he agreed with Augustine's characterization of the human as "a rational and mortal animal," for instance, he disagreed that human rational-

---

[503] Ibid., 21.

[504] Overton, *Man Wholly Mortal* (1675 edition), 122-123.

[505] Browne, *Religio Medici*, "To the Reader." Montaigne makes a similar claim in "To Philosophize is to Learn how to Die."

ity is disembodied and therefore immortal.[506] Overton also defined the human as "a living Rational Creature; whose degrees or excellences of natural Faculties make him in his kind more excellent th[a]n the Beasts," but he maintained that "it doth not follow, that those Faculties together are a Being of themselves immortal."[507] In other words, human excellence does not amount to exceptionalism, such that humans are superior to animals merely "in degree, [not] by kind," as Raphael instructs Adam in book 5 of Milton's *Paradise Lost*, published a quarter century after Man's *Mortalitie*.[508] Overton derived this insight, which emphasizes commonality rather than difference across lifeforms, from several mortalist sources, including Ecclesiastes; Ambroise Paré, the sixteenth-century French barber surgeon to four kings; and Nemesius, the fourth-century Christian philosopher whose work the poet George Wither Englished from the Greek in 1636.[509]

While detractors dehumanized mortalists, Overton argued that immortalism dehumanizes its adherents by dividing their individual nature. He defended mortalism not

---

[506] Augustine, *De civ dei*, 236.

[507] Overton, *Man Wholly Mortal*, 8-9.

[508] John Milton, *Paradise Lost*, *Complete Poems and Major Prose*, 5.490.

[509] Overton, *Man's Mortalitie*, 2. Just as "living-creatures" are compounds of sensible parts (e.g., flesh and sinews) and insensible parts (e.g., bones, fat, and hair), Nemesius posited, so too has the Creator interlinked all species and things, such that there is no stable, essential difference between "creatures void of life," "creatures reasonable," and "inanimate creatures" (*The Nature of Man*, trans. George Wither [London: 1636], 6-7; 10).

to annihilate human identity, but to re-define its terms. "If my being did not distinguish me from an owl and a woodcock, and thy being the same; then an owl and a woodcock were both writer and reader. But an owl and a woodcock is neither writer nor reader."[510] Overton rejected the idea that humans transcend nature and mortality through ostensibly disembodied faculties such as willing, knowing, and ratiocination, which he regarded as no less bodily than the processes of eating, feeling, and growing. He observed that humans (no less than fish, birds, and beasts) reproduce "without any transcendency of nature," so that we are "not halfe mortal, halfe immortal, halfe Angel, halfe man, but compleat man totally mortal: for through mortal organs immortality cannot be conce[iev]d, or therein possibly reside."[511] Where Pomponazzi and others hedged their bets by arguing that humans partake of both mortality and immortality, Overton believed that the ethical and political payoffs of mortalism required being "absolute for death," or in other words, that as long as any part of human nature is ascribed immortality there will be a haven from which to claim unjust prerogative and exceptionalism.

Over a decade after Overton's intervention, Walter Charleton also considered how sovereignty institutes sociopolitical order through immortalism in *The Immortality of the Human Soul* (1657), a fictional dialogue between Athanasius and Lucretius. The former, representing Char-

---

[510] Overton, *Man Wholly Mortal* (1675 edition), 26-27.
[511] Overton, *Man Wholly Mortal*, (London, 1655), 5.

leton's own position, is the early Christian Church father whose name puns on "immortal" (*a-thanatos*) and whom Overton associated with Augustine for his belief that the soul is "intelligent, invisible, immortal, incorporeal, like the angels."[512] Lucretius is the epicurean poet whose name smacked of mortalism in early modern England. Charleton's Athanasius swears that immortalism is a universal and natural belief "as ancient as Humanity itself," but Charleton's Lucretius counters that the idea may have originated, "for ought we know," as a political fiction invented by the first legislators after "observing that the punishments denounced upon capital Delinquents in this life were not sufficient to deterre them from committing enormities destructive to the common right and safety of Societies."[513]

Lucretius supposes that the political myth of immortalism took root, "found a general belief," and eventually became "naturalized," because it appeals to humanity's "desire and love of life."[514] Athanasius retorts that the first legislators already found the belief "set[t]led and radicated in the hearts of the people, from the very beginning of Mankind." He grants that the lawmakers may have instrumentalized the belief for political ends, "but [that this is] no reason, to allow, that therefore it is a meer politique

---

[512] Overton, *Man Wholly Mortal* (1675 edition), 4.
[513] Charleton, *The immortality of the human soul* (London: 1657), 131.
[514] Ibid., 132.

Fiction."[515] Charleton ultimately maintained immortality as an essential truth of humanity as well as an indispensable political fiction, in contrast to Overton who deemed immortalism not a noble but a nefarious lie that corrupts rather than grounds morality.

Charleton imagined immortalism as a tool by which sovereignty can "deterre" criminals—who, like Barnardine, do not fear capital punishment—from violating public safety and encroaching upon the common rights of their fellow citizens. Overton, however, was less concerned with how immortalism deterred criminals than how it enabled sovereigns to encroach upon the common rights of their subjects. Thomas Hobbes realized this concern in *Leviathan* (1651), positing that "*sovereignty* is an artificial *soul*, [which gives] life and motion to the whole body" of the commonwealth.[516] Like Charleton, Hobbes saw the social value of immortalism. While traditionally characterized as a mortalist himself, Hobbes also apprehended the danger of people like Overton, who proliferated "interpretation[s] of the Bible [not] authorized by the commonwealth."

> The maintenance of civil society, depending
> on justice; and justice on the power of life and
> death, and other less rewards and punishments,
> residing in them that have the sovereignty
> of the commonwealth; it is impossible a

---

[515] Ibid., 132-133.

[516] Thomas Hobbes, *Leviathan*, ed. J.C.A. Gaskin (Oxford and New York: Oxford University Press, 2008), 7.

> commonwealth should stand, where any other
> than the sovereign, hath a power of giving
> greater rewards than life, and of inflicting
> greater punishments than death. Now seeing
> *eternal life* is a greater reward than the *life present*,
> and *eternal torment* a greater punishment than
> the *death of nature*; it is a thing worthy to be well
> considered…by obeying authority…what is
> meant in Holy Scripture.[517]

Hobbes followed Overton in placing the preservation of embodied life at the center of the political order. *Leviathan* therefore defines natural right as "the liberty each man hath, to use his own power, as he will himself, for the preservation…of his own life," as opposed to natural law, that "which a man is forbidden to do, that, which is destructive of his life, or taketh away the means of preserving the same."[518] Several years earlier, Overton fought not just for the sanctity of embodied life, but also for the right to come to terms with its finitude.

The only just laws, Overton argued, are those that promote the well-being and safety of the commonwealth, "and this is mans prerogative and no further."[519] In Overton's view, the English church and state overextended their prerogative by sanctioning immortal life as the only life worth living and by encroaching upon the right of individuals

---

[517] Hobbes, *Leviathan*, 297.

[518] Ibid., 86.

[519] Overton, *An Arrow Against All Tyrants*, 4.

to preserve embodied, mortal life. Overton's mortalism thereby tacitly indicted a range of prerogatives that were linked to the prerogative of immortality. It is telling that Guy Holland titled his rebuttal to Overton *THE Prerogative of Man: OR, THE IMMORTALITY OF HUMANE SOULES* (1645), because seventeenth-century Anglicans conceived immortality in precisely these terms. Browne saw mortalism as a challenge to "this prerogative of my Soul."[520] Charleton likewise believed that the Creator elected "man to be his Darling and intimate Favorite," as evidenced by humanity's various "Praeeminences and Praerogatives," including the ability to dominate all other creatures and things under the moon, and "that inestimable propriety, the Immortality of his Soul."[521] On the one hand, Overton's mortalism was just one facet of his larger challenge to prerogative, but on the other hand, Overton saw the doctrine of immortality as the source and origin of other prerogatives, including those of political sovereignty.

In *An Arrow against all Tyrants and Tyranny, shot from the prison of Newgate, into the Prerogative Bowels of the Arbitrary House of Lords* (1646), Overton condemned Presbyterian abuses of power and the "daily encroaching" of the House of Lords on the freedom and liberty of the common people.[522] Overton argued that in a representative and legiti-

---

[520] Browne, *Religio Medici*, 14.

[521] Charleton, *Darknes of Atheism*, 169.

[522] Structures of thought and rhetorical patterns from *Man's Mortalitie*

mate government, "the Soveraigne power...cannot be conveyed by, or derived from [the King] to any...So that his meere prerogative creatures, cannot have that which their Lord and creator never had hath."[523] Overton compared the House of Lords to "spit" from the King's mouth, suggesting the futility of ending monarchy but leaving the prerogatives that sustained it for others to reappropriate in new forms. Claiming the King's former prerogative enabled the Lords to "make incursions & inroads upon the Peoples rights and freedomes, and extend their prerogative pattent beyond their Masters compasse," Overton wrote, but any other group "might as well challenge that prerogative of Soveraignity."[524]

The House of Lords was not the only "prerogative Head" that concerned Overton, who also took aim at the "unnatural, tyranicall, blood-thirsty desires and continuall endevours of the Clergy, against the contrary minded in matters of conscience."[525] He denounced the collusion

_____

appear translated and repurposed in Overton's critique of tyrannical sovereignty. Overton's challenge to the Divine Assembly's assertion that the souls of the dead "immediately return to God who gave them," for example, is consistent with if not constitutive of his argument against the Divine Right of Kings, that "all just humain powers take their original not immediately from God (as Kings usually plead their prerogative) but mediately by the hand of nature, as from the represented to the representors" (*An Arrow Against All Tyrants*, 4).

[523] Overton, *An Arrow Against All Tyrants*, 12.
[524] Ibid.
[525] Ibid.

between Clergy and Parliament, specifically, the "powerfull agitation" of church leaders that compelled members of Parliament to ratify "a most Romish inquisition Ordinance."[526] This refers to Parliament's ordinance against heresy, proposed by Nathaniel Bacon and Zouch Tate.[527] Overton's anti-Catholic characterization of the ordinance evokes the decree that criminalized mortalism and other heresies on the eve of the Reformation. Overton defended religious toleration and freedom, however, and his challenge aimed not at Catholic elements in the Anglican church but at elements of the Anglican church within the English state, an incursion that in turn encroached on Overton's freedom to speak, to publish his ideas in the press, and to not be wrongly imprisoned.

Overton's clandestine printing press was seized by the authorities, and he was committed to Newgate Prison on several occasions, which did little to stem the dissemination of his ideas.[528] In 1647, while at Newgate, Overton

---

[526] Ibid.

[527] See Ann Hughes, *Gangraena and the Struggle for the English Revolution* (Oxford University Press), 381. As church "ministers urged action," against toleration, heresy, and blasphemy, "parliament remained bitterly divided over a proposed ordinance against heresy, introduced in September 1646 by Nathaniel Bacon and Zouch Tate. Tate had overseen the military reorganization that created the New Model Army; his increasing identification with the Presbyterian political programme, driven in large part by his anxiety about religious radicalism [shows] how religious upheaval…contributed to political re-alignment."

[528] The polemical Presbyterian preacher Thomas Edwards reports

managed to publish a petition that he had composed a year earlier on behalf of the inhabitants of Buckinghamshire and Hertfordshire. It "was signed with almost ten thousand hands," and brought to Parliament on February 11, 1646 by "about 500. Gentlemen and yeomen," who were protesting their lack of access to those representing them. From prison, Overton readdressed the petition to the House of Commons, urging them to recognize "the slavish condition, that we the free People of England" have been subjected to "by some prerogative-men of this Kingdom" who, though not elected by the people, yet exercise arbitrary "power over our bodies or Estates." Citing his own false imprisonment as an example of such arbitrary power, Overton implored the House to "free us and our children from the fear and prejudice" of "Prerogative-proceedings" by "Prerogative-men." He signed the petition, "Richard Overton, Prerogative-Prisoner in Newgate."[529]

Overton intuited that the "power over…bodies" exer-

---

with incredulous resentment in *Gangraena* (London: 1646), a catalogue of Protestant sectarianism in the form of an heresiography, that since Overton's imprisonment "there are some wicked railing Pamphlets come out in his name, and sold openly…venting a company of cursed principles," challenging religious and political authority, and demanding popular sovereignty and free speech. Edwards scoffs at Overton's heretical ideas, including his indictment of "the Ordinance for punishing Blasphemies and Heresies" (149).
[529] Richard Overton, *To the right honourable, the betrusted knights, citizens, in the Commons House of Parliament (Englands legall soveraign power): the humble petition of the inhabitants of Buckingham-shire, and Hartfo[rd] shire, whose names are hereunto subscribed* (London: 1647).

cised by unelected "prerogative-men" depended on the prerogative of immortality and its concomitant belief that rational life is disembodied. His mortalism, which reinvested the body with life, bears a potent(ial) political critique: if this "thing the Soul"[530] is just that, a thing, and not an incorporeal property, then it is subject to be instrumentalized by the body no less than the body is by it. Overton weighed the view of the "Soularies"—his strategic neologism for immortalists, which shifted the onus of the controversy onto them—that "the soul, is rationality it selfe; and that rationality is no more of the body, then inke is from the pen."[531] Overton showed how immortalism produced internal contradictions within English orthodoxy, specifically, in matters of criminal justice.

Where soularies from Thomas More to Walter Charleton feared that mortalism's deferral (if not denial) of postmortem justice would undermine social order, Overton instead derived from mortalism a defense of due process and a critique of the death penalty. He remarked, for instance, that since there is no Judgment before Resurrection, and since Resurrection "is not yet brought to pass,"[532] then "execution must goe before Judgment, which in a Commonwealth would be ridiculous injustice,

---

[530] Overton, *Man Wholly Mortal* (1675), 16.

[531] Ibid., 53.

[532] Church of England, *Forty-two Articles of Edward*, quoted in Nathaniel H. Henry, "Milton and Hobbes: Mortalism and the Intermediate State," *Studies in Philology*, vol. 48, no. 2 (April 1951): 234-249; 238.

as first to hang men, and then judge them."[533] If the body
is (as immortalists conceived it) a lifeless tool wielded by
an incorporeal and rational soul, then to punish the body
is as absurd "as if a Magistrate should hang the Hatchet,
and spare the Man that beate a mans braines out with
it."[534] Likewise, if "the body is but an instrument, or as
the pen in the hand of a Writer, to the Soul, whereby it
acts and moves, [and] if the Soul come immediately from
God, [then] that immortall thing, and not our mortall flesh,
is Author of all sinne."[535] It is absurd, in other words, to
punish the body as if it were an agent in a culture that
insists that the body is a mere instrument. Overton's mortalism de-instrumentalized the body and imbued it with
certain rights and liberties that, logically, should be invio-
lable in any culture that claims to value life.[536]

Overton concluded the 1655 postscript of *Man Wholly
Mortal* with a verbatim transcription of what appears to
be Philemon Holland's 1601 translation of the book from
ancient Roman philosopher Pliny's *Natural History* entitled
"Of the ghosts or spirits of men departed." Overton found
in Pliny an ethical analogue of the mortalist theology of
Luther and Tyndale. Overton's attention to this analogue

---

[533] Overton, *Man's Mortalitie*, 25.

[534] Ibid., 5.

[535] Ibid., 44.

[536] See C.B. Macpherson, *The Political Theory of Possessive Individualism:
Hobbes to Locke* (Oxford: Oxford University Press, 1962), 275. "The
individual in market society is human as proprietor of his own
person."

reflects his understanding of mortalism not only as a challenge to local, historically specific forms of authority, but
also as a defense against incursions into embodied life
wherever and whenever immortalism is invoked.

Pliny observed that belief in immortality leads people
to "suppose that the Ghosts sequestred from the Body"
still possess sense, which compels the living to "honour
and worship" the dead. As a pagan writing fifteen hundred
years before the Reformation, Pliny's complaint was not
with abuses of church power but rather with ideologies
that burden the living with the weight of the dead and dis-
place attention from this life to an imagined hereafter. He
remarked that notwithstanding many conflicting opinions
about the state of the soul after the body's burial, it "is
generally held [that] neither Body nor Soul hath any more
sence after our dying day, th[a]n they had before the day
of their nativity."[537]

Immortalism, for Pliny, was symptomatic of the
human "folly and vanity" that extend "even to the future
time," such that "in the very time of death" we flatter
ourselves "with fond imaginations," dreaming of the life
to come.[538] Overton concurred with Pliny that humans
breathe the same breath as "other living Creatures," and
that there are "many other things in the world, that live

---

[537] Overton, *Man Wholly Mortal*, "The Postscript." Cf. *The Historie
of the World*, trans. Philemon Holland (London: 1601), book VII,
chapter LV.
[538] Ibid.

much longer th[a]n men; and yet no man judgeth in them the like immortality."[539] Immortality, for Pliny and hence for Overton, was a "foolish and childish" fiction "devised by men that would fain live alwayes, and never make an end."[540] Seventeenth-century Anglicans approved of Pliny's ethical insight that the *ars moriendi* (art of dying) is inseparable from the *ars vivendi* (art of living), and that to live well requires being "absolute for death."[541] The fierce backlash to Overton's mortalism, however, suggests that many in England had not yet properly grasped this wisdom or come to terms with being mortal.

---

[539] Overton, *Man Wholly Mortal*, "The Postscript."
[540] Ibid.
[541] See Montaigne, "To philosophize is to learn how to die," and Jeremy Taylor's *The Rule and Exercises of Holy Living* (1650) and *The Rule and Exercises of Holy Dying* (1651).

Reviving Vitalism in King Lear

"I know when one is dead and when one lives," Lear howls with Cordelia's corpse in his arms at the close of Shakespeare's *True Chronicle Historie of the life and death of King Lear* (1606), "She's dead as earth" (24.255-256).[542] Lear's analogy is fraught in the world of the play, where human actors summon the latent virtues of dead and inanimate things earnestly if without visible success. In the early modern English worldview more generally, to be dead as earth was not decisively to be dead, as the discourse around autochthony suggests, for example, in its representation of lifeforms born from the earth. Robert Watson has argued that Lear's statement "shows only too keenly how it feels to inhabit a world where the willful mysteries of nature have been turned into a passive object, a mass of materiality."[543] This reading risks foreclosing the play's vitalist discourse, which remains unrealized not because it is superseded by an ostensibly more legitimate paradigm such as seventeenth-century mechanism—which represented matter as Watson has represented Cordelia's body,

---

[542] Greenblatt et al., eds., *The Norton Shakespeare* (New York and London: Norton & Company, 2008).
[543] Robert Watson, *Back to Nature: The Green and the Real in the Late Renaissance* (Philadelphia: University of Pennsylvania Press, 2006), 53.

that is, as passive, objective, and inanimate—but because it is "unpublish'd" (18.18), as Cordelia says of the earth's secret virtues.

Momentarily doubting that Cordelia is in fact dead, Lear performs a series of critical tests to check her for vital signs. Some seventeenth-century audiences and readers may have seen this final uncertainty as a tragic consummation of Lear's folly, insofar as one must be foolish not to know what differentiates the living from the dead. The hermetic philosopher and alchemist Thomas Vaughan asked in 1650, for instance, "who is so stupid as not to know the Difference between Life and Death, the absence, and presence of his Soul?" The rhetorical question is part of Vaughan's challenge to the authority of ancient texts, because one need not read Aristotle to know "that the Soul is the Cause of Life, sense, motion, and understanding."[544]

Many of Shakespeare's contemporaries disagreed, however, with such binary (and what Overton called "soulary") views of life and death; for them, Lear's indecision may have reverberated not as a sign of senility but as a response to a set of decisive questions in early modern English culture, science, and politics—namely, who has the capacity to know, the power to decide, and the authority to declare "when one is dead and when one lives"? I suggest in what follows that Lear's analogy seeks to reclaim not a

---

[544] Thomas Vaughan, "Anima Magica Abscondita," in *The Works of Thomas Vaughan*, ed. Arthur E. Waite (London: Theosophical Publishing House, 1919; first published 1650), 5.

given capacity common to all rational humans but rather a decision-making power that is specific to his role as the sovereign.

The stage directions of the early texts underscore how Shakespeare's play contradicts the modern assumption that the difference between life and death is always obvious. In the 1608 Quarto version of the *True Chronicle Historie of the life and death of King Lear* and the 1623 First Folio edition of *The Tragedie of King Lear*, Lear enters "*with Cordelia in his armes.*"[545] Later play texts, by contrast, determine that Cordelia is dead before the scene begins. In the modern conflated version published by *Norton Shakespeare*, Lear enters "*with* CORDELIA *dead in his arms.*"[546] The editorial decision to pronounce Cordelia dead on arrival elides the play's strategic ambiguity between the living, the dead, and the (in)animate; it also encroaches on Shakespeare's dramaturgical decision to keep Cordelia alive, or at least to keep that possibility alive, long enough for Lear and the audience to decide for themselves.

The previous chapters have examined how decisions about the terms of human life potentially disrupted existing sociopolitical orders and alliances in early modern England. Before Bacon decided that anything nourished qualifies as living, before Overton redefined human life as embodied and mortal, and long before modern editors decided that Cordelia is dead prior to the final scene,

---

[545] Greenblatt et al., eds., *The Norton Shakespeare*, 2487.
[546] Ibid., 2565.

Shakespeare dramatized the proliferation of lifeforms generated by decentered acts of anthropogenesis. The subtle discourse of vitalism in *Lear* represents *in potentia* the opposition to absolute and indivisible sovereignty. That many competing lifeforms and definitions of life in *Lear* remain unauthorized by a legitimate sovereign was perhaps not lost on King James, who in December 1606 was in the audience at Whitehall for the play's earliest known performance.[547]

James believed that the existence and survival of the nation depended on "the will of the sovereign and his absolute power of life and death over his subjects."[548] The same year that James attended the first performance of *Lear*, Richard Knolles translated into English the work of French political philosopher Jean Bodin, whose concept of sovereignty was "the source of confusion that helped prepare the way for the theory of royal absolutism, for he was primarily responsible for introducing the seductive but erroneous notion that sovereignty is indivisible."[549]

---

[547] Grace Ioppolo, ed., *A Routledge Literary Sourcebook on William Shakespeare's King Lear* (New York: Routledge, 2003). "The play's apparently authorised publication in 1608, so soon after its composition in 1606, suggests that *King Lear* was popular enough to draw reading audiences while not compromising the interest of future theatrical audiences (3).

[548] Daniel Juan Gil, *Shakespeare's Anti-Politics: Sovereign Power and the Life of the Flesh* (Houndmills, Basingstoke, Hampshire: Palgrave Macmillan, 2013), 6.

[549] Jean Bodin, *On Sovereignty*, ed. and trans. Julian H. Franklin (Cambridge, 1992), xiii. Quentin Skinner has remarked that Knolles

Bodin argued that it is necessary "in a well ordered Commonweale, to restore vnto parents the power of life and death ouer their children," and by extension, to restore to sovereigns the power of life and death over their subjects, "which by the law of God and nature is giuen them."[550]

Seventeenth-century English authors took issue with Bodin, however, and the reach of James' power was checked not only by parliament but also by technological limitations. The absolute biopower toward which James could have aspired in 1606 was the power to decide whom to let live and whom to kill; just before the advent of new scientific discourses including Bacon's proto-biology and Cartesian mechanism, however, he likely did not foresee that absolute sovereignty would soon also require, first, the power to decide which lives to foster and prolong and which to let die, and second, the knowledge to discern and/ or the authority to declare what lives and what is lifeless.[551]

Criteria for distinguishing the living from the dead were in flux during the seventeenth century as a result of theological, scientific, and political upheaval. French phi-

---

translation of Bodin into English was among the first the concept of "state" emerged "with some consistency in a recognizably modern sense" (*The Foundations of Modern Political Thought*, vol. I: The Renaissance [Cambridge, 1977], ix-x).

[550] Jean Bodin, *The six bookes of a common-weale* (London, 1606), 22.

[551] Again, Foucault has argued that in the seventeenth century the characteristic task of sovereign power "was perhaps no longer to kill, but to invest life through and through" ("Right of Death and Power over Life," *The Foucault Reader*, 262).

losopher René Descartes therefore insisted in *Passions of the Soul* (1649):

> Death never occurs through the absence of
> the soul, but only because one of the principle
> parts of the body decays. And…the difference
> between the body of a living man and that of a
> dead man is just like the difference between, on
> the one hand, a watch or other automaton (that
> is, a self-moving machine) when it is wound up
> and contains in itself the corporeal principle of
> the movements for which it is designed…and,
> on the other hand, the same watch or machine
> when it is broken and the principle of its
> movement ceases to be active.[552]

The analogy between human bodies and automatons epitomizes the seventeenth-century mechanistic world-view, which, as Watson says of Cordelia's dead body, sig-naled for many that "the willful mysteries of nature ha[d] been turned into a passive object." But the difference between living and dead human bodies is arguably "just like" many analogous differences, including that between the earth conceived as an unambiguous marker of dead-ness and the earth conceived as an animate source and symbol of vitality. In the centuries following Descartes, Western thought has fixated on his decisive bifurcation of

---

[552] Descartes, *Passions of the Soul*, in *Descartes: Selected Philosophical Writings*, trans. Cottingham and Stoothoff (New York: Cambridge University Press, 1998), 331.

the Great Chain of Being, which divided human life from lifeless automatons and inanimate things.[553] Preempting the decisive Cartesian split, Shakespeare's *Lear* critically dramatized the transformation of political sovereignty as a negotiation between, on the one hand, the power to decide which lifeforms qualify as living—as worthy of being lived, nourished, protected, and prolonged—and on the other hand, the authority to declare the difference between living and dead bodies and (in)animate things.

Where extant scholarship on seventeenth-century vitalism has generally focused on its oppositional relationship with mechanism, I argue that intimations and invocations of vitalism in *Lear* represent a challenge to an emergent discourse of biopower, which the play stages as the power to let live, to prolong life, to deprive of death, to "know when one is dead and when one lives," and finally, to allow to die. Vitalism, like mortalism, refers to a heterogenous collective of tenets and traditions: some iterations represent all bodies and things as intrinsically endowed with life rather than as dead or inanimate matter infused with

---

[553] Stuart Shanker, "Descartes' Legacy: The Mechanist/Vitalist Debates," in *The Philosophy of Science, Mathematics, and Logic in The Twentieth Century*, ed. Stuart Shanker (New York: Routledge, 1996), 316. See Jones, *The Racial Discourses of Life Philosophy*: "Some would try to restore the continuum by emphasizing that man's higher capacities could be found in lesser degree down the chain, in animals and even inanimate matter; however the opposite attempt became dominant, and the mechanical movement of matter was analogized to reflex actions and then to thought itself" (33).

life from without, for example, by a divine soul or breath; other iterations, by contrast, isolate the phenomena of life as autonomous from and irreducible to their material substrates.[554] Shakespeare's contemporaries did not explicitly name this set of ideologies later defined as "vitalism," I suggest, because it was such an integral part of their lives that it remained "unpublish'd," as it were, hidden in plain sight. *Lear* stages the transformation of vitalism into an idea that can no longer go without saying.

Literary historian John Rogers has remarked that seventeenth-century English vitalism, "known also as animist materialism, holds in its tamest manifestation the inseparability of body and soul and, in its boldest, the infusion of all material substance with the power of reason and self-motion."[555] What I provisionally identify as vitalism in *Lear* describes a constellation of related tropes involving the personification of *virtual* lifeforms represented as morally

---

[554] For Hans Driesch, the "main question of Vitalism" was whether the purposive processes of life result from "a special constellation of factors known already to the sciences of the inorganic," or whether such processes issue from "an autonomy peculiar to the processes themselves" (*The History of Vitalism* [London: Macmillan and Co., 1914], 1). In his essay "Contemporary Vitalism" (1926), Mikhail Bakhtin described the three camps of modern biology: the mechanists, the vitalists, and those who try to accommodate both mechanism and vitalism. The vitalists, he explains, conceive life as autonomous and subject only to its own laws which are unique in nature ("Contemporary Vitalism," in *The crisis in modernism: Bergson and the vitalist controversy*. eds. Frederick Burwick and Paul Douglass [Cambridge University Press, 1992]), 76-77.

[555] Rogers, *Matter of Revolution*, 1.

virtuous, physically potent, and inherently powerful, but also as latent and potential rather than actual or operative. The analogy between Cordelia's virtue and the virtues of the earth accordingly preserves and reasserts a cross-onto-logical continuity between lifeforms and (in)animate things against an opposing tendency in discourses of mechanism and biopower to decisively differentiate rational, human life from creaturely, vegetative, and inanimate bodies.

Several years after the first performance of *Lear*, John Donne published *The First Anniversary* (1611), a eulogy for his patron's young daughter Elizabeth Drury, which "anat-omizes" several themes including the shortness of life and the advent of the new sciences. The poem usefully contex-tualizes both Lear's pronouncement that Cordelia is "dead as earth" as well as subsequent readings of this pronounce-ment as the death knell of vitalism and the harbinger of a new mechanistic world order. While Elizabeth lived, "all things" derived their "verdure" and "lustre" from her, "(For Ayre, and Fire but thick grosse bodies were,/And liueliest stones but drowsie, and pale [compared] to her)" (367-368). After her untimely death, "the world is dead" (7) too, unable to survive without her virtue, which was the vital principle that animated all things. That Elizabeth was the "Cyment which did faithfully compact/And glue all vertues" (49-50) aligns her with the "organic cement" that was thought to bind microcosmic parts to macrocosmic wholes in medieval vitalistic worldviews.[556]

Without Elizabeth, everything is "in peeces, all coherence gone;/All just supply, and all Relation:/Prince, Subject, Father, Sonne, are things forgot" (213-215). This recalls Gloucester's lament in *Lear*, that "love cools, friendship falls off, brothers divide; in cities mutinies, in countries discords, palaces treason, the bond cracked between son and father" (2.99-101). The poem attributes the dissolution of social, political, and ontological orders to the "new Philosophy" (205), the decay of nature, and the death of Elizabeth. Although Elizabeth shared her name with the monarch who had died in 1603, she was herself a subject, not a sovereign. That the death of an individual subject might have such enormous consequences indicates the seventeenth-century transformation of vitalist discourse from, on the one hand, an ideology of absolute sovereignty to, on the other hand, a site for contesting absolutism and imagining the decentralization, if not yet democratization, of sovereignty. I argue, likewise, that Cordelia's death represents not the death of vitalism but a *pièce de résistance* that resists the absolutization of biopower.

If the deaths of Cordelia and Elizabeth nailed the coffin of the vitalist worldview, as some have suggested, they also compelled survivors to reorganize the world that remained. "Let no man say, the world it selfe being dead," Donne enjoined, that it is "labour lost to have discovered/

---

[556] Merchant, *The Death of Nature*, 71.

The worlds infirmities, since there is none/Alive to study this dissection;/For there's a kind of world remaining still,/ Though shee which did inanimate and fill/The world, be gone" (63-69). Elizabeth's "virtue" becomes the "matter and the stuffe" of the "new world" that has emerged "from the carkasse of the old world," while "the forme" of the "new world" is "our practise" (75-78). In other words, Elizabeth's virtue, formerly an immaterial force animating matter with form, itself materializes after her death, while human practice (rather than theory) now gives form to matter that is no longer regarded as self-organizing. The deaths of Elizabeth (and the world) and Cordelia (and the earth) signal not the end of vitalism, then, but the point at which human action must take over from natural agency; the point at which vitalism transforms from a ubiquitous worldview whose operations appear autonomous and self-evident to a position that must be cultivated, defended, and practiced by human actors.

A History of Vitalism

The predominant worldview in medieval Europe regarded nature, the earth, and society—in short, every-thing—as organic and alive. Historian Andrew Mendelsohn has therefore suggested that vitalism did not emerge as a distinctly intelligible position before the sixteenth century, because in a medieval scholastic culture dominated by Aristotelianism, everyone could be described as a vitalist.[557] As Carolyn Merchant has remarked in *The Death of Nature* (1981), it was generally difficult in the Renaissance "to differentiate between living and nonliving things, because of the resemblance in structures. Like plants and animals, minerals and gems were filled with small pores, tublets, cavities, and streaks, through which they seemed to nourish themselves." Under this dispensation, "all things were permeated by life, there being no adequate method by which to designate the inanimate from the animate."[558]

Gail Kern Paster's analysis of psychological materialism further accounts for this early modern methodological perplexity. She has argued that humoralism—the dominant medical paradigm and ontology in the medieval period and into the seventeenth century—emphasized on the shared materiality of humans and "other living things—animate and inanimate."[559] This worldview saw no need for the rigorous ontological separation of living, dead, and (in)animate bodies

---

[557] "Vitalism," Melvyn Bragg, *In Our Time*, BBC (October 16, 2008). With Patricia Fara, Fellow of Clare College and Affiliated Lecturer in the Department of History and Philosophy of Science at Cambridge University; Andrew Mendelsohn, Senior Lecturer in the History of Science and Medicine at Imperial College, University of London and Pietro Corsi, Professor of the History of Science at the University of Oxford.

[558] Carolyn Merchant, *The Death of Nature: Women, Ecology, and the Scientific Revolution* (New York: HarperCollins Publishers, 1980), 27-8.

[559] Gail Kern Paster, *Humoring the Body: Emotions and the Shakespearean Stage* (Chicago and London: The University of Chicago Press, 2004), 19.

that became increasingly crucial in seventeenth-century England.

The capacity to discern and the authority to declare what lives accrued new urgency in the seventeenth century when practical and ideological motives compelled writers to reimagine things such as the earth as lifeless. Merchant has observed that "the image of the earth as a living organism and nurturing mother had served as a cultural constraint restricting the actions of human beings. One does not readily slay a mother, dig into her entrails for gold or mutilate her body, although commercial mining would soon require that."[560] Concomitant with these commercial practices and their conceptual and ecological devitalization of the earth were new theological and scientific paradigms that rigorously distinguished human life from creaturely bodies and material things.[561]

---

[560] Merchant, *The Death of Nature*, 3.

[561] Protestants critiqued what they saw as Catholic idolatry based on the assumption of the liveliness of things—the intercessionary power of images of saints, for example, or the salvific virtues of relics such as wood from the cross, or the bone fragments, hair, and fingernails of saints. Catholics also contributed to the devitalization of matter. According to Steven Shapin, the French theologian and polymath Marin Mersenne, a friend of and major influence on Descartes, "saw very dangerous consequences flowing from the Renaissance revival of the doctrine of the anima mundi, or world soul—the notion that matter was imbued with life and the associated identification of God with nature" (*The Scientific Revolution*, 43-44). Mersenne's concern was that the doctrine legitimated non-Christian practices such as magic and flouted the separation between the natural and the supernatural. For him "the root problem was the

The intellectual historian Arthur Lovejoy, author of *The Great Chain of Being* (1936), remarked over a century ago "that, in the use of the term 'vitalism' and its common antithesis 'mechanism,' a good deal of confusion has arisen" such that the "term vitalism might, with real advantage to both biology and philosophy, be retired from service."[562] Whether or not this holds true can be left to biologists and philosophers. However, relegating vitalism to the dustbin of antiquated ideas is to risk propagating an over-schematized historical narrative at the expense of a more continuist and, I argue, more accurate account of seventeenth-century ideas that regards the shift toward mechanism as neither total nor instantaneous. To regard vitalism as a defunct worldview, moreover, precludes recognition of generative continuities between seventeenth-

---

idea of matter as essentially active, and the root solution was to be an account of matter as completely passive and inert." See also Margaret Wertheim, *Pythagoras' Trousers: God, Physics, and the Gender Wars* (New York: Norton, 1995), 81-103; 92. "For Mersenne, the root heresy lay in the organic philosophy of nature on which magic was based. In particular he objected to the idea that the world had a soul that was the source of its vital activity." In other words, vitalism was the problem and mechanism the solution, a worldview embraced by Descartes and widely disseminated across other fields of thought. Watson has remarked, for example, that "[a]n essential criterion of modern experimental science—that a result can be replicated—implies a loss of the voluntary and subjective character of the universe under both medieval and earlier Renaissance theology" (*Back to Nature*, 23).

[562] Arthur O. Lovejoy, "The Import of Vitalism," *Science*, vol. 34, no. 864 (July 21, 1911): 75-80; 80.

century texts and twenty-first-century critical theory, which both for different reasons have sought to revive the cultural and political virtues afforded by vitalism.

The history of vitalism, like that of autochthony and mortalism, comprises long periods of latency punctuated by moments of intense urgency, and it therefore demands attention to continuity as well as discontinuity. Distinct strains of vitalist thought have arisen throughout history. In the twentieth century, Henri Bergson revived vitalism in part to preserve the freedom and open-endedness of life from the mechanized and deterministic worldview of modern science, while the Nazis instrumentalized "vitalism to justify German conquest of 'less vital' peoples."[563] *Lear* affords us a *nature morte*, or a not-quite-still life, of the vitalism that sprang up in seventeenth-century England, from what many have thought were its death throes, to challenge the emergent paradigms of mechanism and biopower.

Extant accounts of vitalism have glossed too quickly over its seventeenth-century English history. "The triumph of the mechanical philosophy," according to Keith Thomas "meant the end of the animistic conception of the universe."[564] Mikhail Bakhtin has likewise concluded that

---

[563] Jane Bennett, "A Vitalist Stopover," *New Materialisms*, 49.
[564] Keith Thomas, *Religion and the Decline of Magic* (New York: Penguin, 1991), 664. See also Keith Thomas, *Man and the Natural World: changing attitudes in England, 1500-1800* (Oxford: Oxford University Press, 1996).

"the century of Kepler, Galileo, Descartes, and Newton, was not inclined favorably to vitalism," but that since "the very *end* of the nineteenth century…vitalism has returned with new vigor."[565] Bakhtin went without saying, however, that the seventeenth century belonged not only to Kepler, Galileo, Descartes, and Newton, but also to Shakespeare and countless contemporaries who, if they were not inclined favorably toward vitalism, were nevertheless preoccupied with it. Rogers has called vitalism "one of the least understood intellectual movements in early modern England, a short-lived embrace of philosophical idealism"[566] that did not "prove sufficiently strong to withstand its dissipation by the mechanistic philosophies of matter that came to dominate the Scientific Revolution."[567] Seventeenth-century writers that introduced mechanism, however, did so as an alternative to vitalism, such that vitalism structured the thought even of its opponents.

There is a growing consensus among historians of science that vitalism survived and even supported the rise of mechanism. Philosopher David Skrbina has noted "a persistent countercurrent" of non-mechanistic thought during "the emergence and rise to power of the Mechanistic Worldview" around 1600. "Even some of the founders

---

[565] Mikhail Bakhtin, "Contemporary Vitalism" (1927) in Frederick Burwick and Paul Douglass, eds., *The Crisis in Modernism: Bergson and the Vitalist Controversy* (Cambridge: Cambridge University Press, 1992), 8.

[566] Rogers, *Matter of Revolution*, 1.

[567] Ibid., 212.

of mechanistic philosophy...those thinkers who we most associate with advancing this new worldview, harboured doubts about viewing matter as inherently dead, inert, and insensate."[568] Charles Webster has argued that the vitalism of Renaissance philosopher and botanist Paracelsus undergirded Isaac Newton's thought, arguing that "from the historical point of view it is impossible to disregard the sources of evidence suggesting that non-mechanistic modes of scientific expression remained intellectually challenging...into the age supposedly dominated by the mechanical philosophy."[569]

Lear captures "non-mechanistic modes of...expression" that were neither strictly scientific nor merely "intellectually challenging" but also politically disruptive. Merchant has suggested that vitalism's "religious and political dimensions...had not been emphasized" before the English Civil War, at which time "Paracelsian challenges to authority, orthodoxy, and rationalism were held up as an alternative to both the Aristotelian philosophy taught in the universities and the new mechanical philosophy being discussed at Oxford."[570] Accordingly, *Lear* affords perspective on vitalism during a period when it was not "emphasized" not because it was far from English minds,

---

[568] David Skrbina, *Panpsychism in the West* (Cambridge and London: The MIT Press, 2005), 65-66.

[569] Charles Webster, *From Paracelsus to Newton: Magic and the Making of Modern Science* (Cambridge University Press, 1982), 11.

[570] Merchant, *The Death of Nature*, 123.

but because it was still the hegemonic worldview and did not yet need fully to assert and defend itself.

Divine Right and Bio-omnipotence

The vitalist worldview traditionally bolstered early modern sovereignty via the doctrine of the Divine Right of Kings, the notion that the monarch is divinely appointed to rule at the head of the Chain of Being and not subject to any earthly authority. Because it presupposed that all beings support the divinely appointed monarch, this worldview did not emphasize the distinction between the living and the (in)animate that became decisive in the emergent discourses of mechanism and biopower. The seventeenth-century ideologies of sovereignty and vitalism shared a preoccupation with the properties, capacities, and phenomena peculiar to life; the two became incompatible, however, as sovereignty aligned with biopower while vitalism represented a proliferation of potential lifeforms and definitions of life that were unauthorized by sovereignty and beyond its reach.

Shakespeare dramatized this breakdown of the ideological alliance between sovereignty and vitalism in *The life and death of King Richard the Second* (1597). "Feed not thy sovereign's foe, my gentle earth," Richard commands moments before Bolingbroke usurps him. Registering the skepticism of his listeners—who recognize the Divine Right of Kings but who also recognize the superiority of the usurper's forces—Richard defends his vitalist world-view, which attributes to animals, insects, plants, stones, and the earth itself the capacity for self-motion, sense, and reason. "Mock not my senseless conjuration, lords:/ This earth shall have a feeling and these stones/Prove armed soldiers, ere her native king/Shall falter under foul rebellion's arms" (3.2.23-26). That Richard's stones do not spring up to defend him may signal the delegitimization of sovereign power derived from the vitalistic doctrine of Divine Right.[571] Royalists, however, continued to invoke vitalism to support monarchy through the Civil War, the execution of King Charles I in 1649, and the Restoration that returned his son Charles II to the throne in 1660.

Four decades after the first performances of *Lear*, the Welsh physician and Cavalier poet Henry Vaughan (whose brother Thomas deemed "stupid" anyone who does not "know the Difference between Life and Death") took the pulse of vitalism in a poem called "The Stone" (1650), and it appeared alive and well. The speaker is "shown one day in a strange glass/That busie commerce kept between/God and His creatures, though unseen" (19-21).[572] Such com-

---

[571] According to Richard Halpern, it is no coincidence that "it is when his sovereignty collapses that Richard gains full access to [a] figurative register" characterized by mechanistic tropes, and that after his conjuration of earthly lifeforms fails, "Richard is left only with machines—indeed, imagines himself as mechanism" ("The King's Two Buckets: Kantorowicz, *Richard II*, and Fiscal Trauerspiel," *Representations*, vol. 106, no. 1 [Spring 2009]: 67-76; 72).

[572] See M.H. Abrams, ed., *The Norton Anthology of English Literature*

merce refers to life itself. As Eugene Thacker has noted, in medieval and early modern thought, "the concept of life was caught somewhere within the relation between Creator and creature, with the concept of life denoting both the concrete manifestations of living beings, as well as the abstract principle by which living beings are living."[573]

Seeing what was "unseen"—namely, that life is everywhere, that everything is alive—paralyzes the speaker, who characterizes life by its capacity to witness and so no longer knows "where to act, that none shall know,/Where I shall have no cause to fear?/An eye or ear" (2-4). The speaker fears that her or his "dark designs" will be witnessed by "dumb creatures" and "things," which unlike human witnesses, cannot be silenced by bribery. "They hear, see, speak,/And into loud discoveries break,/As loud as blood. Not that God needs/Intelligence, whose spirit feeds/All things with life" (22-26). "Hence sand and dust/Are shak'd for witnesses, and stones/Which some think dead, shall all at once/With one attesting voice detect/Those secret sins we least suspect" (37-41). As in *Lear*, it is not the actual spontaneous animation of creatures and things but rather their imagined potential for life that gives seventeenth-century vitalism its force.

(New York: Norton, 1993). See also Thomas Calhoun, *Henry Vaughan: The Achievement of the Silex Scintillans* (New Jersey: Associated University Presses, Inc. 1981).

[573] Eugene Thacker, *After Life* (Chicago: University of Chicago Press, 2010), 98; 159. The King James Bible is sensitive to this ambiguity, translating *ktiseos* as both "creature" and "creation."

Vaughan's poem alludes to the Old Testament book of Ecclesiastes, which interweaves discourses of vitalism and sovereignty in a warning that even those who curse the king in private are still witnessed by creatures and things. Mid-seventeenth-century biblical exegetes glossed this as a topically relevant admonition against treason, concurring that it is dangerous to oppose the king even secretly, since "God can reveal it by brute creatures; birds, and beasts; by inanimate creatures...Yea, we say, walls, and hedges have ears. And consider the discovery of our hellish Powder-plot."[574] It is less important that the locution "we say" betrays a belief that vitalistic attributions of life (as witnessing-capacity) to inanimate creatures and things are metaphorical figures of speech not to be taken literally; it matters more that "we say" reflects a conventional consensus that, whether they believed it or not, Anglican subjects were expected to act and live in the world *as if* everything were alive.

Notwithstanding such consensus, the vitalist worldview did not neatly align with any one political affiliation or religious creed in seventeenth-century England, where it chafed against the ideology of sovereignty as often as it was invoked to support it. In the 1660s, for instance, Margaret Cavendish challenged those who maintained that animals and vegetables are the only things in nature ani-

---

[574] John Richardson, James Ussher, and Thomas Gataker, *Choice observations and explanations upon the Old Testament* (London, 1655), 330-331.

mated with life, "since Nature consists of a commixture of animate and inanimate matter, and is self-moving, there can be no part or particle…were it an Atome, that may be call'd Inanimate, by reason there is none that has not its share of animate, as well as inanimate matter, and the commixture of these degrees being so close, it is impossible one should be without the other."[575] Cavendish claimed that empirical observation, not religious or political beliefs, led her to conclude that life is "self-moving, sensible and rational, as well as material."[576] Nevertheless, any theory of life in seventeenth-century England was inevitably political. Cavendish was a Royalist, but she espoused vitalism when it no longer unambiguously aligned with the interests of the monarch; and though she never explicitly called for a reorganization of political sovereignty to correspond with her vitalist ontology, that potential inheres in her work.[577]

Like Cavendish, William Harvey, the physician of King Charles I, was a dedicated Royalist whose vitalism vexed the ideology of sovereignty. In *De Motu Cordis* (1628), his study of the heart's movement, Harvey reiterated the commonplace that the heart is the life-source of living creatures, just as the king, analogously conceived as the heart

---

[575] Cavendish, *Observations upon experimental philosophy*, "To the Reader."
[576] Ibid., 233.
[577] Rogers has remarked that Cavendish and William Harvey "were committed Royalists, before and after the Civil Wars, and could not have displayed less interest in seeing the extension of their 'liberal' visions of material organization into corresponding prescriptions for a liberal political state" (*The Matter of Revolution*, 14).

of the body politic, is the life-source of the common-wealth. "*The Heart* of creatures is the foundation of life," Harvey declared in the dedication to Charles, "the Prince of all, the Sun of their Microcosm, on which all vegetation does depend, from whence all vigor and strength does flow. Likewise the King is the...*Heart* of his Common-Wealth, from whence all power and mercy proceeds."[578]

Harvey again construed the heart as the body's central-ized life-source in *De Circulatione Sanguinis* (1628), his study of blood circulation first published the same year as *De Motu Cordis*. In the 1649 version, however, Harvey reimag-ined the blood as the life-source itself rather than as the mere conduit of the heart's vitality.[579] Rogers has suggested a correlation between Harvey's decentralization of the life-source from the heart to the blood and the decentraliza-tion of political agency in seventeenth-century England. It seems more than coincidental, in other words, that Harvey first declared the body's life-source to be decentralized the same year that Charles I was executed and the monarchy temporarily suspended.[580]

Thomas Hobbes was more explicit than Harvey about the difficult interplay between the ideologies of vitalism

[578] William Harvey, *The Anatomical Exercises, De Motu Cordis and De Circulatione Sanguinis in English Translation*, ed. Geoffrey Keynes (New York: Dover Publications, 1995), vii.
[579] Ibid., 170. Rogers has remarked that by midcentury, "Harvey appears to have applied to his understanding of the human body the principal tenets of vitalism" (*Matter of Revolution*, 20).
[580] Rogers, *Matter of Revolution*, 214.

and sovereignty. In *Leviathan* (1651), he mocked the vitalistic attribution of purposiveness to inanimate objects derived from Aristotelian physics, which, as Shapin has noted, was modeled on biology and which employed "explanatory categories similar to those used to comprehend living things."[581] Hobbes' mechanistic critique of the biological character of Aristotelian physics informed his theory of absolutist sovereignty, which does not stop at mechanizing inanimate bodies. *Leviathan* begins with the infamous claims that human "life is but a motion of the limbs," and that "*sovereignty* is an artificial *soul*, [which gives] life and motion to the whole body" of the commonwealth.[582]

The notion that sovereignty gives life not only to the body politic but also to the human bodies that constitute it appears more concretely in Hobbes' discussion of freedom and liberty, which "signifieth (properly) the absence of opposition...and may be applied no less to irratio-

---

[581] Shapin, *The Scientific Revolution*, 29. "For that reason one may loosely refer to such traditional views of matter as 'animistic,' attributing soul-like properties (the Latin anima means soul) to natural objects and processes."

[582] J.C.A. Gaskin, introduction to *Leviathan*, ed. J.C.A. Gaskin (Oxford and New York: Oxford University Press, 2008), 7. This corroborates Foucault's thesis that before the seventeenth century, "[f]or millennia, man remained what he was for Aristotle: a living animal with the additional capacity for political existence; [whereas] modern man is an animal whose politics places his existence as a living being into question" ("Right of Death and Power over Life," *The Foucault Reader*, 265).

nal, and inanimate creatures, than to rational."[583] Hobbes remarked that people are "absurd" to demand liberty, "if we take "liberty [as] an exemption from laws," because such liberty would make "all other men…masters of their lives."[584] Because laws are necessary to protect life, Hobbes argued, "[t]he liberty of a subject" can consist "only in those things, which in regulating their actions, the sovereign hath praetermitted: such as liberty…to choose their own abode, their own diet, [and] their own trade of life."[585]

The tradeoff of such curtailed liberty is the preservation of the subject's life, which the sovereign protects from the potential violence of other subjects. But such truncated liberty also leaves subjects vulnerable to violence sanctioned by the sovereign or the state. Hobbes insisted that "the sovereign power of life and death, is [n]either abolished, [n]or limited" by the subject's liberty because "nothing the sovereign representative can do to a subject, on what pretence soever, can properly be called injustice, or injury; because every subject is author of every act the sovereign doth."[586] The sovereign power of life and death is authorized by those subject to it, which becomes problematic when sovereignty seeks to represent, and exercise power over, subjects incapable of such authorization.

Bruno Latour has suggested that Hobbes' theory of

---

[583] Hobbes, *Leviathan*, 139.

[584] Ibid.

[585] Ibid.

[586] Ibid, 141.

absolute sovereignty, like the new mechanistic worldview, hinged on the belief that bodies and things are inanimate, because to regard matter as inherently (if potentially) living or vital, Hobbes thought, was to dissipate the authority otherwise consolidated in the sovereign, the commonwealth, or the state.[587] "Inanimate things," according to Hobbes, such "as a church, an hospital, a bridge, may be personated by a rector, master, or overseer. But things inanimate, cannot be authors, nor therefore give authority to their actors."[588] During the seventeenth-century rise of rationalism, which increasingly characterized life that is human and worth living by its capacity for reason, irrational living creatures were reductively grouped with inanimate things. Hobbes thus extended his argument about a church, hospital, and bridge to "children, fools, and madmen that have no use of reason, [who] may be personated by guardians… but can be no authors…of any action done by them," until

---

[587] Ventriloquizing Hobbes, Latour remarked that egalitarian radical groups such as the Levellers and the Diggers are most dangerous "when they invoke the active powers of matter and the free interpretation of the Bible in order to disobey their legitimate princes." Accordingly, "[i]nert and mechanical matter is as essential to civil peace as a purely symbolic interpretation of the Bible. In both cases, it behooves us to avoid at all costs the possibility that the factions may invoke a higher Entity—Nature or God—which the Sovereign does not fully control" (*We Have Never Been Modern*, trans. Catherine Porter [Cambridge, Massachusetts: Harvard University Press, 1991], 19).

[588] Hobbes, *Leviathan*, 108.

they are judged to be "reasonable."[589] On the one hand, *Leviathan* appears to dehumanize, thingify, and devitalize subjects deemed irrational. On the other hand, it may be read to humanize through personification things deemed inanimate.[590] In either case, the unauthorized personifications of (in)animate things in *Lear* represent a metatheatrical correlate of Shakespeare's authorization of actors to represent the potentially (non)rational lives of madmen, fools, suicides, those that are too young, and those that are too old. Four decades after the first performance of Lear, Hobbes suggested that "such things cannot be person-

---

[589] Ibid.

[590] See Samantha Frost, *Lessons from a Materialist Thinker: Hobbesian Reflections on Ethics and Politics* (Stanford: Stanford University Press, 2008). According to Frost's New Materialist reading, Hobbes' reduction of human life to matter-in-motion does not devitalize human life but rather recognizes the vitality of bodies. She argues that Hobbes conceived "some forms of matter…as alive or thoughtful without the liveliness or capacity for thought somehow 'added' onto an inert substrate" ("Fear and The Illusion of Autonomy," *New Materialisms*, 159-160). Frost grants that regarding human life as absolutely embodied risks limiting subjects to determined, mechanical actions, but only insofar as matter is seen as inherently lifeless. Contrariwise, to preserve an immaterial component of the human being such as Descartes' disembodied res cogitans is to interpellate a subject capable of acting unilaterally on otherwise inert matter, thereby encouraging what Frost calls "the illusion of individual autonomous agency" (*New Materialisms*, 160). Instead, recognizing matter's inherent vitality reveals "the impossibility of self-sovereignty" and compels us to accept that "our interdependence is the condition for our effective actions," that true agency emerges not from autonomy but rather from heteronomy.

ated, before there be some state of civil government."[591]
Set amidst a fictional war and a crisis of sovereignty, then,
the vitalist personifications in *Lear* represent both a timely
challenge to James' aspirational bio-omnipotence and a
preemptive contestation of the absolute sovereignty later
codified by Hobbes.

The emergent form of sovereignty depicted in *Lear*
shares with vitalism its attention to phenomena peculiar
to life; it requires living bodies as subjects, hence its interest in the conditions of longevity, its renegotiation of
capital punishment, and its prohibition of suicide, all of
which Shakespeare dramatizes through characters whose
lives appear absolutely subject to biopower. Kent, for
instance, stakes his life between Lear's wrath and Cordelia:
"answer my life my judgment," he implores Lear, and in
the exchange that follows, Kent's life becomes thingified
"as a pawn" in a game, the primary object of which is to
protect the king's life at all costs. Lear rages, "Kent, on
thy life, no more." Kent replies, "My life I never held but
as a pawn to wage against thy enemies; nor fear to lose it,
thy safety being the motive" (1.144-146).[592] Speaking as the
interim sovereign at the end of the play, Albany decides
that "we will resign, during the life of this old majesty, to

---

[591] Hobbes, *Leviathan*, 108.

[592] This aligns with the "power of life and death" described by
Foucault, which "was not an absolute privilege [but] was conditioned
by the defense of the sovereign, and his own survival" ("Right of
Death and Power over Life," *Foucault Reader*, 258).

him [Lear] our absolute power; [*to EDGAR and KENT*] you to your rights" (24.292-294). This is little more than a symbolic gesture given that Lear is on death's doorstep, and Albany does not announce what will become of the "rights" of Edgar and Kent to live and die once Lear passes and Albany arrogates "absolute power" once again.

As a counterpoint to such representations of absolute power over life, the play repeatedly depicts life as it eludes the sovereign's reach. This occurs both thematically and rhetorically; in the latter case, where characters' empty oaths evacuate "life" of any determinate meaning. Gonoril, for instance, swears that she loves Lear "no less than life" (1.50), and as Edmund frames Edgar with a counterfeit letter intimating patricide, he tells their father Gloucester, "I dare pawn down my life for him he hath wrote this to feel my affection to your honour" (2.80-82), which is a lie since it was Edmund who composed it. Such rhetorical indetermination of "life" was already at play in the anonymous version of *Leir* that served as one of Shakespeare's sources, as was the discourse of biopower that dramatized suicide, state-sanctioned murder, life-prolongation, and decisions about the worthiness of certain lives to live.[593]

Shakespeare's revision of the earlier play is more critical of biopower, and it articulates the underside of the sovereign power to let live and foster life, namely, the power to make live and to prevent from dying. As James Shapiro

---

[593] Anon, *King Leir*, ed. Tiffany Stern (London: Nick Hern Books, 2002).

has remarked, the title page of Shakespeare's printed *Lear* "distinguish[es] the new play from the old one by emphasizing that it is about both the lives *and* the deaths of Lear and his three daughters."[594] Daniel Juan Gil has suggested that *Lear* concludes "with raw matter that is animated and yet is not fully captured by the sovereign power that imposes stable socio-symbolic identities."[595] Gil has found this animate "raw matter" epitomized by "the final tableau of (socially) dead but (biologically) living bodies with which the play ends."[596] In addition to the raw animate matter of human bodies, however, *Lear* confronts us with an array of nonliving things imagined to possess vitality. These things may not spring to life in the way that characters hope, but their very inertia produces effects, moving human actors to act, and moving spectators to feel, what they might not act or feel in a world regarded as dead.

---

[594] James Shapiro, *The Year of Lear: Shakespeare in 1606* (New York: Simon & Schuster, 2015), 49.

[595] Gil, *Shakespeare's Anti-Politics*, 122.

[596] Ibid., 122.

Gloucester's Beard

The play's latent vitalism surfaces on scene when Regan and Cornwall torture Gloucester.[597] Cornwall finds himself constrained by the law, or rather by a failure to give murder the appearance of legality, recognizing that without absolute sovereignty he lacks the right to take Gloucester's life. "Though well we may not pass upon his life without the form of justice," Cornwall reasons, "yet our power shall do a courtesy to our wrath, which men may blame, but not control" (14.22-25). In other words, it is reprehensible but not illegal to torture Gloucester, a loophole Cornwall uses to satisfy his "revenge" (12.1) and "displeasure" (14.4). Before gouging out one of Gloucester's eyes, Regan plucks his white beard, which like Lear's beard, recurs throughout the play as a no-longer-venerated symbol of old age.

At the nadir of vulnerability and impotence, Gloucester conjures his uprooted beard to thwart the transgression of the laws of hospitality and veneration of the old. "Naughty lady," he chides Regan, "these hairs, which thou dost ravish from my chin, will quicken, and accuse thee: I am your host: with robbers' hands my hospitable favours you should not ruffle thus. What will you do?" (14.35-

---

[597] Gil remarks "a strange, luminous quality" in this scene, "because it points to a transformed foundation for common life; namely the flesh that is the precondition of any functioning sovereign power, and that Cornwall makes visible by losing his temper on the body of Gloucester" (*Shakespeare's Anti-Politics*, 116).

39).[598] Gloucester's conjuration fails in that his plucked hairs do not "quicken" or come to life to "accuse" Regan; but the plea arguably succeeds in rousing Regan's servant to intervene on Gloucester's behalf, breaking the law of obedience by killing his master Cornwall in adherence to a different bond—one grounded in a concept of shared life that is both no longer and not yet articulate—whose alliances are yet unformed and whose limits remain indeterminate enough to include the potential life of (in)animate things.

To be sure, the servant does not react immediately to Gloucester's vitalist plea but rather, it seems, in response to Gloucester's second, more anthropocentric appeal: "He that will think to live till he be old give me some help!" (14.66-67). The vitalistic hope that matter will spring to life gives way to the paradigm of longevity as a model for human action, according to which virtue is rewarded with long life and vice punished with short life. Another servant

---

[598] That Gloucester's vitalism arises from the violation of his "hospitable favours" recalls a similarly latent vitalism in Shakespeare's *Macbeth*, where en route to kill the king the eponymous character hesitates because he is Duncan's "host, who should against the murderer shut the door not bear the knife myself." Feeling guilty for being a regicide and a bad host, Macbeth observes that in his half of the world "nature seems dead," and yet he commands the "sure and firm-set earth" not to hear his "steps which way they walk, for fear/ Thy very stones prate of my whereabout" (2.1.56-58). The stones do not prate (loudly enough) to save Duncan from Macbeth's knife, but the belief that they might continues to haunt Macbeth with the anticipation of vitalistic justice: "It will have blood, they say. Blood will have blood./Stones have been known to move, and trees to speak" (3.4.121-122).

standing by submits that if Regan "live long and in the end meet the old course of death, women will all turn monsters" (14.97-99). The emphasis remains on life's length in relation to virtue or vice, with the implication that if one as evil as Regan should reach old age, then all women, presumably desiring long life, will follow her bad example to be rewarded in kind.

Fatally wounded, Cornwall slays the rebellious servant and then removes the prisoner's remaining eye. "Out, vile jelly! Where is thy lustre now?" he asks Gloucester, who reasserts rather than abandons his vitalistic hope: "All dark and comfortless. Where's my son Edmund? Edmund, enkindle all the sparks of nature, to quit this horrid act" (14.80-84). After Gloucester is avenged not by his beard but rather by Cornwall's servant (apparently inspired by the beard's personification), his second conjuration recognizes that vitalist potential must be actualized by human practice. The performance of Gloucester's torture finally represents a "form of justice" beyond the cynical sense in which Cornwall uses that phrase (i.e., justice as a façade for murder). Gloucester's beard fails to quicken quickly enough to prevent his enucleation, but the scene depicts vitalism's success in failure, where the suggestion of material vitality, succeeded by an appeal to common life that is worth preserving, inspires the servant to act.

The subtle work performed by the vitalism in this scene, and in Shakespeare's play more generally, is brought into sharper focus by its absence in the 1681 "Reviv'd"

King Lear authored by Nahum Tate, who was born the year the Civil Wars ended and named poet laureate of England in 1692. Tate disregarded Shakespeare's portrayal of latent vitality as a failure of representation,[599] which accords with his omission of Gloucester's beard from the torture scene. Shakespeare's characters personify the vitality of things amidst a crisis of sovereignty that is exacerbated, if not enacted in the first place, by the proliferation of unauthorized personifications. By contrast, because Tate sought to reinforce rather than deconstruct the ideology of absolute sovereign biopower, his *Lear* reduces material vitality to mere metaphor.

Where Edgar and Cordelia never exchange words in Shakespeare's play, for example, Tate's Cordelia amorously entices Edgar into her arms, an action that belies her virtue as Shakespeare represents it. "Is't possible?" Tate's Edgar wonders, to which Cordelia responds with a vitiated, bathetic simulacrum of vitalism: "By the dear Vital Stream that baths my Heart, these hallow'd Rags of Thine, and naked Vertue, these abject Tassels, these fantastick Shreds (Ridiculous ev'n to the meanest Clown) to me are dearer

---

[599] He described *Lear* as "a Heap of Jewels, unstrung and unpolisht; yet so dazling in their Disorder," and as a "Heap of Flow'rs" grown in Shakespeare's "soil" yet lacking the arrangement needed to activate its potential virtue. This compels Tate to interject scenes to provide the play with an organizing principle: "Why shou'd these Scenes lie hid, in which we find/What may at Once divert and teach the Mind?" Tate asks, invoking the Roman poet Horace's dictum that poetry should "instruct and delight," which Shakespeare's *Lear*, in Tate's view, fails to do ("Dedicatory Epistle").

than the richest Pomp of purple Monarchs" (3.2.443-448). By depicting vitality springing unilaterally from Cordelia to the rags, tassels, and shreds, Tate precluded the possibility that these things might have a life of their own. Tate's *Lear* took precedence on the stage for more than a century and a half, in part because audiences could not stomach the final heap of bodies in Shakespeare's version that seemed gratuitous to many,[600] including the eighteenth-century author and critic Samuel Johnson, who wrote of Shakespeare's *Lear*:

> A play in which the wicked prosper, and the
> virtuous miscarry, may doubtless be good,
> because it is a just representation of the
> common events of human life: but since all
> reasonable beings naturally love justice, I cannot
> easily be persuaded, that the observation of
> justice makes a play worse; or, that if other
> excellencies are equal, the audience will not
> always rise better pleased from the final triumph
> of persecuted virtue.[601]

---

[600] Nahum Tate, *The History of King Lear* (London: Cornmarket Press, 1969). See also Peter L. Sharkey, "Performing Nahum Tate's King Lear: Coming Hither by Going Hence," *QJS* 54, 4 (December 1968): 398-403; 400; Steven Urkowitz, *Shakespeare's Revision of "King Lear"* (Princeton: Princeton Univ. Press, 1980); Christopher Spencer, "A Word for Tate's *King Lear*," *SEL* 3, 2 (Spring 1969): 241-51; Nahum Tate (New York: Twayne, 1972).

[601] Arthur Sherbo, ed., *Johnson on Shakespeare*, in *The Yale Edition of the Works of Samuel Johnson*, vol. 8 (New Haven: Yale University Press, 1968), 659-705.

Johnson approved of Shakespeare's realism for its "just representation" of injustice, that is, but he censured what he saw as the play's failure to make justice observable. According to Maynard Mack, "eighteenth-century *King Lears* with their benign ending were perhaps the natural product of an age which held that under the appearances of things lay an order of justice which it was the job of literature to imitate, not to hide."[602] Shakespeare's *Lear* does in fact imitate rather than hide an order of justice, but because that order is linked to a residual vitalism latent within emergent world orders competing to replace it, its imitation required (the representation of) concealment, recalcitrance, and inaction.[603] Shakespeare's play continually invokes, without staging, the animation of lifeless things alongside the activation of justice for "undivulgèd crimes unwhipped of justice" (9.51-52). The inertia—or apathy—of Gloucester's beard and the demise of virtuous characters do not represent the failure of justice (or the successful portrayal of injustice) in Shakespeare's *Lear*; they gesture rather toward a "form of justice" that counteracts the absolutization of sovereign biopower by personifying inanimate things whose life remains virtual and hence difficult to capture.

---

[602] Maynard Mack, *King Lear in Our Time* (Berkeley and Los Angeles: University of California Press, 1972), 25.

[603] See James Shapiro, *The Year of Lear*, 52. "Call it what you will—resistance, refusal, denial, rejection, repudiation—this insistent and almost apocalyptic negativity becomes a recurring drumbeat, the bass line of the play."

The Unpublished Virtues of the Earth

Lear stages virtue—both the moral quality of persons and the inherent capacity or property of things to produce effects—as an unpublished latency that not everyone is able or authorized to declare. In the play's opening scene, Burgundy abandons his courtship of Cordelia after Lear, who has a "will to publish our daughters' several dowers" (*The Tragedy*, 1.41-42), excludes her from his will. The King of France, by contrast, recognizes Cordelia as "herself a dowry" (1.229). When Cordelia's silence prompts Lear to wish that she had never been born, France asks, "is it no more but this—a tardiness in nature, that often leaves the history unspoke that it intends to do?" (1.224-226). In light of the play's vitalist context, France's recognition of Cordelia's inner virtue—"thee and thy virtues here I seize upon" (1.240)—evokes the specialized knowledge of the Paracelsian physician who discovers the hidden medicinal virtues of plants and herbs by reading the "exterior and visible" signs that indicate "their internal virtue, which has been given to them by heaven as a natural dowry."[604] That Cordelia's dowry remains unpublished signals for France the latency rather than the lifelessness of nature, which Cordelia discovers again in scene 18.

Scene 18 proleptically complicates Lear's decision that Cordelia is "dead as earth" by drawing attention to the earth's latent vitality. Embroiled in war, at the French camp

---

[604] Quoted in Foucault, *The Order of Things*, 30.

near Dover, Cordelia organizes a search party for Lear, who is reportedly too ashamed to show himself. Where in *The History* Cordelia enters with a doctor and others, in *The Tragedy* she enters with a gentleman and soldiers.[605] This crucial discrepancy calls attention to the decentralization of seventeenth-century sovereignty as it is displaced from the political theology of the divinely appointed monarch to the medical expertise of doctors, to the social authority of gentlemen, and to the sheer power of soldiers.[606] Cordelia orders the others to "search every acre in the high-grown field" for her father, whom she last saw camouflaged and "crowned with rank fumiter and furrow weeds, with bur-docks, hemlock, nettles, cuckoo-flowers, darnel, and all the idle weeds that grow in our sustaining corn" (18.3-5).[607] Such flora—unlike Ophelia's "rosemary,

---

[605] Greenblatt et al., eds., *The Norton Shakespeare*, 2446-2447.

[606] This distribution of sovereignty corroborates Agamben's argument that the integration of medicine and politics constitutes "one of the essential characteristics of modern biopolitics," according to which "the sovereign decision on bare life comes to be displaced from strictly political motivations and areas to a more ambiguous terrain in which the physician and the sovereign seem to exchange roles" (*Homo Sacer*, 143). Lear appears to resist this displacement even as he abdicates, provoking Kent to equate his banishment with Lear's killing his "physician" (1.150).

[607] Shakespeare cites Cordelia's list of idle weeds almost verbatim but in reverse in *Henry V* (1600), also in the context of Anglo-French hostility. In that play's final scene, where the victorious Henry lays out the conditions of peace before the French royal palace, a bitter Duke of Burgundy complains that war has devastated "this best garden of the world our fertile France," leaving its hedges

that's for remembrance" and "pansies, that's for thoughts" in *Hamlet*—seem on the surface to do nothing. That they are "idle weeds" suggests both that they grow without human labor and that they are useless, possessing no active properties or virtues. The "idle weeds" represent the vegetative or nutritive lifeforms that grow autonomously and cannot easily be instrumentalized by sovereignty because, unlike "our sustaining corn," they do not participate in the human-ordered hierarchy of things.

Cordelia initially fails to see that the latent virtues of the "idle weeds" with which Lear is "crowned" are, as her metaphor betrays, key to restoring Lear's sovereignty. She asks the doctor how "man's wisdom" (18.8) might restore Lear, but the doctor shifts focus from human power back toward the "foster-nurse of nature" and the "many simples operative, whose power will close the eye of anguish" (18.12-16). Lear just needs "repose" (18.12), the doctor says, which can be "provoke[d]" (18.13) with "simples" (herbal medicines) that are "operative" (active or capable of acting). Cordelia describes them as "unpublish'd" (18.17),

---

untrimmed like the "wildly overgrown" hair of prisoners. "The darnel, hemlock and rank fumitory" take root in the arable land, Burgundy complains, "while that the coulter rusts that should deracinate such savagery." The fallow land, which once yielded "freckled cowslip, burnet and green clover," now "conceives by idleness and nothing teems but hateful docks, rough thistles, kecksies, burs, losing both beauty and utility" (*Henry V*, 5.2.36-53). Remarkably, in both *Henry V* and *Lear* it is the character Burgundy who fails to recognize latent virtue when it is not conspicuously marked with a signature or accompanied by an external dowry.

but these potentially operative virtues became more widely legible through seventeenth-century herbals such as medical reformer Nicholas Culpeper's *The English Physitian* (1652), a catalogue of natural remedies to preserve readers' health and cure their diseases "for three pence charge, and with such things only as grow in England."[608]

With the doctor's knowledge at her command, Cordelia personifies the earth to summon its hidden power: "All blest secrets, all you unpublish'd virtues of the earth,

---

[608] Nicholas Culpeper, *The English Physitian* (London, 1652), frontispiece. Culpeper listed numerous "vertues" for the plants cited by Cordelia. Hemlock, for example, "may safely be applied" to inflammations and tumors "in any part of the Body (save the Privy parts)" (63). Fittingly in the context of *Lear*, where tears and blindness abound, hemlock is also a remedy for swollen, red eyes, and it "is a tried Medicine" for treating certain eye diseases. The juice of nettles, Culpeper advises, acts as an expectorant, cures inflammation and soreness of the mouth and throat, expels kidney stones, cleanses "old rotten and stinking sores, or Fistulaes and Gangrenes," remedies "the stinging of Venemous Creatures," and counteracts the poisonous effects of hemlock, among other active properties (89). Burr leaves are analgesic, good for sciatica, and taken with wine they "wonderfully help the bitings of any Serpents"— which may be useful for Lear, since he knows "how sharper than a serpent's tooth it is to have a thankless child" (4.266-267). Fumitory is "very effectual" for purging obstructions in the liver and spleen, treating jaundice, curing melancholy, clearing eyesight, and "clarifying the Blood" of excessive humors, which early modern medicine held as the root of illness (57). Darnel, like nettle juice, slows gangrene and similar "fretting and eating Cankers, and putrid Sores." Bathing in darnel, Culpepper recommends, "is profitable" for sciatica, the painful spinal condition for which Lear's burr leaves are also indicated as treatment (42-43).

spring with my tears! Be aidant and remediate in the good man's distress! Seek, seek for him; lest his ungovern'd rage dissolve the life that wants the means to lead it" (18.16-21). This potentially legible and operative but latent and unpublished virtue further affiliates scene 18 with the vitalism of Paracelsus, who asserted that "all herbs, plants, trees and other things issuing from the bowels of the earth are so many magic books and signs" that "speak to the curious physician through their signatures, discovering to him…their inner virtues hidden beneath nature's veil of silence."[609] As with Gloucester's beard, what matters is not that the earth actually "spring" to life, but rather that recognizing the potential virtues and vitality of things that are autonomous from the order of "man's wisdom" revitalizes human practice, for example, by tempering the ideology of

---

[609] Foucault, *The Order of Things*, 18. Cordelia's conjuration also aligns with the vitalist worldview to which Jane Bennett, four centuries later, has proposed a return. Specifically, the "virtues of the earth" anticipate Bennett's concept of "vibrant matter," which she defines as "an active, earthy, not-quite-human capaciousness" whose self-organizing energy is not accommodated by a mechanistic account of matter (*Vibrant Matter*, 3). Cordelia's earthly virtues also resemble the "virtue" that Julia Reinhard Lupton has characterized "as both the excellences practiced in civic humanism and as those capacities that subsist in things, whether animal, vegetable, or mineral." The difference between these two kinds of virtue, according to Lupton, is that "political virtues are fundamentally active, existing only in their practice, while vital virtues subsist as latencies and tendencies with the power to burst into flower or die still born" (*Thinking with Shakespeare: Essays on Politics and Life* [Chicago: University of Chicago Press, 2011], 10).

absolute sovereignty and its fantasy of bio-omnipotence.

Cordelia's invocation is a political act that anticipates mid-seventeenth-century English radicals including Richard Overton and Gerrard Winstanley, who according to Rogers figured political revolution "as a vegetabilization of humanity,"[610] as they imagined with myriad "monists, mortalists, and hermeticists" during the English Civil Wars "that the labor required to institute the millennium [was] not human labor only but the labor also of the animal and vegetative forces of nature."[611] In *Fire in the Bush* (1650), for instance, Winstanley critiqued the injustices of private property and enclosure, prophesying that "the spirit of truth" will "fetch Earth up to live in that life, that is a life above objects...the life, that will bring in true community; and destroy murdering propriety."[612] He appealed to "universall Love, which our age calls...pure Reason; or the Seed of life that lies under the clods of Earth."[613] Winstanley shared with Cordelia and Gloucester a glaring disadvantage and impotence in the anthropocentric political order, which may partly explain his pivot from observable human agency toward hidden subterranean sources of action. However, Winstanley also shared with Shake-

---

[610] Rogers, *Matter of Revolution*, 44.

[611] Ibid., 63-4.

[612] Gerrard Winstanley, *Fire in the Bush: the spirit burning, not consuming, but purging mankind, or, the Great Battell of God Almighty, between Michaell, the seed of life, and the great red dragon, the curse fought within the spirit of man* (London: 1650), 5.

[613] Ibid., 5-6.

speare's characters what appears to be a genuine recognition, or attempt to recognize, the reason, intentionality, and subjectivity—in short, the life—of things that were increasingly pronounced dead or inanimate by English authorities.

Like Winstanley's failed political revolution, Cordelia's failure does not quash hopes of future success. The potential for earthly virtues to become published and legible to those other than the sovereign was actualized when seventeenth-century proto-scientists shifted their gaze from texts to what they called the Book of Nature. Harvey, for instance, argued "how unsafe, and degenerate a thing it is, to be tutored by other mens commentaries, without making tryal of the things themselves: especially, since Natures Book is so open, and legible."[614] Such open legibility posed a threat to royal sovereignty, even from within the state-sanctioned laboratories of the Royal Society.[615] Half a century earlier, Shakespeare fabricated subversive agen-

---

[614] William Harvey, *Anatomical exercitations concerning the generation of living creatures* (1653), "The Preface."

[615] Latour has imagined Hobbes' reaction to such challenges to royal absolutism: "And here we are again, Hobbes worries, right in the middle of a civil war! We are no longer to be subjected to the Levellers and Diggers, who challenged the King's authority in the name of their personal interpretation of God and of the properties of matter (they have been properly exterminated), but we are going to have to put up with this new clique of scholars who are going to start challenging everyone's authority in the name of Nature by invoking wholly fabricated laboratory events!" (*We Have Never Been Modern*, 20).

cies in the laboratory of the theater by staging things—including Gloucester's beard, the earth, and the bodies of actors—that fluctuate between life, death, and animacy.[616] In scene 18, however, the vitalistic hope that the earth will spring to life appears to yield to biopower. Under the care of the doctor and Cordelia, Lear survives for a time, but in a play preoccupied with the tragedy of overliving, prolonging Lear's life does not represent a good or virtuous act. Indeed, upon reviving he says as much to Cordelia: "You do me wrong to take me out o' th' grave" (21.43). *Lear* most explicitly articulates biopower's wrongful prolongation of life through Gloucester's thwarted suicide attempt, to which I now turn.

Suicide and Sovereignty

Regan comes to regret Cornwall's self-restraint, if it can be so called, in torturing but not killing Gloucester: "It was great ignorance, Gloucester's eyes being out, to let him live: where he arrives he moves all hearts against us" (19.9-11). She consoles herself, however, that Edmund "is gone, in pity of [Gloucester's] misery, to dispatch his nighted life" (19.9-13). Although for different reasons, Gloucester agrees with Regan that it was wrong to let (or rather to make) him live. Where she worries that as a living martyr Gloucester is a political liability, he wants to end his life

---

[616] For the idea of the stage as a laboratory, see Michael Witmore, *Shakespearean Metaphysics*, 20.

because he cannot "bear it longer" (20.37). Scholars have read Gloucester's stymied suicide as a meta-commentary on theatrical illusion, as a faithful adherence to orthodox ethical and theological injunctions against suicide, and even as a moral exemplum to emulate.[617] I argue that Gloucester's suicide attempt constitutes a political act that elaborates the play's ongoing articulation of sovereignty through the discourses of vitalism and biopower.[618]

En route to the cliffs at Dover, Gloucester encounters Edgar, who is still disguised in speech and garb as Poor Tom. Rather than reveal himself to console his father, Edgar stages an elaborate mock suicide to revive Gloucester's will to live, to "trifle" with his "despair" in order "to cure it" (20.33-34). Edgar's ruse has been read as an expo-

---

[617] Henry S. Pancoast remarked roughly a century ago that "in Lear, more than in all other plays, we are moved and purified by the sense that life itself is tragic. We must accept this mysterious burden of life, this weight of misery that is laid upon us, and we must…'endure' it, until the gods shall give us leave to lay it down" ("Note on King Lear," *Modern Language Notes*, 40, no. 7, [November 1925]: 407). Sean Lawrence has read "the difficulty of dying" in Lear as evidence that the play is not "an existential tragedy" about individual authenticity but rather an "ethical tragedy" primarily concerned with the acknowledgment of others ("The Difficulty of Dying in King Lear," *ESC: English Studies in Canada*, 31, no. 4 [December 2005]: 35-52).
[618] Suicide, according to Foucault, "testified to the individual and private right to die, at the borders and in the interstices of power that was exercised over life. This determination to die…was one of the first astonishments of a society in which political power had assigned itself the task of administering life" ("Right of Death and Power over Life," *Foucault Reader*, 261).

sition of the dramaturgical illusions that are ubiquitous but concealed throughout the play and indeed throughout all plays. Stephen Orgel has argued that because all theater presents the imaginary as real, it follows that "the Dover Cliff scene is a paradigm not simply for Shakespeare's stage, but for all theater."[619] Emily Sun has concurred with Orgel that the scene represents the limits of representation, adding that Dover Cliff, as the geopolitical "bourne of Britain" and "the terminus of the lives of most of the characters," represents "the principle of the limit. The limit Gloucester intends to cross there is that between life and death."[620]

Even if the cliff were "real" in the play—that is, if Edgar were to succeed in deceiving the audience as well as Gloucester with his theatrical illusion, as Harry Levin has suggested[621]—then Gloucester's death would still be a performance by the body of a living actor. Gil has therefore argued that Gloucester's failed suicide "puts his body in a state of suspended animation,"[622] while reflecting "a fact about the medium, the theater, in which a strange, ineradi-

---

[619] Stephen Orgel, "Shakespeare Imagines a Theater," *Poetics Today*, vol. 5, no. 3, Medieval and Renaissance Representation: New Reflections (1984): 549-561; 557.

[620] Emily Sun, *Succeeding King Lear: Literature, Exposure, and the Possibility of Politics* (Fordham University Press, 2010), 67.

[621] Harry Levin, "The Heights and the Depths: A Scene from *King Lear*," in *Shakespeare and the Revolution of the Times* (New York: Oxford University Press, 1958 [1976]): 162-186.

[622] Gil, *Shakespeare's Anti-Politics*, 117.

cable life within the character is aligned with the life that emanates from…the dimension of the real world in which characters are really actors playing parts."[623] Shakespeare's meta-theatrical representation of Gloucester's suicide attempt establishes critical distance between the staged action and audience's reaction, while it disarticulates the performance of life from the biological life of the performer.

This de-alignment draws attention away from Edgar's power over Gloucester, toward Shakespeare's dramaturgical authority over his characters, and back again. However subliminally it is experienced, this oscillation between layers of illusion provokes the audience to participate in decentered sovereign decisions about what actually lives and what only seems to be alive. Where Gloucester's earlier prosopopoeia raises questions about the animacy of his beard, Edgar's filial exercise of biopower—which inverts Bodin's advice to reinstitute *parents'* power of life and death over their children—raises questions about whether the characters themselves are alive or dead. "If Edgar live," Gloucester wavers with dramatic irony on the imagined precipice, "O, bless him!" (20.40). As Gloucester jumps toward what he expects will be his death, Edgar wonders how mere thoughts can drive one to suicide considering that life inevitably ends on its own: "I know not how conceit may rob the treasury of life, when life itself

---

[623] Ibid., 118.

yields to the theft: had he been where he thought, by this, had thought been past. Alive or dead? Ho, you sir! Friend! Hear you, sir! Speak! Thus might he pass indeed: yet he revives. What are you sir?" (20.42-48).[624]

From the perspective of a culture that privileges the sanctity and preservation of life, it is not immediately clear why Edgar's well-intended cure poses a political as well as a dramaturgical problem. But Edgar fails or refuses to accept Gloucester's express and persistent wish to die, inveigling the old man to see that "life's a miracle" (20.55). And yet Gloucester shows that life is not (only) a miracle but also a theatrical performance, a state hardly distinguishable from death, characterized by "wretchedness," and subject to biopower. Edgar may have virtuous intentions—he later reaffirms his conviction that even a life burdened by pain and knowledge of mortality is worth living: "O, our lives' sweetness! That we the pain of death would hourly die rather than die at once!" (24.180-182). However, Edgar is blind to his father's experience of life, the individuality of which is obfuscated by the plurality of "our lives." When he first sees his father led by another old man, Edgar

---

[624] Compare with Trinculo's similar inquiry of Caliban ("a man or a fish? dead or alive?"). Again, Caliban's earthliness, signaling an earthly form of bare life, renders him subject to Prospero's sovereignty to a greater degree than the non-"autochthonous" shipwrecked Europeans. Gloucester's suicide attempt likewise renders his life bare and ontologically ambiguous. Both Prospero and Edgar exercise power not by letting Caliban and Gloucester live but by making them live.

acknowledges the allure of suicide—"World, world, O world! But that thy strange mutations make us hate thee, life would not yield to age"—but even here he imagines that life should be prolonged indefinitely, that not even old age would kill, if only the world's "strange mutations" did not make us, or rather the subject "life," give way.

Denied the right to end his own suffering, Gloucester asks, "is wretchedness deprived that benefit, to end itself by death? 'Twas yet some comfort, when misery could beguile the tyrant's rage, and frustrate his proud will" (20.61-64). Gloucester refers not to the personified abstraction of death, which was frequently described as a tyrant in medieval funerary poetry.[625] The tyranny he wishes to beguile is rather the biopower that was first exercised by Regan and Cornwall, who tortured him but "let him live," and which is now exercised by Edgar, who makes him live by preventing his suicide. Such tyranny was recognizable to seventeenth-century English audiences, who were routinely reminded by state and church authorities of the prohibition against suicide.[626]

---

[625] Joshua Scodel, *The English Poetic Epitaph: Commemoration and Conflict from Jonson to Wordsworth* (Ithaca and London: Cornell University Press, 1991), 213.

[626] Legal author Michael Dalton, for instance, voices the hegemonic view in early modern England when he condemns "the heinousness" of suicide as "an offence against God, against King, and against Nature" (*The Countrey Justice: Containing the Practice of the Justices of the Peace* [London, 1655], 297). Punishments for suicide were rarely enforced before 1500 and after 1660, as Michael MacDonald has observed, while early-seventeenth-century England witnessed "[t]

Edgar prevails, temporarily convincing Gloucester to "bear affliction till it do cry out itself 'enough, enough,' and die" (20.75-77). But Edgar fails to allow Gloucester the "benefit" of *euthanasia*, and readings of the scene fail if they fail to recognize that Gloucester is not the author of his resolution to live. Gloucester's survival is not a virtuous act performed autonomously by his reformed character but rather an exercise of the tyrannical biopower to which he is subject.

"Away, and let me die" (20.48), Gloucester begs Edgar, as if speaking on behalf of all the characters who are deprived of the right to die. It is worth remarking that Spenser's version of the Lear story in *The Faerie Queene* (1596) concludes with Cordelia's suicide. She restores the crown to Lear, who eventually dies of old age and returns sovereignty back to her. Cordelia rules for a "long time" until the children of Goneril and Regan mature, rebel, and imprison her, where, "weary of that wretched life, her selfe she hong."[627] At the close of Shakespeare's play, by contrast, Edmund reveals the plot "to hang Cordelia in the prison, and to lay the blame upon her own despair, that she fordid herself" (24.248-250). On one reading, Shakespeare arguably saves Cordelia's virtue by preserving her as one

---

he era of greatest severity toward self-murder...the product of concatenated political and religious changes" (John Sym, *Lifes Preservative Against Self-Killing* [1637], ed., Michael MacDonald [London and New York: Routledge, 1998], xi).

[627] Spenser, *The Faerie Queene*, II.x.32.

who chooses life over death.[628] Read alongside Gloucester's prohibited suicide, however, Shakespeare's revision
arguably makes a virtue of Cordelia's death, where prolonging her life would have been the real injustice.

Moments after Gloucester resolves to live, Lear arrives
on scene to reclaim sovereignty. "I am the King himself"
(20.83-84), he declares, but his notion of kingship has
undergone a sea-change following at least two correlated
realizations: that nature eludes his dominion—"the thun-
der would not peace at my bidding" (20.99-100)—and
that he is mortal, which flatterers had formerly concealed
from him: "They told me I was everything; 'tis a lie, I am
not ague-proof" (20.101-102).[629] Despite these revela-
tions, Lear's sovereign identity is revived when Glouces-

---

[628] Reading *Lear* through the lens of his own historical moment, for
instance, R.W. Chambers noted in a lecture from November 1939
that "the message has been smuggled out of Concentration Camps:
'You will be told that I committed suicide: it will not be true.' The
sender of the message has wished to save his reputation from what
he feels would be a slur upon it…Shakespeare feels this about
Cordelia" (*King Lear*, The First W.P. Ker Memorial Lecture Delivered
at the University of Glasgow, 22-23).

[629] The latter insight constitutes a collapse of the separation of the
king's two bodies—the idea that the sovereign has both a natural
body that lives and dies and a symbolic body that survives the
succession of rulers—which according to Agamben (following
Kantorowicz), "culminates in the principle so often repeated by
medieval jurists that 'dignity never dies' (dignitas non moritur, Le
roi ne meurt jamais [the king never dies])" (Agamben, *Remnants of
Auschwitz*, 66-67).

ter recognizes his voice as that of the king. Having just established that natural phenomena are beyond his control, however, Lear shifts his gaze to the phenomena of human life, where he intends to reinstitute his rule.

With his resuscitated sense of sovereignty, Lear first imagines pardoning an adulterer whose crime is punishable by death: "When I do stare, see how the subject quakes! I pardon that man's life. What was thy cause? Adultery? Thou shalt not die: die for adultery! No: the wren goes to 't, and the small gilded fly does lecher in my sight" (20.105-109). Although he has not yet recognized him, the man whose life Lear imagines pardoning may indeed be Gloucester, whom the play's opening dialogue establishes as a fornicator and possibly an adulterer. In this case, on the heels of Edgar's dubious lifesaving ploy, Lear's pardon appears less than merciful, because, again, Gloucester does not want to live. Lear justifies the pardon by supposing that he also pardons lechery in nature; or rather, because he now recognizes that nonhuman lifeforms evade his sovereignty, and that forms of justice such as capital punishment are delegitimized by the absence of a corresponding law in nature.

Lear's pardon results not from a humanitarian impulse or a desire to show mercy but from a strategy to foster lives over which he can exercise sovereignty. "Let copulation thrive...To 't, luxury, pell-mell! for I lack soldiers" (20.110-113). No longer secured by Divine Right and incapable of commanding nature, Lear reconfigures his sovereignty as biopower extorted from the living bodies of his subjects, who are born to die, allowed to live in order to be exposed to death. This reflects the same logic of life-preservation that Regan and Cornwall apply to Gloucester when they "let him live"; the same that leads Cordelia and the physician to "wrong" Lear by taking him "out o' th' grave"; the same that prevents Gloucester from committing suicide; and the same that obliges Lear to pardon the adulterer's life.[630]

Lear's reconfigured sovereignty compels him to confront his own mortality anew. "I will die bravely," he announces unsolicited, "like a bridegroom. What! I will be jovial: come, come; I am a king, my masters, know you that" (20.184-186). An attending gentleman confirms that Lear is "a royal one" who commands obedience, to which Lear replies with an indeterminate pronoun: "Then there's life in't" (20.187-188). Here, as in the play's culminating scene, the audience is left to wonder in *what* Lear sees life. The preposition conjoined with a reifying pronoun ("in't") raises the question of whether Lear imagines sovereignty as the life-source of otherwise lifeless things, or rather if

---

[630] Lear's pardon substantiates Foucault's observation that beginning in the seventeenth century, when "power gave itself the function of administering life," capital punishment became increasingly indefensible: "How could power exercise its highest prerogatives by putting people to death, when its main role was to ensure, sustain, and multiply life, to put this life in order?" ("Right of Death and Power over Life," 260).

he recognizes life inhering in "the thing itself," that is, in the human body that, once socially "unaccommodated" in the wilderness, appears to him as "a poor, bare forked animal" (11.90-92).

Lear's determination to "die bravely, like a bridegroom" recalls Claudio's similar claim in *Measure for Measure*, as he waits in prison to be executed by the state. Duke Vincentio has just advised Claudio to "reason…with life" as "a thing" that only "fools would keep" (3.1.6-8), and Claudio's sister Isabella has arrived with more righteous advice for the condemned. Preserving Claudio's life by sleeping with the corrupt vice-duke Angelo will cost Isabella her virtue, and she fears that Claudio nevertheless wishes "a feverous life [to] entertain, and six or seven winters more respect than a perpetual honour. Darest thou die?" she asks rhetorically, prompting the affirmative answer she expects: "If I must die," Claudio consents, "I will encounter darkness as a bride, and hug it in mine arms" (3.1.73-83). "Yes," Isabella approves, "thou must die: thou art too noble to conserve a life in base appliances" (3.1.85-87). The moral weight of this scene tends toward the Duke and Isabella, who both insist that "worldly life" (3.1.129) is not worth preserving at all costs, and that capital punishment must be accepted—even if the condemned is family and even if the judge is openly corrupt—as a better alternative than preserving life through ignoble means only to survive with shame.

Lear, by contrast, with its biopolitical commitment to

fostering life, disallows such "noble" forfeiture of self-preservation. When Regan suggests that Lear return to Goneril, for instance, he replies that he "could as well be brought to knee [at France's] throne, and, squire-like; pension beg to keep base life afoot" (7.365-367). The irony is that, until the very end, Lear and others do "keep base life afoot" even as they reiterate their wish to die. The evolution from Lear's contempt for undignified "base life" in scene 7 to his exclusive focus on such embodied, mortal life in scene 20 parallels the transformation of his concept of sovereignty from the power to kill to the power to let or make live.

As Lear himself lies dying at the play's end, Edgar's initial reaction, which aligns with his handling of Gloucester's suicide attempt, is to revive him: "Look up, my lord" (24.306). But Kent, the surrogate sovereign who has best served Lear's interests all along, intervenes: "Vex not his ghost: O, let him pass! he hates him much that would upon the rack of this tough world stretch him out longer" (24.307-309). Edgar cedes that Lear already "is gone," to which Kent, unastonished, adds, "the wonder is, he hath endured so long: he but usurp'd his life" (24.310-311). That Lear "usurp'd" or wrongfully appropriated life suggests that he was in Kent's opinion on borrowed time, as it were, having overlived the point where he should have died.

Before Kent urges Edgar to let Lear die, Cordelia predicts for Kent that she will not live long enough to recompense his virtue, thereby signaling her opposition to or at least her abandonment of the paradigm of life-prolongation that is arguably a greater source of tragedy in *Lear* than the death of characters: "O thou good Kent, how shall I live and work to match thy goodness? My life will be too short, and every measure fail me" (21.1-3). After Lear is finally allowed to pass, Albany in *The History* and Edgar in *The Tragedy* deliver the play's consummating lines, a couplet reasserting that the lives of the young generation will be shorter than those of their predecessors: "The oldest have borne most. We that are young shall never see so much, nor live so long [*Exeunt, carrying the bodies*]" (24.320-321). Shakespeare's *Lear* thus cogently questions sovereign biopower by depicting the limits of life-preservation, which is of a piece with the play's subtle articulation of a vitalism that recognizes potential lifeforms outside the human order of things.

The biopolitical paradigm of life-administering sovereignty, which emerged around the same time as the earliest performances of *Lear*, appears to have become naturalized in Tate's "Reviv'd" version seven decades later. Tate maintained that it is better, albeit more challenging, to save life than it is to kill or to allow to die. It is no "Trivial an Undertaking to make a Tragedy end happily," he congratulated himself in the introductory epistle, "for 'tis more difficult to Save than 'tis to Kill: The Dagger and Cup of Poyson are always in Readiness: but to bring the Action to the last Extremity, and then by probable Means to recover All, will require the Art and Judgment of a Writer, and cost him many a Pang in the Performance."[631] Tate, the lifesaving writer, is only too happy to dispense with this cost, because he wants to "divert" the minds of the audience, not shock them with scenes causing emotional anguish or sudden sharp feelings of any kind.

In the final moments of Tate's *Lear*, Gloster asks the "gentle Gods" once more to "give Gloster his Discharge." "No, Gloster," Lear responds, having forgotten or never learned Shakespeare's lesson about the tragedy of life-prolongation, "Thou hast Business yet for Life" (Act V). Tate arguably mistakes his own acquiescence to the paradigm of biopower for a dramaturgical standard; conversely, it is arguable that such lifesaving aesthetic in the theater, already manifest in the anonymous *Leir*, preceded English culture's predilection for life-prolongation.

In either case, Tate's "Reviv'd" *Lear* ends with the revival of Cordelia and other virtuous characters. He was determined to make "the Tale conclude in a Success to the innocent distrest Persons: Otherwise I must have incumbred the Stage with dead Bodies, which Conduct makes many Tragedies conclude with unseasonable Jests."[632] Tate's impulse to keep his characters alive aligns with his desire to keep them under his dramaturgical authority, which in turn aligns with the paradigm of biopower that involves decisions about which lifeforms represent "Persons" and are therefore worth preserving. Just as Tate deactivated

---

[631] Tate, *King Lear*, "The Epistle Dedicatory."
[632] Ibid.

and buried the latent vitalism of Shakespeare's play, he also presumed too quickly that the bodies encumbering the stage at its conclusion are dead. In fact, Shakespeare's *Lear* represents bodies and things hanging ambiguously between life, death, and animacy, thereby inviting the audience to partake, or rather to learn that we already partake, in sovereign decisions about what lives and what is dead.

So Long Lives This, and This Gives Life to Thee

That Regan, Goneril, Gloucester, and Cordelia all die off stage suggests that Shakespeare sought to remove corpses from the stage, not to encumber it as Tate believed. The first to die is Gloucester. Edgar's account of his death is interrupted by a gentleman with a bloody knife screaming for help. "What means that bloody knife?" Edgar asks, a locution that is more than mere metaphor in a play that repeatedly gestures toward the latent vitality of bodies and things, representing a worldview wherein objects such as knives can indeed "mean" or be intentional apart from human subjects.[633] "'Tis hot, it smokes," answers the Gen-

---

[633] Margreta de Grazia has productively complicated relations between subjects and objects in Lear, arguing that Shakespeare articulates something altogether different from either, on the one hand, Jacob Burckhardt's notion of the Renaissance subject who is autonomous from objects, or, on the other hand, Karl Marx's notion of the "Early Modern object, the commodity, [which] denies its relation to persons by effacing its origin in social production" ("The

tleman, still fixated on the knife rather than revealing the human actor who presumably must have wielded it: "It came even from the heart of—O, she's dead!" (24.218-219; *Tragedy*, 5.3.198-199). That the knife itself "came" from Goneril's heart obfuscates the human actor that put it there, allowing the object subjectivity and potential personhood, as if to suggest that knives, not people, kill people.

However rhetorical and contrafactual it is, the suggestion that the knife is self-moving and intentional performs vital work. It does not so much absolve human actors of ethical and political responsibility for their actions as it does revive an alternative ecology that recognizes the interdependence and shared life of humans, creatures, and things.[634] Personifying the vitality of things can become ridiculous if taken *ad absurdum*, as when Lear performs a mock trial for a "joint-stool" in place of his daughter. "Arraign her first. 'Tis Goneril. I here take my oath before this honourable assembly she kicked the poor King her father" (13.40-41). When the Fool asks the stool if its name

Ideology of Superfluous Things," 18). Instead of the Burkhardtian or Marxist views of mutually autonomous subjects and objects that allow for social and historical mobility, de Grazia argues that Lear, by representing persons and things as inseparable, "blocks the mobility identified since the nineteenth century with the Modern…in an attempt to withstand flux or fluidity, superflux or superfluity" (21).
[634] Jane Bennett has weighed the payoffs of recognizing "the power of human-nonhuman assemblages"—which include resistance to "a politics of blame"—against the pitfalls of persisting "with a strategic understatement of material agency in the hopes of enhancing the accountability of specific humans" (*Vibrant Matter*, 38).

is Goneril, Lear rightly interjects that "she cannot deny it" (13.42-43). Teeming beneath the absurdity of this scene, however, is the play's serious inquiry into the potential vitality of things such as beards, the earth, human corpses, knives, and stools, which characters animate through rhetorical devices such as personification, prosopopoeia, and apostrophe. The scene becomes still less comic in light of subsequent models of absolute sovereignty, such as that articulated by Hobbes, which reduced the lives of fools and other ostensibly irrational humans to the same ontological, political, and juridical status as inanimate things.

When Hobbes posited that "things inanimate," as well as "children, fools, and madmen that have no use of reason, may be personated by" those with the authority to impersonate them, he remarked that "few things... are incapable of being represented by fiction."[635] Shakespeare's inclusion of (in)animate things within the human dispensation of law and order was not strictly fictional, then, or rather, such fictions were included in English legal and political discourse before they were represented in the theater. Deodands, for instance, the name for inanimate things and irrational creatures that caused injury or death to rational humans, were included in English common law from the eleventh to the nineteenth century. Such actants as animals, boiling pots of water, falling trees and church bells implicated in violent incidents were "to be given to

---

[635] Hobbes, *Leviathan*, 108.

God, that is, to be sold and distributed to the Poor, by the Kings Almoner, for expiation of this dreadful event, though effected by unreasonable, yea, sensless and dead creatures."[636]

The civil lawyer John Cowell included deodands in *The Interpreter* (1607), his legal dictionary that "caused an uproar in the parliament of 1610, which was marked by a general fear of royal absolutism."[637] Cowell defined a deodand as "a thing given or forfeited (as it were) to God for the pacification of his wrath in a case of misadventure, whereby any Christian soule commeth to violent ende, without the fault of any reasonable creature."[638] It is remarkable that in 1607 Cowell reserved deodand status for things, because later iterations of the law came to include irrational creatures including human beings.

In *Institutes of the Laws of England* (1628), lawyer and politician Edward Coke defined a deodand as "any moveable thing inanimate, or beast animate [that causes] the untimely death of any reasonable creature by mischance… without the will, offence, or fault of himself, or of any

---

[636] Thomas Blount, *Nomo-lexikon, a law-dictionary interpreting such difficult and obscure words and terms as are found either in our common or statute, ancient or modern lawes* (In the Savoy [London], 1670).

[637] Brian P. Levack, s.v. "Cowell, John (1554–1611)." In *Oxford Dictionary of National Biography*, online, ed. David Cannadine (Oxford: Oxford University Press, 2004-. Accessed March 25, 2017, [http://www.oxforddnb.com.turing.library.northwestern.edu/view/article/6490.

[638] John Cowell, *The Interpreter* (Cambridge, 1607).

person."[639] Cowell's version of *The Institutes of the Laws of England* (1651) added that "bruit Beasts, and things inanimate, by which a man happens to be slain…this, whatsoever it be, is in a manner sacred unless it belong to the King.)"[640] Cowell's specification in his definition from 1607—that a "thing" had to harm a "*Christian* soule" to be deemed a deodand—already intimated the question of whether irrational and non-Christian humans could qualify as deodands; by 1651, Cowell's answer was unequivocally affirmative, such that either "Servants or Catell" could become "in a manner sacred,"[641] which is to say, at once holy and accursed, consecrated and sacrificial, protected from and exposed to violence.[642]

During the English Civil Wars, Andrew Marvell conjured deodands in a poem entitled "The Nymph Complaining for the Death of Her Fawn" (circa 1650), which Rogers has called "the finest and most sustained elegy for

---

[639] Quoted in Anna Pervukhin, "Deodands: A Study in the Creation of Common Law Rules," *The American Journal of Legal History*, vol. 47, no. 3 (July, 2005): 237-258; 252. See also R.F. Hunnisett, *The Medieval Coroner* (Cambridge: Cambridge University Press, 1961), 32-33.

[640] John Cowell, *The Institutes of the Laws of England* (London, 1651), 229.

[641] Ibid., 229.

[642] Cowell's definition evokes the figure from ancient Roman law that Agamben has associated with "bare life, that is, the life of *homo sacer* (sacred man), who may be killed and yet not sacrificed" (Giorgio Agamben, *Homo Sacer: Sovereign Power and Bare Life*, trans. Daniel Heller-Roazen [Stanford: Stanford University Press, 1998], 8).

vitalism."[643] The nymph—a beautiful young woman who calls to mind the semi-divine spirit in classical mythology thought to inhabit rivers, mountains, and trees—mourns her fawn as it lays dying after being shot for no apparent reason by passing soldiers who recall the New Model Army: "The wanton troopers riding by/Have shot my fawn, and it will die./Ungentle men! They cannot thrive/Who killed thee/Thou ne'er didst alive/Them any harm, alas! Nor could/Thy death yet do them any good" (1-6). The fawn's murder represents the failure of vitalism to uphold justice on behalf of divine sovereignty: "It cannot die so. Heaven's king/Keeps register of everything" (12-13). However, rather than read the poem as an "elegy for vitalism," I suggest that it represents a transformation of vitalism in the vein of Donne's *The First Anniversary* and Shakespeare's *Lear*.

The transformation is marked, first, by a decentralization of sovereignty and a recognition that animal life is no less worth living and preserving than the life of sovereigns and their human subjects; second, by Marvell's suggestion that although the slaying of "sacred" creatures is not punishable as murder—because such victims are not

---

[643] Rogers, *Matter of Revolution*, 213. Marvell shares with Winstanley, with a few other Puritan radicals, and with vitalist philosophers such as William Harvey and Jean Baptiste van Helmont a conceptualization of agency that defies the orthodoxies of providential Calvinism and mechanistic Hobbesianism through an engagement of a revolutionary doctrine of animist materialism" (*Matter of Revolution*, 43).

deemed alive to begin with—justice is nevertheless served by recategorizing the murderers themselves as dead, inanimate things: "nothing may we use in vain;/Even beasts must be with justice slain,/Else men are made their deodands" (15-17). Marvell thus turned the traditional logic of deodand law on its head by positing that rational, human, and Christian lives are equally eligible to be forfeited as the things and creatures they unjustly use.

Lear's mock trial for the "joint-stool," then, draws attention to the potential deodand status not only of stage props such as knives represented as agents in their own right, but also of the characters who kill unjustly, as well as the actors who are not themselves authors of their actions but personified by Shakespeare's authority. If indeed Shakespeare's early audiences recognized any of these as deodands, they may have experienced cognitive dissonance in deciding to whom or what these personified things, traditionally "given to God" or the earthly sovereign, were to be given in the context of a pagan, polytheistic play-world where the king himself has been deemed irrational.

The mock trial may also be read as a trial of the audience's capacity to discern what lives from what is dead, a capacity brought to crisis by the play's final scene. When Albany learns that Goneril has poisoned Regan before stabbing herself, he gives a surprising, almost dramaturgical order: "Produce their bodies, be they alive or dead" (24.224). Recalling Gloucester's body, which is ambiguously "alive or dead" in the Dover Cliff scene, Albany's indecision or indifference as to whether the bodies are alive or dead is problematically redundant because the gentleman has already announced that Goneril and Regan are dead. Similarly, when Kent informs Lear that his "eldest daughters have fordone themselves, and desperately are dead," Lear replies with a peculiar indecision that seems to reduce Kent's knowledge to mere opinion: "So think I, too" (24.285-287).[644] Lear agrees with Kent but without conviction, leaving unarticulated the sovereign decision about what lives and what is dead.

What Kent calls "the promised end" (24.259) of Shakespeare's play culminates in Cordelia's body as it hangs ambiguously between life and death. After his chthonic analogy announces how dead Cordelia is, Lear scarcely pauses for breath before checking her body for vital signs. "She's dead as earth. Lend me a looking-glass; if that her breath will mist or stain the stone, why, then she lives" (24.256-258).[645] He discovers the life of Cordelia's body only by its absence: "No, no, no life! Why should a dog, a horse, a rat, have life, and thou no breath at all?"

---

[644] "Where is your servant Caius?" Kent, no longer disguised as Caius, asks Lear. "He's a good fellow," Lear answers, "I can tell you that; he'll strike, and quickly too: he's dead and rotten" (24.278-279).

[645] In *Urn Burial* (1658), Thomas Browne describes such "critical tests of death, by apposition of feathers, glasses, and reflection of figures, which dead eyes represent not: which, however not strictly verifiable in fresh and warm cadavers, could hardly elude the test, in corpses of four or five days" (chapter IV).

(24.299-301).[646] This consummating question marks Lear's recognition of the virtual cross-ontological vitality that is central to the play.

Earlier, Lear declared that human life is exceptional because its needs exceed the biological requirements for sustaining bare animal life: "Allow not nature more than nature needs," he stipulated, then "man's life is cheap as beast's" (7.419-420). The question on Lear's dying breath, by contrast, shifts focus from superfluous needs to the more basic faculty of respiration, which humans share at least with animals and plants, and in early modern vitalist worldviews, also with minerals.[647] Lear may not descend lower than dogs, horses, and rats in his litany of lifeforms that survive Cordelia, but his emphasis on breath invokes the shared life and mutual interdependence of all creatures and things, including the earth itself.[648]

---

[646] The question recalls the anti-human-exceptionalist argument from *Ecclesiastes* (3:19) that Overton elected as the epigraph to *Mans Mortalitie*: that the same thing "befalleth" humans and beasts, "as the one dieth, so dieth the other; yea, they have all one breath: so that Man hath no pre-eminence above a Beast: for all is vanity."

[647] In *Observations upon experimental philosophy* (1666), Margaret Cavendish defines respiration as "a kind of Reception of forreign Matter," accompanied by an "emission" of matter proper to the breathing subject or object. For Cavendish, breathing constitutes not only the process "which in Man, and other animal Creatures, is performed by the lungs, but [also] a dividing and uniting, or separating and joyning of parts...of the exterior from and to the interior" of all (in)animate things (14-15).

[648] In the first century of the common era, the Roman author Seneca, whose work was a bedrock of early modern English culture, asked

Lear's question carries the seeds of subsequent seventeenth-century English rebuttals of Descartes' mechanistic philosophy, particularly the infamous "beast-machine hypothesis" that characterized animals as lifeless automatons. Platonist philosopher Henry More, for example, took Descartes to task for "that deadly and murderous sentiment…whereby you snatch away, or rather withhold, life and sense from all animals, for you would never conceive that they really live."[649] Inspired by Cordelia's breathless

---

rhetorically, "How could she [the earth] nourish all the different roots that sink into the soil in one place and another, had she not an abundant supply of the breath of life?" (Quoted in Merchant, *The Death of Nature*, 23). See Lucius Seneca, *Physical Science in the Time of Nero; Being a Translation of the Quaestiones Naturales of Seneca*, trans. John Clarke (London: Macmillian, 1910), 244-45; 126-127.

[649] Henry More, "Henry More to Descartes 11 December 1648," in Leonara D. Cohen, "Descartes and Henry More on the Beast-Machine-A Translation of their Correspondence Pertaining to Animal Automatism," *Annals of Science* 1 (1936): 50. See also Erica Fudge, *Brutal Reasoning*, 156. Recently a wide range of scholars in political theory, literary criticism, and the new materialisms have justly critiqued Cartesian philosophy anew, in large part because of its conceptual devitalization of nonhuman and purportedly irrational forms of life. See, for example, Lakoff and Johnson, *Philosophy in the Flesh* (New York: Basic Books, 1999); Diana Coole and Samantha Frost, eds., *New Materialisms* (Duke University Press, 2010); Laurie Shannon, *The Accommodated Animal* (University of Chicago Press, 2013); and Garrett Sullivan, *Sleep, Romance and Human Embodiment: Vitality from Spenser to Milton* (University of Cambridge Press, 2012), 23. Sullivan notes, for instance, that Descartes could not have located human life in thought (cogito) without first erasing or "banishing the vegetable and sensitive souls," which constitute plant life and animal life, respectively.

body, Lear ends by acknowledging, however resentfully, that animals partake of the same life as human beings.

That Cordelia no longer shares this common life represents what Laurie Shannon has identified in *Lear* as "human negative exceptionalism," which characterizes the human as a privative case rather than paragon of the animal.[650] Descartes posited that the difference between living and dead human bodies is "just like the difference between" working and broken machines, and that a disembodied, immortal faculty of reason distinguishes human life from creaturely mortality and thingly inanimacy. By contrast, Lear's isolation of breath as that which differentiates the living from the dead preserves a worldview that does not "withhold life" from nonhumans but instead recognizes the potential vitality of all bodies and things.

The play's final scene dramatically politicizes the ancient saying, still commonplace in seventeenth-century England, that "all things conspire." Early moderns understood conspiracy (from the Latin *conspīrāre*, "to breathe together") in its metaphorical senses, to signify both covert plotting and cooperation more generally.[651] Pursuing the breath

---

[650] Shannon, "Poor, Bare, Forked: Animal Sovereignty, Human Negative Exceptionalism, and the Natural History of *King Lear*," *Shakespeare Quarterly* 60, no. 2 (Summer 2009): 168-196; 175.

[651] John Roberts begins *The compleat cannoniere* (London, 1639), a treatise on the art of gunning, with a list of philosophical principles, including that the "perfection" and "conservation" of nature results "when all things conspire" such that "the action that commeth from the Agent, as the passion from the patient hath proportion" (1-2).

that passes between Cordelia and a menagerie of animals and things including the earth and a looking-glass or stone, Lear articulates a conspiracy that finally overflows the stage to inspire audiences as they take in the expiration of staged corpses. This articulation represents not only the limits of sovereign biopower to preserve life and decisively to "know when one is dead and when one lives," but also an alternative anthropogenesis that intimates, if it does not yet enact, new modes of sociopolitical organization and cohesion around a (discourse of) shared vitality.

Useful for understanding this process is Walter Benjamin's concept of conspiracy—"a conspiracy with texts and images, with the objects that we fetishize"—which political theorist James Martel has revived in order to conceive a politics based "on alien forms of hope and alliances with objects," but without presupposing "an active and self-conscious political subject...who maximizes her or his will and desires through an engagement with other political actors."[652] *Lear* insists on such "alien forms of hope and alliances with objects," including Gloucester's beard and the bodies of living actors playing "alive or dead."

The last object of Lear's conspiracy is a breath-blown feather that produces an anamorphosis between life and death. "The feather stirs; she lives! If it be so, it is a chance which does redeem all sorrows that ever I have felt" (24.260-262). The play does not offer such redemp-

---

[652] James R. Martel, *Textual Conspiracies: Walter Benjamin, Idolatry, and Political Theory* (Ann Arbor: University of Michigan Press, 2011), 4; 17.

tion, but here it compels the audience to rethink the motive agency that Lear tacitly associates with the (in)transitive verb "stirs," which might be Cordelia's breath or the feather itself. Michael Cody has suggested that "only Lear's animalistic presence can sense the feather," where "for the audience, the feather drifts only in Lear's imagination, and we, yielding to the medium of the drama, only have access to the sounds and images presented us....and the tragedy has brushed against its medium's limit once again."[653] This is not strictly true, especially if Shakespeare has successfully incorporated us into the same animalistic or vitalistic presence as Lear.

Even if audiences are not prepared to entertain that the feather stirs of its own vitality, we may still see it stir as a result of wind blowing through an open-air stage, a draught coursing through an indoor theater, or by the breath of the living actor who is only playing dead. Rather than brush against the medium's limit, the stirring feather moved by breath of uncertain provenance momentarily dissolves that limit to include us in the play's conspiracy. And readers breathe together with the written text no less than audiences breathe together with actors during a live performance, a fact that Shakespeare already underscores in the final couplet of Sonnet 18: "So long as men can breathe, or eyes can see,/So long lives this, and this gives

---

[653] Michael C. Clody, "The Mirror and the Feather: Tragedy and Animal Voice in *King Lear*," *ELH* 80, no. 3 (Fall 2013): 661-680; 674.

life to thee."[654] Likewise, though she be "dead as earth," Cordelia lives as long as the earth lives and as long as readers, actors, and audiences decide to revive her.

---

[654] William Shakespeare, *Shakespeare's Sonnets*, ed. Stephen Booth (New Haven and London: Yale University Press, 2000).

And There's An End

This book has pursued life in unlikely places, not in the forest, field, zoo, or Petri dish, but in old texts written by authors who have been dead for centuries. After observing, describing, and where possible reasoning with a menagerie of seventeenth-century lifeforms—including autochthonous lives, vegetative and creaturely lives, short and prolonged lives, lives worth living and lives deemed unworthy of life, nonhuman and dehumanized lives, (im)mortal lives, individual and collective lives, past lives, actual lives, and potential lives—my pursuit has made a quietus with Cordelia's dying breath. If this sprawling chase of life has finally yielded mere breath, I should pause to breathe, if not to concede with Thomas Wyatt that "in a net I seek to hold the wind."[655]

Early modern wisdom on life and death teaches that it is vital to make an end, ideally a good one, and to come to terms with finitude. Recall, for instance, Overton's agreement with Pliny that immortality is a "foolish and childish" fiction "devised by men that would fain live always, and never make an end."[656] The same corpus of wisdom

---

[655] Thomas Wyatt, "Whoso List To Hunt," *The Columbia Anthology of British Poetry*, ed. Carl Woodring and James Shapiro (New York: Columbia University Press, 1995), 29.
[656] Richard Overton, "The Postscript," *Man Wholly Mortal* (London,

also teaches, however, that ends are messy and incomplete, offering inadequate closure to the lives that overflow their appointed and determined boundaries, limits, and definitions. For example, Ophelia's response to her father's death—"they say he made a good end" (*Hamlet*, 4.5.181)—is a tragically dubious claim given that Polonius was stabbed to death, mistaken for someone else while hiding behind an arras. Instead of closure, his end opens a gaping hiatus that engulfs those who survive him. The preceding chapters have dwelt on the hiatuses through which early modern life escapes the enclosures that would delineate it, enclosures including the borders of sovereign territory, the limits of longevity, the strictures of orthodoxy, the ontological categories of race and species, the periodization of history, and, of course, death.

The anthropologist Clifford Geertz claimed of human beings that "one of the most significant facts about us may finally be that we all begin with the natural equipment to live a thousand kinds of life but end in the end having lived only one."[657] For Geertz, life's potential plurality, its pluripotency, is gradually singularized as it approaches death, which finally reduces life to an absolute singularity. This linear view of life is just one way to narrate, historicize, and make sense of the countless (in)decisions made during a lifetime, imagining each as a point on a line that

---

1655).

[657] Clifford Geertz, *The Interpretation of Cultures: Selected Essays* (New York: Basic Books, 1973), 45.

actualizes "only one" possibility while leaving all other potentials unrealized.[658] Alternative views, already current in early modern texts, have reemerged in the decades since Geertz's claim about the "facts" of human life.

"It is of the essence of life that it does not begin here or end there," anthropologist Tim Ingold contends, "or connect a point of origin with a final destination, but rather that it keeps on going, finding a way through the myriad of things that form, persist and break up in its currents. Life, in short, is a movement of opening, not of closure."[659] The work of tracing and retracing life's movement in early modern texts has hopefully further opened readers of this book to the unactualized potential of outmoded ideas, ideologies, words, and worldviews, or in other words, to what Aby Warburg called the Nachleben or afterlife of the Renaissance.[660] I have not tried to revive remnants from

---

[658] Cf. Giovanni Pico della Mirandola, "Oration on the Dignity of Man," trans. Elizabeth Livermore Forbes, in *The Renaissance Philosophy of Man*, ed. Ernst Cassirer, Paul Oskar Kristeller, and John Herman Randall, Jr. (Chicago and London: The University of Chicago Press, 1948), 223-254. "On man when he came into life the Father conferred seeds of all kinds and the germs of every way of life. Whatever seeds each man cultivates will grow to maturity and bear him their own fruit. If they be vegetative, he will be like a plant. If sensitive, he will become brutish. If rational, he will grow into a heavenly being. If intellectual, he will be an angel and the son of God....Who would not admire this our chameleon?" (225).

[659] Tim Ingold, *Being Alive: Essays on Movement, Knowledge and Description* (New York: Routledge, 2011), 3-4.

[660] For a discussion of Agamben's use of Aby Warburg's term Nachleben, see Leland de la Durantaye, *Giorgio Agamben: A Critical*

the "dead" past, because, after all, their residual and urgent emergence bares a kind of life. I have tried rather to tap into the unexpired potency of texts that manifest and embody forms and characteristics of life.[661]

One of the threads suturing the preceding chapters is an attention to the "as if" and the "what if"—that is, to potentialities, latencies, and counterfactuals. Caliban, for example, is not actually autochthonous, though Chapter 1 followed the consequences of Prospero's suggestion that he might be. Human individuals do not, and presumably cannot, live for hundreds of years, but Chapter 2 found Bacon wondering if—and how—they might. The dominant culture in early modern England believed or professed to believe that the human soul is immortal and independent from the body, but Chapter 3 caught Overton entertaining the mortality of the soul, and in the process, realizing the body's potential vitality. Early moderns may no more have believed than we (who have never been modern) believe that beards can spontaneously quicken, or that inanimate

---

Introduction (Stanford: Stanford University Press, 2009), 71. "Warburg used the term Nachleben...to understand the life and afterlife of images—to study images as 'charged' with psychic energies or symbolic life. The correlate of this conception was that images from our cultural past are not dead, gone, or extinguished; they are at most dormant and remain infused or 'charged' with the energies that cultures have invested in them—a dynamic potential that they retain even when they lie forgotten for decades, centuries, or even longer."
[661] Cf. Giorgio Agamben, *Potentialities: Collected Essays in Philosophy*, trans. Daniel Heller-Roazen (Stanford: Stanford University Press, 1999), 177.

things can stand trial as accused and accusing legal subjects, but Chapter 4 interrogated Shakespeare's enactment of such possibilities.

The inoperative early modern potentials I have described oscillate between the historiographical categories identified by Raymond Williams as "residual" and "emergent," both of which account for historical possibilities and human capabilities that remain unactualized by the "dominant" social order.[662] Williams regarded as "emergent" those "new meanings and values, new practices, new relationships and kinds of relationship [that] are continually being created."[663] By "residual," he meant not "an element of the past...to be consciously 'revived' in a deliberately specializing way," but rather "an effective element of the present...still active in the cultural process."[664] From the perspective of Williams' dialectic, my work to actualize the residual and emergent potential of past lives represents a predictable stage of dominant culture.

---

[662] Raymond Williams, *Marxism and Literature* (Oxford and New York: Oxford University Press, 1977), 124. "[N]o...dominant social order and therefore no dominant culture ever in reality includes or exhausts all human practice, human energy, and human intention. This is not merely a negative proposition, allowing us to account for significant things which happen outside or against the dominant mode. On the contrary it is a fact about the modes of domination, that they select from and consequently exclude the full range of human practice."
[663] Ibid., 123.
[664] Ibid., 122.

> In the subsequent default of a particular phase
> of a dominant culture there is…a reaching back
> to those meanings and values which were created
> in actual societies and actual situations in the past,
> and which still seem to have significance because
> they represent areas of human experience,
> aspiration, and achievement which the dominant
> culture neglects, undervalues, opposes, represses,
> or even cannot recognize.[665]

I have focused in particular on what has been neglected, undervalued, and unrecognized by dominant cultures including seventeenth-century English culture, contemporary American culture, the culture of human exceptionalism, and the culture of life. This includes both outlandish and antiquated ideas such as autochthony, as well as familiar but widely repressed ideas such as those surrounding mortality.

Thomas Browne remarked that physicians and others "whose study is life and death, who daily behold examples of mortality," have less need than others for *memento mori*, "or coffins by our bed side, to mind us of our graves."[666] Quotidian examples of mortality were more conspicuous to Browne's contemporaries than they are to most people living in the West today. Notwithstanding the early modern

---

[665] Ibid., 123-124.

[666] Thomas Browne, *Religio Medici and Urne Buriall*, ed. Stephen Greenblatt and Ramie Targoff (New York: New York Review Books, 2012), 94.

instances of death-denial, including Gloucester's stymied suicide and the backlash to Overton's mortalism, there was generally less denial of death in seventeenth-century England than there is in our culture.

The surgeon and author Atul Gawande insists that twenty-first century physicians no less than laypeople urgently need such reminders of mortality as early moderns including Browne beheld everywhere.

> Modern scientific capability has profoundly altered the course of human life. People live longer and better than at any other time in history. But scientific advances have turned the processes of aging and dying into medical experiences, matters to be managed by health care professionals. And we in the medical world have proved alarmingly unprepared for it.[667]

The medicalization of death—the underbelly of the medicalization of life which Chapter 2 placed in Bacon's new science of life-prolongation—has increasingly denied Americans the kind of death that most report to prefer: namely, death with dignity and without needless suffering, at home or in hospice rather than in the sterile, anesthetic environment of an Intensive Care Unit following a series of heroic but ultimately futile life-saving, or death-delaying, measures.[668]

---

[667] Atul Gawande, *Being Mortal: Medicine and What Matters in the End* (New York: Metropolitan Books, 2014), 6.

[668] See Mary O'Hara, "Death and Dying Continues to be Seen as a Big Taboo," *The Guardian*, May 9, 2017, https://www.theguardian.

The denial and the medicalization of death have not only relegated the experience of dying from the home to the hospital; they have also deferred critical dialogue about death to the end of life. Having difficult conversations about mortality earlier in life can potentially bring into closer alignment how, on the one hand, people claim they want to die with, on the other hand, how most in our culture actually die.

Early modern texts, this project has insisted, promote such conversations, which can in turn enrich our *ars moriendi* (art or technique of dying) and the *ars vivendi* (art or technique of living) that is inseparable from it. More immediately, early modern texts can help us to clarify, by historicizing, the ways we value and evaluate life as well as the terms we use in coming to terms with our ends. An effective response to the medicalization of life and death, for instance, demands vigorous conceptions of what life and death were before they were medicalized; of what other transformations they have undergone in addition

---

com/society/2017/may/09/death-dying-big-taboo-bj-miller. See also "How To Have A Better Death," *The Economist*, April 29, 2017, http://www.economist.com/news/leaders/21721371-death-inevitable-bad-death-not-how-have-better-death. The article cites a 1662 book by a "London haberdasher" named John Graunt as "the first quantitative account of death," which gives "a glimpse of the suddenness and terror of death before modern medicine. It came early, too: until the 20th century the average human lived about as long as a chimpanzee. Today science and economic growth mean that no land mammal live longer. Yet an unintended consequence has been to turn dying into a medical experience."

to medicalization, including rationalization, politicization, incorporation, economization, and (de)humanization; and of how life and death might be imagined and experienced in a future where they are no longer, or less, medicalized.

My analysis of anthropogenesis as a process by which sovereignty institutes sociopolitical order has suggested that the articulation of heterodox or unconventional ideas about life and death challenges the status quo of dominant culture. In *The Denial of Death* (1973), Ernest Becker likewise argued,

> Society wants to be the one to decide how
> people are to transcend death; it will tolerate the
> *causa-sui* project only if it fits into the standard
> social project. Otherwise there is the alarm
> of 'Anarchy!' This is one of the reasons for
> bigotry and censorship of all kinds over personal
> morality: people fear that the standard morality
> will be undermined—another way of saying that
> they fear they will no longer be able to control
> life and death.[669]

One lesson gleaned from the story surrounding the mid-seventeenth-century emergence of Overton's *Man's Mortalitie* is that alternative anthropogenic claims—for example, that humans are wholly embodied and absolutely mortal—do not necessarily imply an anarchic dissolution of social morality. On the contrary, such claims can rein-

---

[669] Ernest Becker, *The Denial of Death* (New York: Simon & Schuster, 1973), 46.

vigorate existing social bonds by opening them to new, more humane alliances, forms of organization, and cultural projects. It should therefore be possible to cultivate a more robust discourse surrounding matters of life and death, not to break ties with past tradition or to undermine present practice, but to reconceive what is and has been actual and to plant the seeds for a potentially better future.

To that end, this project has identified a number of key (dis)continuities between "our life" and early modern lives. For example, a constitutive task of both early modern and modern sovereignty has been to institute sociopolitical order through anthropogenic decisions. Notwithstanding its eventual instrumentalization, however, early modern anthropogenesis was speculative and theoretical, whereas the practical applications of modern anthropogenesis are more urgently immediate. Even as he overturned orthodox modes of anthropogenesis, Overton was confident in the stability of ontological categories: "If my being did not distinguish me from an owl and a woodcock, and thy being the same," he speculated, "then an owl and a woodcock were both writer and reader. But an owl and a woodcock is neither writer nor reader."[670] Today, by contrast, scientific advancements such as gene-editing, artificial gestation, and stem cell research have promised, or threatened, to actualize the potential collapse of ontological boundaries separating humans from other living creatures.[671]

---

[670] Richard Overton, *Man Wholly Mortal* (London, 1675), 26-27.

[671] See David Robson, "The Birth of Half-Human, Half-Animal

To recapitulate a final locus of (dis)continuity: present-day researchers are continuing Bacon's project of life-prolongation, and despite centuries of progress, the potential for superlongevity remains virtually as unactualized for us as it did for Bacon.[672] This line of continuity is disjoined, however, insofar as scientists disregard the long tradition in which they are working, and insofar as Bacon enacted a medicalization of theology while twenty-first-century longevity research has been shaped by an economic capitalization of medicine.[673]

My attention to (dis)continuity has yielded a literary-intellectual history that is sporadic (from the Greek for "scattering" or "sowing") in both form and content—in content, because the concepts of autochthony, life-prolongation, mortalism, and vitalism each appear intermittently throughout history; in form, because the convergence of these four disparate discourses, loosely connected by their pertinence to the study of life and death in early modern England, generated a book that is itself scattered and

Chimeras," *BBC*, January 5, 2017, http://www.bbc.com/earth/story/20170104-the-birth-of-the-human-animal-chimeras. See also Olga Khazan, "Babies Floating in Fluid-Filled Bags," *The Atlantic*, April 25, 2017, https://www.theatlantic.com/health/archive/2017/04/preemies-floating-in-fluid-filled-bags/524181/.
[672] See, for example, Sarah Plumridge, "The Quest to Lengthen Quality Life," *Northwestern Medicine Magazine*, vol. 3, no. 4 (Fall 2016): 15-17.
[673] See, for example, Tad Friend, "Silicon Valley's Quest to Live Forever," *The New Yorker*, April 3, 2017, http://www.newyorker.com/magazine/2017/04/03/silicon-valleys-quest-to-live-forever.

dispersed, which may be a virtue in the dissemination of knowledge.

Any innovation of this sporadic history, conceived not as a necromantic revival of the dead past but as a critical actualization of past and present potentials, springs not from a search for novelty but rather from re-tracing the footsteps of scholars along trodden paths of tradition. In other words, I have worked to actualize potentials through what Thomas Kuhn termed "normal science," which "consists in…an actualization achieved by extending the knowledge of those facts that [a] paradigm displays as particularly revealing, by increasing the extent of the match between those facts and the paradigm's predictions, and by further articulation of the paradigm itself."[674]

I unfolded paradigms of biopower—such as Foucault's thesis that the ancient sovereign power to kill yielded in the seventeenth century to a power to foster life and to make live by denying death—by extending knowledge not of "facts" that corroborate the paradigms but of polysemous bits of textual evidence that elucidate as well as vex their predications. "By focusing attention upon a small range of relatively esoteric problems," Kuhn argued, "the paradigm forces scientists to investigate some part of nature in a detail and depth that would otherwise be unimaginable."[675] It was not my departure from

---

[674] Thomas S. Kuhn, *The Structure of Scientific Revolutions* (London and Chicago: The University of Chicago Press, 2012), 24.
[675] Ibid., 25.

but my adherence to established paradigms that led me to discover "relatively esoteric" concepts such as autochthony, mortalism, and vitalism, which represent lifeforms at the outer limits of what is imaginable and allowable within hegemonic cultures of life.

I have learned from many who, as Victoria Kahn has remarked, "find in the early modern period...a break with an older form of political theology construed as the theological legitimation of the state, a new emphasis on a secular notion of human agency, and most important, a new preoccupation with the ways art and fiction reoccupy the terrain of religion."[676] I have followed those for whom "political theology names...the persistent haunting of liberal modernity by something in excess of the law, an exception that is then analogized not only to the miracle, grace, or some other figure of transcendence but also, in the register of immanence, to mere life, creaturely life, biopower or bios."[677] Kahn's innovation was to introduce poiesis—"the principle, first advocated by Hobbes and Vico, that we can know only what we make ourselves"—as "the missing third term in both early modern and contemporary debates about politics and religion."[678] My intervention may be conceived as "normal" research

---

[676] Victoria Kahn, *The Future of Illusion: Political Theology and Early Modern Texts* (Chicago and London: The University of Chicago Press, 2014), 2-3.

[677] Ibid., 4.

[678] Ibid., 3.

into the historical symbiosis between poiesis and bios, a process whereby the latter emerges as both subject and object of the former. For early moderns, what might be termed bio-poiesis involved the power to foster life and to make live. Contemporary bio-poiesis, by contrast, increasingly also involves the power to make life and to produce new lifeforms.

Nikolas Rose argues that "we are inhabiting an emergent form of life" in the twenty-first century, as a result of new technologies and styles of thinking that have disrupted normative ideas about what it means to be human and about what it means to be alive.[679] *Early Modern Matters of Life and Death* aimed at an historical ethics or ethical

---

[679] Nikolas Rose, *The Politics of Life Itself: Biomedicine, Power, and Subjectivity in the Twenty-First Century* (Princeton and Oxford: Princeton University Press, 2009), 5-7. Rose cites several "mutations" that have contributed to this emergent form of life, including: "First, moleculariazation: The 'style of thought' of contemporary biomedicine [that] envisages life...as a set of intelligible vital mechanisms among molecular entities that can be identified, isolated, manipulated, mobilized, recombined, in new practices of intervention...Second, optimization. Contemporary technologies of life...seek to act in the present in order to secure the best possible future for those who are their subjects. Hence, of course, these technologies embody disputed visions of what, in individual and or collective human life, may indeed be an optimal state. Third, subjectification. We are seeing the emergence of new ideas of what human beings are, what they should do, and what they can hope for. Novel conceptions of 'biological citizenship' have taken shape that recode the duties, rights, and expectations of human beings in relation to their sickness, and also to their life itself, reorganize the relations between individuals and their biomedical authorities."

historicism that would look to the past for perspective on matters of vital concern today.

These days, one only needs to turn on the nightly news to observe sovereignty entrenching itself with anthropogenic decisions along the frontlines of life and death. In his recent speech on Islam in Saudi Arabia, United States President Donald Trump reiterated his campaign promise "that America will not seek to impose our way of life on others."[680] Presupposing that "our way of life" signifies a coherent, unifed category, Trump went on to reduce the plurality of global actors, alliances, and conflicts to a binary opposition between those who value life and those who do not.

> Terrorists...worship death. If we do not act...
> Terrorism's devastation of life will continue
> to spread. Peaceful societies will become
> engulfed by violence. And the futures of many
> generations will be sadly squandered.... This
> is not a battle between different faiths...or
> different civilizations. This is a battle between
> barbaric criminals who seek to obliterate human
> life, and decent people of all religions who seek
> to protect it.... If you choose the path of terror,
> your life will be empty, your life will be brief,
> and your soul will be condemned.[681]

[680] Uri Friedman and Emma Green, "Trump's Speech on Islam, Annotated," *The Atlantic*, May 21, 2017, https://www.theatlantic.com/international/archive/2017/05/trump-saudi-speech-islam/527535/.
[681] Ibid.

Such characterization of what is "barbaric" (i.e., foreign) and "criminal" (i.e., not state-sanctioned) by its opposition to human life epitomizes sovereignty's attempt to institute sociopolitical order through authorized anthropogenic declarations. Here, however, Trump's intention to redraw national, sectarian, and cultural boundaries along the ontological borders of human life and death is mere fantasy given that the American "way of life" still accommodates "decent" (i.e., tolerable, respectable, or fitting to special circumstances) people who worship or simply respect death without being terrorists, people for whom the protection and prolongation of life is not the be all and end all.

If this book has delivered more questions than answers concerning the meanings of life, may it at least serve as a reminder that disavowing outlandish or "repugnant" ideas is a sure way to squander the potential of our lives. Still, there is no prescription for living long or living well. Instead, every generation, every moment, we must again decide for ourselves the meanings of life.

Our Philosophy

We believe that life-writing is essential to living; that writing life is a privilege, right, and responsibility; that written words captivate the atmosphere of lived experience; that there are as many styles of life-writing as there are lives.

We are zealous preservers of memories and legacies. Preservation is not just the recollection of ancestors and origins, but also pre-serving: a proactive form of service for family, community, and posterity. Our mission is to create narratives that enlighten, entertain, and inspire while preserving stories that are vital to life.

bioGraphbook.com

Printed in the USA
CPSIA information can be obtained
at www.ICGtesting.com
LVHW091617080424
776763LV00003B/625